Norma Cranko was born in 1933 in Durban, South Africa. She lived with her wealthy Jewish parents until their separation, when Norma was sent as a boarder to Redhill school in Johannesburg. At fourteen years old, she left her mother's house to work as a secretary for a gold-mining company in Odendaalsrus, an experience which reinforced her sense of the injustices in her homeland. She moved back to Johannesburg to join other anti-apartheid activists and in 1953 became a member of the Congress of Democrats – the white wing of the African National Congress.

In 1955, Norma went to London before attending the Warsaw Youth Festival, and there met David Kitson, whom she married the following year. The Kitsons returned to Johannesburg in 1959 to continue their anti-apartheid work, which led to David Kitson's arrest in 1964 – he was sentenced to twenty years' imprisonment. Norma, too, was arrested and tortured, and in 1966 was forced to flee to London with her two children, Steven and Amandla. The story of her youth, her struggle to support her children on her own in London (where she started her own typesetting company), the formation of the City of London Anti-Apartheid Group, and her ill-treatment on her returns to South Africa to visit David make harrowing and inspiring reading in this, her first book.

The ceaseless work of Norma Kitson, her children and the City of London Anti-Apartheid Group ensured that attention was focused on political prisoners, including David Kitson, who was freed eight months before his sentence was due to end. The Kitson family continue to fight for the cause of freedom in South Africa, most recently as central figures on the non-stop picket outside South Africa House calling for the release of Nelson Mandela and all Southern African political prisoners.

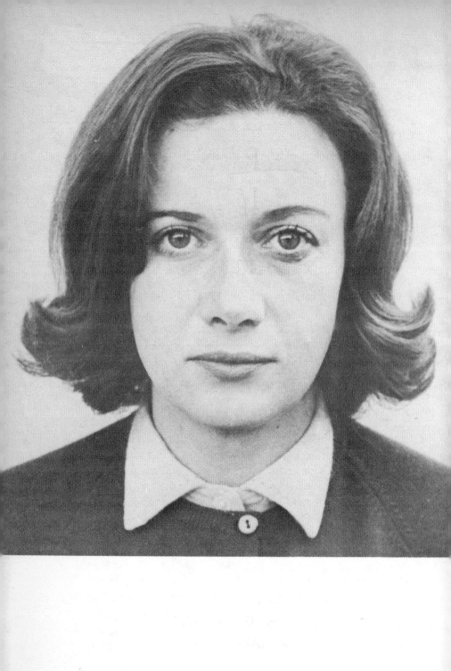

WHERE SIXPENCE LIVES

Norma Kitson

THE HOGARTH PRESS
LONDON

Published in 1987 by
The Hogarth Press
Chatto & Windus Ltd
30 Bedford Square, London WC1B 3RP

First published in Great Britain by Chatto & Windus Ltd 1986
Hogarth edition offset from original Chatto edition
Copyright © Norma Kitson 1985, 1986

British Library Cataloguing in Publication Data

Kitson, Norma
Where sixpence lives
1. Kitson, Norma 2. Radicals – South Africa – Biography
I. Title
322.4'4'0924   DT779.955.K5/

Typeset by Red Lion Setters
Printed in Great Britain by
Cox & Wyman Ltd
Reading, Berkshire

For David,
Steven and Amandla

Our dearest possession is Life.
It is given to us but once.
And we must live it so as to feel
no torturing regrets for wasted years,
never know the burning shame
of a mean and petty past;
so live, that dying, we might say:
'all my life
all my strength
were given to the finest cause in all the world –
the fight for the Liberation of Humankind.'

Nikolai Ostrovsky *How the Steel was Tempered*

ILLUSTRATIONS

· 1 ·

'The moles are wrecking the tennis court again,' my father said, as he was carving the Sunday chicken.

My mother looked up, her dark blue eyes pained, and impatiently flicked her beautiful long fingers towards her face. Turning her diamond rings to the front of her fingers, her habit when tense, she said, 'I thought you'd dealt with all that last week, Bill. *Not* on the right, Jim' – she turned on our black waiter who was hovering over us with the plates of food – 'I've told you a *hundred* times. Serve on the *left*.'

'I simply can't understand it. They burrow where the gravel is soft and mixed with earth at the edges of the court – that's where I find mounds. I suppose they can't get at the hard surface. Jim rolls it nearly every day. It's a funny place for moles to choose. Anyway, I thought we'd got rid of them for ever – we put some poison down last week.'

'Well,' said my mother, 'you know we're playing next Sunday. I've got a whole crowd coming over – all the family. I hope you'll see to it that the court is flat by then.'

I pulled my legs up onto the chair and then suddenly stood up on it. As my mother started to protest, I made a cockle-doodle-doo sound and jumped to the ground and, racing to the top of the table, flung myself at my father, throwing my arms around his neck.

'Come on, Normie,' he said, disentangling himself and holding me away by my forearms. 'Behave yourself. Go and sit down and eat your dinner.'

'Not hungry,' I said. I went back to my place. I did not want them talking about the tennis court. I didn't want them to find out my secret and I didn't want my father to look so worried.

1

My sister Joan kicked my brother Ronnie under the table and they began to giggle.

'Well, just sit down,' Dad said. 'Behave yourself at the table or you'll have to eat all your meals in the children's dining room. If you want to eat with us, you'll have to behave like a big girl.'

I was seven years old. We ate Sunday lunch with the grown-ups. The rest of our meals we had in the breakfast room, ruled by our hated Nurse McGrath. I would have screamed blue murder if I had been sent out. I didn't want to miss being with my family. But I hated the long time everything took to be served, I didn't like eating and I could never sit still.

I jumped up and down on my chair.

'Vroom, vroom goes the dynamo,' my brother Ronnie said with approval, nodding at me.

'That child is so *provocative*,' my mother said peevishly.

'It's all right,' said my dad.

'All right? All right! If you only knew, Bill, what I have to put up with. The constant irritations, the draining. She doesn't know how to behave, she loses everything and she never listens to anything I say.'

'What's she lost?'

'Oh, you name it! She just drops her clothes anywhere, tearing around the neighbourhood with Ronnie. And Nurse McGrath tells me her new doll has disappeared. So far as I can gather she has now lost *all* her dolls.'

'But she loves her dolls! Do you mean the one we gave her for her birthday is lost? That was very expensive.' My father was always thinking about the cost of things: my mother never did. Turning to me he asked:

'Where is it? Don't you remember? Where's your new doll? I saw you playing with it only a couple of days ago.'

I ground my fork into the pumpkin and then mashed it to the side of my plate. I speared my potato and stood the fork up in it.

'Will you eat *properly* at the table.' My mother gave a sigh of self-pity and despair. 'Bill, look what she's doing *now*.'

I felt sick. If they made me eat one single bit of it, I would vomit. If I vomited on the new purple carpet that matched the new purple velvet curtains, my mother would never forgive me. She had had a terrible time getting the décor she wanted. Everything had gone wrong: the stuff had taken months to arrive from overseas and you couldn't get decent labour these days, she had said. She had talked for weeks about the colour. My father didn't really care all that much about colours but– 'Purple!' he had said unbelievingly.

When she made their bedroom green because she was going to set a fashion trend, he just smiled. 'Everyone's superstitious about green,' my mother explained. 'They don't wear it and they won't have it in the house. So it's bound to catch on.' My mother saw herself as the Durban trendsetter and 'overseas' representative of good taste in décor, dress and make-up. 'I was the first one to wear slacks in Durban and look how they caught on. Everyone wears them now.'

But my father seemed fazed by the thought of purple. 'Purple! It's a royal mourning colour,' he murmured almost to himself. 'But is it a colour for a lounge?'

'They're all doing it overseas.' My mother quashed any objection from my dad. He never had any answer to that except to scratch his head. Everyone knew that 'overseas' meant London or Paris and if they advertised purple furnishings it meant that they were the latest fashion– and no one could argue against that.

I looked at my plate of food and felt sick. If I vomited, Ronnie would laugh and Joan would give me a look of pity. My jaws began to ache and I felt my mouth fill with spit. I must have gone pale.

'Are you ill again?' my mother asked.

'You can see she's not well,' Dad said. 'What have you been eating?'

'Nothing,' I said truthfully. I was thinking about my dolls. They were quite safe but I didn't want anyone talking about them being missing.

'Someone's eaten my peppermint crisp,' Joan offered.

'Well, don't be such a bitch,' Ronnie said. 'It wasn't her, it was me. You took my chocolate log– remember!'

3

'If you two start fighting at the table,' my mother said between her teeth, 'I shall call Nurse McGrath to take you away.'

'I don't care,' said Ronnie. 'I'd *rather* eat in our dining room. I hate it when you're all moaning. I like moles and I hate it when people come to tennis.' He threw his thoroughbred Doberman, Dort Rex Blackblankenberg, a chicken bone.

My mother gasped with horror. 'You *see!*' she pleaded with my father. 'You see what I have to put up with all the time. The children have no *manners*.' Giving Ronnie a pained look she rose. 'I've got a headache. I'm going to have my rest. Are you going to take the children for a drive, Bill?'

'No,' my father said. 'I'm meeting the crew. The yacht needs scraping down and painting.' His yacht, *Ripple*, had been turned upside down in the garden ever since the war began, when it had to be taken out of the harbour because of the warships.

'But Nannie's going off at two,' Mom said, 'and the girl's away because she says her mother has died *again*. You simply *must* take the kids. There'll be so much noise I won't be able to rest. And *do* do something about the tennis court.'

I made a loud bub-bub-bub sound with my hand hitting my mouth, to shut out her words.

'Oh! *That child!*' my mother said as she left the dining room.

'I don't want looking after,' Ronnie said to our father. 'I'm going to see Dennis.'

'I don't want you playing with that Essenwood Road gang,' Dad said to him. 'You'll get into trouble mixing with those boys.' Then he thought about his own plans. 'Well, just this once, then. And what about you, Joan? What are you going to do?'

Joan, who was twelve, paused and gave us a Bette Davis look which I had seen her practising in front of the mirror in our room. But with her round cheeks and big electric blue eyes and her frizzy golden hair bushed out, she looked more like Shirley Temple. 'Oh, I'm OK. I have some homework to do. You go and paint your yacht, Dad. I'll look after her. She can come and read my new magazine.'

4

We started to get up from the table. Jim – whose real name was Phineas, but most houseboys were called 'Jim' – eyed us from the sideboard where he was standing, silent, watching, in his white suit and blue waiter's ribbon. In a suitable pause, he asked, 'You finished, master?'

'Yes, you can clear away now. And tell the servants to be quiet. The madam is sleeping.'

As we rounded the bend in the stairs, Joan said, 'What's wrong with you? Why didn't you want them talking about the tennis court?'

'I'll tell on you,' I screamed. 'I'll bloody tell on you. I'll tell them all you practise film stars in your mirror. I'll tell them you've got a lipstick. I'll tell them a boy phoned you the other day.' I jumped on the banister and slid down to the bottom. I felt threatened and isolated.

Joan looked down at me over the stairwell. 'Come here, you silly! I'm not going to hurt you. I want to help you! I'll tell you what: you tell me your secret and I'll let you put on my new lipstick. Come on. Come up now. If you make a noise, Mom will send us outside.'

Dragging myself step by step and hanging on to the banister rail, I went upstairs, this time carefully avoiding the blue lines on the carpet.

'I haven't got a secret,' I said. 'And I don't like lipstick.'

My big sister looked at me kindly. 'What's wrong?' she asked, putting her arms around me.

'I don't know. Everything!'

'I'm unhappy too, you know,' Joan said.

I looked at her in disbelief. Joan, who knew about everything; who could explain everyone's moods and feelings; who was so pretty: how could she be unhappy? 'Why?' I asked her.

'Just look how fat I am. No boy will ever want to take *me* out.'

'Everybody says the boys are mad about you,' I said, quoting my mother. 'And you're always talking to boys on the phone.'

'Yes,' she said, 'but not to ones I like. Only ones who like me.'

'No one likes *me*,' I said, forgetting her problems.

Joan cuddled me close. 'Everyone *loves* you.'

5

'Just look at my frizzy hair,' I said to her.

'Well, gosh! Just look at mine,' she said, grabbing a bunch of her frizz.

'Yes, but yours is *blonde* and mine's only brown and my eyes are only brown, too.'

'We get our hair from Dad's side of the family,' Joan said. 'Dad puts Vitalis on his hair every morning after he wets it and then he combs it straight and wipes it with his hand to make it lie down flat, but by the time he's had breakfast, it's all crinkled up again – I don't think he knows! Anyway, it's not what you look like, it's what's inside you that counts.'

'I haven't got anything inside,' I said.

'Of course you have. You're not *empty*.'

'I don't care,' was all I could think of to say.

'When I came home from school on Friday, I saw you in the garden playing with your dolls. What have you done with them?' Joan asked.

'Nothing,' I said. 'I don't ask you about your things all the time.'

'Well, you better find them,' Joan said, 'or you won't have anything to play with, will you?'

I thought of my cousin Wendy's tricycle, doll's house, tea set, silver skipping rope and real little shop with samples of Robin starch, Dreen shampoo, Colgate toothpaste, Joko coffee and Five Roses tea. Everybody gave me dolls because they wanted me to be more like a girl instead of playing with Ronnie's gang, and I had a little cooker with an oven door that opened. My usual playing place was screened from view near the servants' quarters behind a row of banana trees. I'd make sure I was quite alone, put the cooker on a stone, seat my dolls around it, and chop up leaves and flowers into dishes made from the silver paper from Mom's CTC cigarette packs. I would feed the dolls, read to them and give them 'lectures'.

My father bought me lots of books. McGrath said I would go blind reading and my mom didn't like it either. 'You'll get a long nose reading books,' she'd threaten. And I did. I passed on to my dolls my school studies, told them my father's stories and gave them my brother's moral lectures. And I always told them, 'You don't want to grow up like me, do you? So just be good, or you will.'

But now I didn't want to talk to my dolls any more.

Joan and I were whispering at the top of the stairs, but my mother was a very light sleeper.

'*Will* you children go out and play?' she called.

'We're just going to our room, Mom,' Joan said.

Our baby brother gave a yell when he heard our voices.

'Go *out*,' Mom said. 'You'll disturb me. And see what's bothering Markie. I'm playing cards with the Sipsers tonight and I have to get some rest.'

Nothing was more important in my mother's life than playing cards. She was Durban winner in the World Bridge Olympics, she played rummy most afternoons and poker most nights. She usually lost at poker and she and my dad had rows about her extravagance. My mother used to boast how one night, in a bad streak, she had lost a thousand pounds. 'Nothing I did was right,' she said laughing. 'None of my bluffs came off and I didn't get one decent hand. Well, when you play with bad players, what do you expect – they never bluff!'

My father was furious. 'That's a year of my pay. I work bloody hard for my money. How can you throw your father's money around like that? My God! Haven't you got any sense?'

'Oh, Bill! Don't be such a stick-in-the-mud. Don't be so boring, for God's sake.'

My father had buried his nose deep in a book. Listening to them, it sounded as if they were tuned in to different radio stations.

They were so different, there was hardly any ground they shared. If my father said anything about his work, my mother would groan with boredom. He was a voracious reader. I think he read everything that was ever printed. He was a champion chess player and a yachtsman – commodore and then president of the Point Yacht Club. There was a separate club for the gentiles in Durban where he wasn't allowed – the Royal Yacht

Club – but the Jewish people kept to themselves anyway. Most of the people we mixed with were our family. There were very few other, even Jewish, families that my mother thought were good enough for us.

My dad was an early-to-bed, early-to-rise man all his life. He was a warden during the war and he knitted socks on four needles. I didn't bring friends home from school because I was scared they'd see him knitting. He was a quiet, almost mysterious man, who came from a very poor family. His father had died in the Boer War in a cattle truck on his way to join his wife and six children in Krugersdorp outside Johannesburg. Dad was the youngest in his family. His brothers lived in Johannesburg but Dad had to live by the sea because of his yachting.

Joan explained to me years later that my father was a homosexual, frightened of women because of his mother. Belle Cranko was a five-foot martinet, adored by her five sons and feared by everyone else. But I don't think my father was frightened of women. He adored my mother. He would sometimes gaze at her with astonished adoration as if he did not know how such a beautiful butterfly could have landed so close to him. They never had much to talk about and she complained that he kept her like an ornament in a glass case. But he would not have a word said against her and made the servants and us tiptoe around the house when she was having 'her rest'. He took us on drives and in his yacht to the Bluff to 'give her a break' and her needs were sacrosanct in our house. Although she often drove him to hair-tearing frustration, he seemed to admire her illogicalities and impulsiveness with a worshipful awe. He thought it was charming that she did not read. Sometimes he would raise his hand and ever so gently stroke her hair, careful not to disarrange it, and a soft look would come into his eyes.

My mother used to tell us our father was 'of Spanish extraction'. Then, when they wrote a biography of my cousin John, they said the Crankos were Hollanders – something *European*. But you can still see Cranko Road in Cape Town and you can still see them all lying buried in the Coloured cemetery there. And where did I get my frizzy hair from?

Unlike the other men in my family, who owned factories and hotels, my dad always worked in a job. He had been a brilliant student who matriculated at thirteen and at eighteen he was a fully qualified chemist. He had gone to England to pass his exams as there was no pharmacy college in South Africa then. He studied the plants at Kew Gardens and learned how to roll pills. During the First World War, he told me, after he had returned to South Africa, he set up a corrugated tin roof in an alley off Smith Street. It wasn't such a main street then. Now it's almost as important as West Street that runs right through the town to the sea. He ordered a small quantity of drugs from England and then sold them to the local retail chemists. He made lifelong friends with the Durban chemists, as far out as Pinetown – that was where mostly Indians lived. His orders got bigger and bigger and eventually he ordered a large shipment of supplies from England. When this shipment was under way, the Second World War broke out and the drug companies could not send further supplies to South Africa. The rich wholesale chemists, South African Druggists in Johannesburg, wanted to get their hands on both his order and his clients, so they offered him a job and a directorship. They built a Durban office in Smith Street and my father remained there until he retired.

My mother was from a Polish family who prided themselves on being aristocrats. My mother and her sisters never worked. My grandfather, Mark Stiller, had emigrated from Lodz as a young man. On his way to South Africa, he met my grandmother, Bertha Zeffert, a Polish Jewess, in London. When he was settled, he sent for her to join him. The Polish Jews considered themselves superior to German Jews – although Russian Jews were the best. The Stillers had the reputation of being dead rich, well known for their millions – houses, factories and hotels. My mother lived for parties, cards and coffee mornings. She would spend hours in the bath, painting her finger- and toenails, putting on face masks, shaving her legs, creaming her skin. She loved to gossip and spent hours on the phone to her sisters and friends exchanging chitchat, and was always irritated when my father showed no interest. She slept during the day and went out every night and my parents passed each other, uneasily, until the ritual Sunday lunch of roast chicken with the children.

I know that my mother felt she suffered terribly from the war. We couldn't get white flour and we had to have government sugar. That spoiled all the recipes. But the worst thing was brown bread because you couldn't get white flour. My mother hated it. And she couldn't buy Wrigley's spearmint chewing gum, which she loved and chewed often to sweeten her breath. Even her CTC cigarettes were sometimes out of stock in the shops. And Dad was always nagging her to save petrol. Eventually, she befriended an American family who visited Durban and so she got supplies of the things she missed most. She and my father would argue about this when they thought we weren't listening. He thought we should just get on with it and that it was unprincipled to make an issue of the things we had to do without. After all, he said, 'There's a *war* on!' But it was a matter of pride with my mother that she should always manage to get the unobtainable.

But my mother did do her bit for the war effort. Every Tuesday afternoon she had volunteer war-work women in the garden knitting for the 'boys'. They made thick white waterproof sweaters for English sailors. I remember my mother saying, 'They can sit in the garden – I will not have them in the house. And if it rains they can sit on the stoep.'

'Why?' my father asked.

'My God, you should just see some of them!' she said. 'Honestly, you don't know where some of those women have been.'

My father held his head with both his hands and scratched his scalp.

'What have I said? What did I say?' my mother asked shrilly. 'It's true. You haven't met them, have you?' My father had no answer. He would shrug in amazement, pick up a book and go and sit on the stoep and read or disappear in his old green Dodge.

My mother also helped hostess at the Durban Jewish Club,

which ran a canteen for British servicemen, and at one time our huge house in Essenwood Road became a convalescent home, when a shipful of wounded Scots landed in Durban. They slept in a long row on the front stoep and VAD nurses would come and look after them – wheel them around the garden and read to them. My mother did first aid for a long time and I was ashamed of her because, although I had passed from first grade to second grade at school, she never passed into second aid.

I thought our home was quite normal, as children do. Once I stole some white sugar to give to Phineas because it was a treat.

'*Ai kona!*' [Oh, no!] he said. 'I don't want no white sugar. There's people dying in the war, Miss Norma.'

'That's got nothing to do with sugar,' I said, feeling hurt. 'I got it for you specially.'

Phineas looked at me sadly. 'It *is* about the sugar and about all the good things – this war's about all those things, Miss Norma,' he said.

Phineas was my friend and he was always saying funny things like that.

Edith was an old black woman with no teeth who ran our house: ordered the food and looked after the linen and cooked for the servants. She was passed on to us by my mother's oldest sister, Auntie Ettie. She had married Uncle Cyril who owned KO Bang the wholesale fisheries, so they were rich. Auntie Ettie graduated to getting a Coloured woman, who cost more. You couldn't talk to Edith properly because she was scared of losing her job. She would say 'Hau! Miss Norma,' in horror, admiration, shock or interest. When she laughed she put her apron over her mouth so we couldn't see that she had no teeth. Sometimes, in the kitchen, I would hear her speaking loudly to the other servants in Zulu and it sounded as if she was complaining. She was frightened of my mother, who was always threatening the servants with the sack. Nurse McGrath complained constantly that Edith ordered too much food for the servants. 'They go through the mealie meal like a dose of salts,' she'd tell my mother, who would flick her hand dismissively and say, 'Oh, do sort it out, McGrath.' Edith's husband had died many years before, as had her five children. Once she showed me her shrunken breasts when she was explaining how her milk dried up and one of her babies died. She hit her breast with her hand as if blaming it for letting her down. She used to go to church whenever it was her 'off' because she was very religious.

A 'girl' came in to do the washing and ironing every day. She wasn't a live-in servant and there was a new 'girl' every few weeks, usually a woman with a baby tied to her back. Sometimes they came straight from the *kraal* – village – wearing bangles around their ankles and beads around their necks. Some didn't have proper English names yet. I remember one wash girl called Ntembi who came with her baby. I crouched behind the banana trees watching as she bent over the zinc wash tub and scrubbed on the rubbing board with Sunlight soap. Her skin gleamed and her baby slept in the sun on her back and she sang to it, and every now and then she would untie the baby and swing it round and look deeply at it, croon and cuddle it. I don't think she had learned yet to be frightened of white people because when Nurse McGrath gave her her money one day, Ntembi started yelling and screaming and holding her baby up and Phineas rushed up to translate.

'Madam, she says the madam said she would get more for a day's work. Madam, she says her child is hungry and she cannot feed the baby with this money.'

Nurse McGrath looked at Phineas icily. 'Tell her if she is not satisfied, she can go. I have no power to increase the wages.'

When Phineas had transmitted this news to Ntembi she spat on the ground near McGrath and shouted loudly at her and walked away.

But the following week she was back. Her skin looked dusty and the baby was sleeping with its eyes half-open. She had taken the bangles off her feet and the beads from around her throat and Sarah gave her an apron so that she looked like a proper servant. When Nurse McGrath handed over her money, she dipped her knee and raised her hands together to her head.

But after a few weeks there was another wash girl scrubbing at the rubbing board.

12

Sarah did the cleaning and was my mother's maid. She took my mother's breakfast up to her in bed every morning at 11.30 and would stand by while my mother ate bits off the tray. A mouthful of an avocado from the garden, a teaspoonful of egg, a bite of toast, a peeled apple quarter, a spoonful of grapefruit, a biscuit with Joseph's home-made cumquat preserve.

Sarah was in charge of our mother's clothes. She was an angry young woman who banged about a lot when she wasn't with my mother. She aped my mother behind her back, catching her mannerisms and foibles in a move or a look. She was resentful and fearful of losing her job. Every day my mother would try on this dress and that scarf, these shoes and those stockings, with that hat. She discarded dresses, shoes and scarves here and there while Sarah picked them up and brought new ones from the cupboards, and the heap of cast-offs mounted on the green velvet chaise longue. Posing in front of the mirror, my mother would ask her, 'How does this look?'

'Very nice, madam.'

'Nice? These are the wrong shade of stockings with this dress. Get me the navy dress with the white spotted belt.'

'Yes, madam.'

'No, dammit! Not *that* navy dress. Don't tell me my lovely navy dress has been pinched. Oh, yes, *that's* the one. Well, but maybe I should wear red today, what d'you think?'

'Yes, madam.'

Then my mother would say 'Oh, you stupid girl,' but I knew that Sarah was very clever because she knew how to keep her job.

This would go on for about an hour every morning and then Sarah would go down to the kitchen for her lunch and regale the servants with the morning's events, tinged with humour and fraught with bitterness.

Sarah was always at war with the ironing girl. She had to be sure that there was not a single crease in anything that went in my mother's drawers and cupboards, so she would inspect each garment and then harangue the 'girl' to improve her ironing. It was a petty, fruitless existence for intelligent Sarah and she was totally dependent on it to keep her children. Meek and un-responsive as she was with my mother, she was sometimes rough and angry with Ronnie and me. I think we were a constant reminder to her of her own children and that she was unable to be with them while they were growing up.

Phineas did the floors and the garden and was our waiter. He was cheerful, friendly and helpful to everyone. He would sit outside his tin room in the full heat of the sun and make sandals out of old car tyres so that he wouldn't have to go barefoot. He had learned to do it when he was a ricksha boy on the Durban beach. Zulus used to be famous warriors led by their king, Tshaka, and wore beautiful headdresses, beads and skins, and carried shields. Their skins shone and they were very tall and strong. Now they did not have enough to eat and many looked puny, with discoloured skins. Now the Durban Corporation licensed them to act like horses, carrying tourists in their carts. But they liked them to wear their warrior clothes – for the photographs. Phineas had to give it up because his chest got sore. My dad said ricksha boys only lived till they were thirty-five. They died from the strain of it. Phineas sometimes disappeared for a couple of hours and we would see him sitting on a kerb in the neighbourhood, playing his guitar and singing.

Sixpence, Sarah's eldest child, came for a few weeks a year and helped everybody. He was a shy, solemn boy, seven years older than I, whose delight was to polish my mother's blue Wolseley car. When he was with us he did jobs for everyone, cleaning shoes, emptying the dirty water from the tin washing basin, carrying buckets of water from the garden tap to the servants' rooms, helping my brother Ronnie catch frogs to sell to the snake park, running to the shops for everyone – although he was not paid, he spent his holiday with his mother working very hard for our family. He used to make me lucky-bean bracelets and necklaces.

The servants lived in tin rooms behind the tennis courts. A grove of banana trees screened their quarters from view. Ronnie used to carve buddhas out of the banana trees and then we'd pray to them and the servants would laugh at us. We'd kneel down and say 'Allah! Allah be praised!' and touch the ground with our heads. Ronnie said a man told him it was good for our souls.

When I wanted to be near people I would sit on the tomato boxes by the banana trees near the servants' rooms, where it was cool and there was always someone to talk to. They missed their families and often talked about not having enough money. I used to say, thinking about Mom's Dimple Haig bottle with her tickey (threepenny bit) collection, 'Ask my mom, she'll give you some.' They'd smile and pat me on the head and Edith would sweep me onto her lap and say, 'Haai, Miss Norma!' as if I had used bad language. Sarah missed her other three children – Sixpence was the only one who ever came to our house. I often told her to let them come and live with us and she'd say, 'Haai! You spoiled kids!' and slap my leg.

Sarah was Joan's friend. She washed Joan's hair and spent ages sitting by the pawpaw tree patiently combing through the tangles, chatting with her. Joan used to give her clothes and get into trouble with Nurse McGrath.

'There are lots of *white* children who don't have enough clothes, Joan. And anyway your things are far too big for Sarah or her children. It's just a waste. I shall tell your mother.' She never threatened to tell my father. She was terrified of him. He was usually the mildest of men but he had once lost his temper with McGrath and had shouted a whole lot of things at her:

'Who would believe that *your* father was a Fenian, the way you go on?' my father had said, all red in the face. 'You're a damned disgrace of a woman!' She never forgot how angry he could get.

Joan had few words for McGrath. 'Go away,' she'd say. And if McGrath threatened her she said, 'Go away or I'll tell my father on you.'

'What a nasty, fat little girl it is,' Nurse McGrath would say.

Nurse McGrath was a nightmare in our young lives. She was cruel and hard. She punished us relentlessly and we never understood what she wanted from us. She operated a code that was unknown even to herself so she was inconsistent and she

15

was a troublemaker, always telling our mother fanciful stories of our wrongdoings in order to get us punished. She threatened me with the bogeyman and used to lock me in the linen cupboard when I was naughty. Joan usually got me out by having a tantrum and raging up and down the house until someone unlocked me. I was so frightened in that cupboard that sometimes I could hardly breathe and I thought I would be left there for ever. It was pitch-dark – the switch was outside the door – and to this day the smell of ironing makes me feel sick. Joan said she was locked in that cupboard half her life by Nurse McGrath.

Nurse MacGrath, being white, was very sharp with the servants. Grandpa Mark had her brought out from Ireland when my mother first got pregnant because he didn't trust a black woman to look after his grandchild. She was remote with us and spent most of her time in her room at the back of the house downstairs. She used to try and ingratiate herself with my mother and do everything to please her but my mother was either bored with McGrath or did not want to confront any of the household issues, and hated having to speak with her.

Joseph was the thin, wiry old cook and wore a fishbone in his hair. Everybody asked his advice. My mother would call down to the kitchen:

'*Joseph!* Is it going to rain today?'

'Yes, Miss Millie,' he would say, running like a streak up the stairs. 'At four o'clock.' Then, having got halfway up the stairs, he would run back to the kitchen.

Joseph was always right. He used to help me with my sums. He could produce a meal for thirty unexpected guests and would whistle through his teeth with dislike for McGrath as he went through the menus with her each day. He had been the cook in my grandparents' home when my mother was little; he still cooked her special delicacies and sent decorated trays to her room, and, unlike the other servants, who only called her 'madam', he called her 'Miss Millie'.

The servants never fought over things as we did. When Nurse McGrath gave Joseph a piece of leftover cake, he shared it out with the others – and they always gave Sixpence the biggest.

16

On Saturdays when we got our pocket money, we gave them some of our sweets. They never ate them in front of us but we had seen them bite pieces off to share when they were all together. They protected each other and if one of them got into trouble, the others would vehemently deny the culprit's wrongdoing. They had a strong wall of solidarity. They were also friends with all the other servants up the street. They weren't allowed to visit each other in their rooms but they would shout across the hedges when they thought their madams were out.

The chauffeur, Philemon, waited in the kitchen, picking his teeth, talking to Edith, until my mother needed him. He was very fat and very senior because he was the driver. He had a black suit and tie and wore a special peaked cap. When my mother went out in the car with him he was very proud and swept open the door for her. But when he took us for drives, he was jovial and would take off his cap, loosen his tie and undo the top button of his shirt. He would stop at a café and ask us to buy him a Coke and then he'd hand it round to us all to have a drink, although my mother wouldn't let us drink out of the same things as the servants. He knew everything that was happening in the neighbourhood and he used to laugh at my brother Ronnie, who was a member of the Essenwood Road gang, and warn him that he would get into trouble one day. He knew all the other servants in the houses roundabout and he used to stop the car and have chats with them.

Philemon despised Nurse MacGrath but he was the only one of the servants she would converse with. He never gave her any of the information about my mother that she sought. He lounged with his back propped up on the fridge or the kitchen table, looking at her sideways, fiddling with a piece of stick between his teeth, and jeered at her. 'What's a woman like you want to know about whether Mrs Cranko won at the horse races for? You a bit nosey, eh? You just take care of that baby – because you the nurse, isn't it?' Then he would give a big bellow of a laugh and walk out through the kitchen door, swinging his legs.

Philemon often took Ronnie and me to Mr Tshabalala's

house in Pinetown. He was black but he was a very important man. He used to shake our hands and he called me 'Norma'. He never said 'Miss Norma' as black people usually did. And he used to call Ronnie 'You scallywag!' and ruffle his hair. We played wonderful games of hide-and-seek and bok-bok with the piccaninnies and Indian children in the back while the black and Indian men had a meeting in the little house. Mrs Tshabalala gave us green lemonade and iced pink cakes for tea and she never minded if I didn't eat them. On the way home Philemon would say, 'If you tell where we went, I won't take you for drives no more.'

'What do you all talk about?' Ronnie once asked him.

'About business,' Philemon said.

'Are you going to get the land back?' Ronnie asked, remembering our father's bedtime stories.

Philemon laughed. 'You kids know a lot, don't you? You just hush up, eh?'

Of course we never told. We loved going to Mr Tshabalala's and it was our secret.

'Don't you feel,' I asked Joan, when we were in our bedroom, 'that everything's coming to an end?'

'What? What's ending?'

'I don't know,' I said. 'Now, every day when I wake up, it feels as if it isn't going to last.'

'What?'

'Everything.'

'Well, that's silly,' said my big sister.

'Maybe I'm going to die of my blood,' I ventured, thinking of Grandma Belle, after whom I was named, who had died of pernicious anaemia.

'There's nothing wrong with your blood.'

'Mom says I look anaemic.'

'You look OK to me.'

But these days I felt everything was tinged with sadness. I had a premonition of my death and would go up close to the bathroom mirror and stare at myself without recognition. And I thought that everybody around me was getting sadder and sadder as if they knew something that I didn't. When he was reading, my dad would frown, and sometimes he wasn't looking at his book. He folded himself right into the chair and his brown eyes always looked anxious. Joan stopped bringing friends home from Durban Girls' College, and she spent more and more time in our bedroom eating chocolates and getting fat. Sometimes at night I heard her sniffling and it frightened me. My baby brother Markie, whom we called Mangelwurzel, was two, and never seemed to stop crying. I thought about my mom and how she was going out more and more, sleeping later every morning and resting every afternoon. I felt I wanted to be with her all the time but I hardly saw her. And when I was with her, I loved her so much that I would go silent. I felt awkward and bumbling and, when I went to kiss her, she would say, 'Don't mess up my hair.' Then I hated her and I knew my feelings were all wrong.

At night or in the early hours of the morning, when she came home, she would tiptoe into our room and bend down and kiss me. I loved the smell of her perfume – always Chanel No. 5 – and the feel of her soft mink fur, worn even in the stifling Durban heat, brushing against my face. It was the best moment of every one of my days. Recently, she had twice forgotten to come. I felt that she was getting further away from me. But I couldn't explain to Joan what I felt – I couldn't explain my feeling that everything was coming to an end.

I went down to the kitchen. The servants had finished clearing and washing up the lunch things and Phineas was taking off his waiter's clothes. Edith was putting the leftover food away in the huge fridge and Sixpence was stirring a pot on the cooker for their lunch.

The servants didn't eat our kind of food. They ate mealie meal and *samp* (boiled husked corn pips) and stew with a lot of tomatoes. I told them they'd get sick. The doctor said I was too thin and had to eat a lot of fruit and meat and have Radio Malt every day. Except for Edith and Philemon, who were fat, the servants were very thin and I told them what the doctor had said to me. Phineas laughed. 'Where we going to get that kind of

19

food from, Miss Norma?' he asked me.

I told my mom that the servants were very thin as well so they must also need lots of fruit and meat.

'Don't be silly, Norma darling,' she said. 'They're not like us. They don't eat things like that.'

'They do, they do, they do,' I said. 'Just ask them, you'll see.'

'Go and play,' my mother had said. 'There are lots of things you don't know about. Don't be silly about it.'

I looked at skinny Phineas now, such a funny, lovely friend.

'Where's Sarah?' I asked.

'She's gone to her mother's funeral,' Phineas said.

'You can't have two funerals,' I said. 'She went to her mother's funeral last month, Mom said.'

'Hau! You white people,' said Phineas. 'You can only have one mother!' He picked me up and sat me on the table. 'All the aunties who look after Sarah's children are mothers. We have many mothers. Look! Who's going to look after Sarah's babies while she's here in Durban working?'

'Well, why are they always dying, then?' I asked him.

'Poor people die a lot, Miss Norma.'

'Why?' I asked. 'What of?'

'Of having no money,' Phineas said.

'Well, my mom thinks she's gone to see her boyfriend,' I said tartly.

Phineas looked sad. 'Why were you so naughty in the dining room today, Miss Norma?' he asked. I swung my legs and didn't answer him. 'You children must have respect for your parents.'

'Why?'

'Hau!' he said. 'Because they your *elders*. Look at Sixpence, how he listens to his mother. He can only visit here for a few weeks every year. The rest of the time he must stay with his other mothers, his aunts. Sixpence can't have a house like you. He doesn't have food like you. He doesn't have anything like you. Where Sixpence lives is nothing. Not much water, no toys, no books. Sixpence doesn't treat his mother like you. You know, you a very lucky girl.'

'I don't feel lucky,' I said.

20

Edith called everyone to go out to the back to eat their lunch and they went, leaving Phineas and myself in the kitchen.

'The master's worried about the moles in the tennis court, Miss Norma,' he said.

A cold terror struck me. I jumped off the table and tried to run out of the kitchen but Phineas swept me back onto the table.

'You sit there, Miss Norma,' he said. 'I want to show you something.' He went to the cleaning cupboard and came out with his hands behind his back. Then he swept them forward in front of my face. 'Here's your new doll. I found it!'

I gasped. I felt my face going red. My secret was out. My nightly diggings in the tennis court had been discovered.

'You make a lot of trouble for everyone, Miss Norma. Why you do this?'

'Oh, Phineas,' I said, beginning to cry, 'don't tell on me.' What if they all found out that it was because I was so naughty that everything was going wrong with the family? McGrath was always taking my dolls away to punish me because she said I was bad. I had to put them somewhere safe, where only I could find them: in case I suddenly had to run away. How could I explain this to Phineas?

'I not tell, Miss Norma,' said Phineas. 'But why you do this?'

Unable to express my insecurity and unhappiness, I looked at him through a blur of tears. 'I don't know,' I said. 'We're all dying.'

Phineas picked me up and rocked me in his arms. 'Poor little girl,' he crooned. 'Never mind. Phineas will look after you. Look! Phineas looks after all your dolls.'

And there behind the old carpet in the cleaning cupboard he showed me them – all my dolls sitting in a row on the floor! When he rolled the tennis court and 'de-moled' it, he had kept my secret. He had unburied my dolls and he was looking after them.

'Will you always work for us, Phineas?' I asked him.

'We don't know, Miss Norma,' he said. 'We try.'

· 2 ·

I never spoke much to my brother Ronnie after his first son was born. After that we didn't know quite what to say to each other.

But when we were kids, Ronnie was my best friend. He was my moral adviser and the authority in my life that I obeyed. He was two years older than I and he belonged to the Essenwood Road gang. They didn't admit girls but Ronnie persuaded them to let me come along as a nurse, so I ran all over the Berea with them.

The Berea was the posh part of Durban where all the rich people lived. It was high on a crest with streets leading off central, steep Marriott Road down to the race course at the bottom. From the upstairs veranda of our house, we could see over the town, where West Street led straight through the shopping centre down to the beach. On the other side, where Grandpa Mark owned Gray Street, the Indians had their shopping centre and the big Indian market. But our family mostly lived in Essenwood, Musgrave or Springfield Roads, off Marriott Road. Our grandparents' house was in Ridge Road, right at the top of the crest, where everyone could see it.

In subtropical Durban the vegetation was lush and the houses had huge gardens with a profusion of plants – mango and avocado trees, great hydrangea bushes, bougainvillea, lilies, creepers and huge coloured flowers of all kinds. Our auntie Thel won the Durban garden competition almost every year, but sometimes Auntie Ettie won it. Some people had two gardeners – a good gardener was a real prize. Our aunties often spoke about swapping them the way I swapped comics with my friends.

Our gang was well known by all the servants in the Berea and they used to shake their heads and call to us as we raced down the back streets where they had their *kias* (rooms) at the back of the houses, beyond the kitchen gardens. I tagged behind the gang, carrying a bottle of ST37 antiseptic and a wad of cotton wool. I had to use them quite often. Apart from splinters and scratches from tree-climbing and cart-making – with stolen pram wheels, tomato boxes, nails and tools – the boys carried knives, and when they met the Sydenham Road gang, the fighting was sometimes serious and resulted in slashes. Then I'd try to run home in terror but I usually got lost on the way. I hid in places where Ronnie would be sure to find me, pretending to be busily engaged in a game of my own. He'd stand looking at me for a moment or two with a concerned look on his face and then either take me back to the gang or home with him. Or, if he was too busy to come and get me, he would send his dog, Dort Rex, to lead me back to wherever he was.

But Ronnie became too ashamed of this behaviour and he said, 'Look, you can't come with us if you're scared. I can't have *my* sister being skitzy. Either come with us and cut the tears or else stay at home.'

So after that I had to pretend not to be scared. This was difficult. I had to think about it a lot, mainly at night in bed when I would swear resolutions and imagine myself not being frightened of anything. I would conjure up terrifying situations and often I was so scared by my own imaginings that I was unable to sleep.

But I did learn to widen my eyes instead of screwing them up; keep my hands at my sides instead of raising them to my face; smile and shake my shoulders nonchalantly instead of flinching. Inside I churned and trembled with fear. I was frightened of the punch-ups and knife fights of the gang, of spiders in martingulu bushes and banana trees, of being caught when we broke into houses and stole Cokes from strange fridges, of being drowned or getting sunstroke when we went swimming in the blistering heat at South Beach, of the group of black men who collected in Overport Drive in the evenings and drank skokiaan and shouted drunkenly at us as we passed, and of the strange dogs barking at us from nearly every gate, trained to kill intruders. Life with the gang was hot, fast and exciting.

Their everyday activity was playing marbles and the object was to get the opponent's goens by nabbing (winning) ten of their glassies – which would win you their ironie – and five ironies won you a goen. My brother Ronnie was the Durban champion marble-player and I was very proud of him.

There were usually about eight of us in our gang. Lots of local boys tried to join and our boys would set them tasks: 'Run across the racecourse during a race and you can join – OK?' 'You can join if you break into the Campbells' house in Musgrave Road – and bring evidence.' 'You can join if you win three goens in a week.' Of course no one could ever do any one of these impossible tasks and admissions were made on more secret criteria, of friendship and trust.

The gang shared pocket money, sweets, comics and condensed milk and had competitions to see who could pee on a wall from the greatest distance. Dennis always won – by miles. He would stand behind the boy who could do it from the farthest point, whip out his willie and not only hit target, but the stream would go up in a great boastful arc before it hit the wall. Furious with my impotence, I would chant:

> 'My friend Billie has a four foot willie
> And he showed it to the girl next door.
> She thought it was a snake
> So she hit it with a rake
> And now it's only two foot four!'

I hoped they squirmed at their little two-inch jobs, and it made me feel better.

Our gang tolerated me without much enthusiasm, and the Sydenham boys ignored me altogether.

Every Saturday morning Ronnie would take me to a ten o'clock film at a café bio in West Street. This was sometimes more frightening than the real knife-life of the neighbourhood. I remember seeing a film about concentration camps with thin walking skeletons in striped pyjamas. One of them died and the other cut a piece out of his leg and ate it. They got a dirty tin of fat from somewhere, scraped it out with their fingers and ate that. I could never eat fat or butter after that.

Ronnie was the gang leader but his position was often threatened by Dennis. So Ronnie had constantly to prove his superiority. One night he woke me up and dressed me. Joan and I shared a bedroom and Ronnie slept on the stoep leading off it. Mangelwurzel slept, or rather cried, in Nurse McGrath's room. Joan woke up when she heard us getting dressed.

'What you doing?'

'I'm taking her out for a walk,' Ronnie said.

'It's too late to go walking now. It's pitch-dark outside and you may get hit on the head.'

'She'll be all right with me,' Ronnie said with all the authority of his nine years. 'D'you want to come?'

'Where you going?'

'To get an ice cream.'

'No,' said Joan sleepily. 'It's too far, and I'd better stay here in case anyone comes in. Mom's not home yet. But you shouldn't take her.'

'She's got to grow up *some time*,' Ronnie said.

'OK.' Joan, at twelve, accepted this. Between them they shared responsibility for my development. 'Well, it'll be good for her. But you'll get into bad trouble if anyone hears you,' Joan said, 'specially Nurse McGrath. Be careful.'

We crept out of the house and walked down to the beach. It was a black starry night with the velvety subtropical feel that is special to Durban – warm and blue after the sweaty heat of the day. The mosquitoes whined around us as we walked down steep Marriott Road on our way to the beach, passing houses with much smaller gardens than ours, built up on one side to be straight. It was so steep that if I ran down, I felt I couldn't stop; as if I would tip head over heels right down to the bottom. We passed the racecourse, and then faced the long walk down the whole of West Street, past John Orrs, Payne Brothers and all the big stores with their lighted windows full of shiny new things.

I felt proud and grown-up to be walking with Ronnie, though it was a long way and he walked very fast and I was sleepy. Ronnie was in a hurry. The strap of one of my sandals broke in the middle of West Street, so I threw them both into the doorway of a shop and went on barefoot to the very end of West Street, to the South Beach.

Ronnie broke a window and climbed into the Cooey Tearoom. I waited outside as I was too short to jump up, my heart thumping with terror, nervously looking around to see if there was anyone about. The sound of the sea was a roar as I strained for any noise that would mean possible detection. I began to shake and thought of calling out to Ronnie but I knew if I did he would be angry. I shivered and felt myself go cold from stress as I waited for him. Then I saw his legs come out of the window. His arm stretched down to me. 'Psst, take these,' he said. He'd got us each an Eskimo Pie and he climbed down carefully carrying a Kandycone for Joan – which immediately began to melt.

On the way home Ronnie ate all three ice creams – as usual I didn't feel like eating and Joan's wouldn't have lasted the long walk home. We weren't in a hurry to get back and Ronnie took the opportunity, as he often did, to give me a lecture.

'You shouldn't be frightened of things like that – windows, grown-ups, blood and things. Just don't do *wrong* things. I paid for them. I put three tickeys on the counter for the man. You shouldn't make people suffer. You just have to pay for what you do. And most of the blood you see is at the bioscope, isn't it? It's just tomato sauce, OK?'

'OK.'

'And you shouldn't call Phineas "Jim" like the others do. You should use his real name. I know he's black and everyone thinks they can't be friends. But they can. Dad thinks so too.'

'Why?'

'Because black people are people just like us.'

'Well, why does everyone call him Jim then?'

'Because they're arseholes.'

My brother Ronnie was something of a feminist and I was never allowed to make excuses for things because I was a girl.

'You can do anything – even maths.'

'Why?'

'Don't always say "why", you stupid. Being a girl isn't anything different. People only think it is. That's why they make them wear dresses. It's because girls can climb trees and do everything boys can but if they're in a dress they don't want people to see their broeks.'

'Boys always laugh if they see girls' broeks,' I said.

'Well, that's it, isn't it? If grown-ups didn't put boys in trousers and girls in dresses, boys couldn't laugh, could they? And if they gave girls penknives they'd practise and wouldn't cut themselves. So you can do anything boys can – even marbles if you practised. You just remember that, OK?'

My brother Ronnie was a very strong influence in my life. But there was an even stronger one.

At night Dad came to tuck us up. He took over from Nurse McGrath, who would say, 'It's too late, Mr Cranko, to keep the children up,' in her generally disapproving way. Dad just ignored her or frowned at her and she would bustle out, her white starched uniform rustling. Then he sat at the end of my bed.

'Tell me the one about Europe, Ireup and Syrup and everyone had to eat potatoes and then they had none left, and they went to America.'

'But I told you that one last night.'

'OK, tell me about the good king.'

'I've told you that one often. There are lots of stories.'

'Oh, go *on*, Dad. *Please!*'

'Well, once there was a king. He wasn't the usual sort of king, like Elizabeth and Margaret's father. He was a real king, a black king. He had lots of land and lots of people and lots of wives.'

'Why?'

'Why! Lots of land to grow food on for the people and let cattle graze, so they could have meat and milk and fur. Lots of people because they loved him and lots of wives so they could all be friends and share the work and the babies.'

'So then?'

'So then the rich white people wanted his people's land and he wouldn't sell it to them.'

'Why?'

'Because land was the best thing to have. The rich whites wanted to give him money. But money is only important because it buys things and the king's people had all the things they needed. They had houses, specially built for the weather. They had lots of good food and milk, fresh and ready to take when they wanted it. They had beautiful beads and feathers. They were healthy and had special doctors. They didn't even have to have Radio Malt every day. They had lots of friends and sang wonderful songs and danced beautiful dances and played very special music. And they had good rules to live by and so they were happy. They didn't need money. That's only pieces of tin and paper. You can't do anything with *actual* money, you have to change it for something you want.'

'Why?'

'Say you were hungry and I gave you a carrot in one hand and a sixpence in the other. You couldn't eat the sixpence. You'd want the carrot, wouldn't you?'

'So then what?' I asked, thinking I'd rather have my pocket money than a carrot.

'So then the whites decided to fight the king and his people for their land.'

'That's not fair!'

'No, it's not. There's quite a lot of things that aren't fair, aren't there? What can you do about that? You can say "It's not fair" and get very cross, or you can just do nothing about it and then it'll *never* get fair. Or you can say "It's not fair and *I'm* always going to try to make it fair".'

'So then what? Tell me about the guns,' I said, trying to duck the homily.

'So then the rich whites got guns. The black people didn't have guns, you see. They didn't want anyone else's things so they didn't bother to invent them. And they raided the people and the people fought back and over four thousand of them got killed.'

'And then what happened to the king?' I asked, shivering with what was to come.

28

'They cut his head off, thinking that would show all the other black people how powerful they were and that they didn't care that he was a king.'

'Well, then the goodies just lost.'

'The story isn't finished,' Dad said. 'Those people will always care about their king. Those people still want their land back and ever since then they have been planning to get it back. And one day they will.'

'When?'

'When you are a big woman.'

'Why?'

It was the story of King Bambata and the 250 years of resistance which resulted in the 1906 Rebellion. I thought my father made his stories up, but I was to learn that they were lessons in history – a progressive brand of history, which was not to be found in our South African school textbooks.

After our foray into the Cooey, and the very long walk uphill home to the Berea, Ronnie and I climbed up the drainpipe to the stoep and crept back to bed.

There was a dreadful fuss the next day. The police came to question Ron. Dad had to come home from his office. Mom was crying with shame, and Nurse McGrath kept on saying over and over, 'Oh, my dear, oh, my dear, what a pity it is.' And she kept on telling my mother that my shoes were lost.

But Ronnie was the hero of the neighbourhood and his position as gang leader was secure for a long time after that.

Dort Rex Blackblankenberg obeyed everything Ronnie said. He waited outside school all day for Ronnie and then lay quite still under the avocado tree in the garden while Ronnie propped his books on Dort Rex's stomach and did his homework. He slept on Ronnie's bed, sat at Ronnie's feet and tolerated the rest of the family. When Ronnie said, 'Fetch Norma,' Dort Rex would find me and tug me by my dress so that I had to follow him back to Ronnie.

Ronnie built a house in the avocado tree and only he and I were allowed in it. Joan used to go up with him but, at twelve, she was now too grown-up. Not even members of his gang were allowed. He stocked it with tins of food pinched from the kitchen, knives, comics and lots of screws and nails. Once up there I had to keep dead silent. It was a reading place and Ronnie would say a hundred times a week in response to my chatter or questions:

'Shut up and read your book. Do you want to grow up *ignorant?*'

Ronnie had a 'stinks cupboard' where he and his friends made concoctions of chemicals. I wasn't allowed in there because I was too young. It was upstairs, next to the linen cupboard. Once when Nurse McGrath had locked Ronnie in the linen cupboard for being naughty he got a very bad asthma attack in there and the doctor had to be called.

In July our second cousins, Alan and John, used to visit us from Johannesburg. They used to make stink bombs and throw them off the stoep and try to hit the grown-ups when they were going out at night. And they used to run strings about six inches from the floor so the grown-ups would trip up. It was very exciting. They turned our bedrooms into 'ghost trains' – put red paper on the lights, made weird faces and masks and put torches in them for eyes. When Alan and John were in the house, everything became lively and full of excitement. We went on trips to the beach, fishing, on picnics, and everyone in the house would show off – even our parents. We would apple-pie Nurse McGrath's bed, knowing that the grown-ups didn't want to punish us in front of visitors, so we got a month off scot-free for our wrongdoings.

Alan was a great joke-teller. I never understood jokes when I was little but I used to laugh anyway. Some of our jokes lasted for years and were like a conspiracy against grown-ups.

'What happens if you cross a man with a sheep?' Alan once asked us all, sitting in the breakfast room.

'Don't know,' shouted John, Joan, Ron and I.

'You get a baby boy called Baaa-zil!'

Everyone roared with laughter, and we all went round for days saying 'Baaa-zil, Baaa-zil'. Whenever anyone called Basil came to the house, or if anyone referred to someone called Basil, Joan, Ronnie and I would scream with laughter and say 'Baa-baa-baa-zil!' and we would be sent to our rooms for being rude.

And from then on, if Ronnie ever wanted to make me laugh, he'd say 'Baa-zil' and I'd double up in spasms of laughter.

After I turned seven, Ronnie took me everywhere with him: to the fair at the beach, on the big wheel, the bumper cars, in the ghost train and on the switchback. He also knew a jazz band and when our parents were out on Saturday nights we would creep out and go down to the Geek Club near the harbour and sit with the band and they would buy us Cokes. He called *me* Vroom-Vroom the Dynamo but he lived his days packed with activity and incident, bunking school whenever he chose – somehow keeping up with the work – racing around the neighbourhood and beyond, getting to know people in the town and at the fun-fair, selling his silkworms in the Indian market and bringing home strange-smelling herbs and magic potions. He always had large projects on the go: building radio sets, carts, boxes and rabbit- and chameleon-hutches. We would lie on our tummies watching the chameleons, putting coloured bits of paper and cloth underneath them to see them change colour. Ronnie would let them out of their cages to wander about but we caught flies for them in case they weren't getting enough to eat. Under his bed on the stoep, Ronnie kept shoe boxes with holes punched in the lids for silkworms, caterpillars and spiders, and he once had a big cardboard box with a green snake which was his pet. Joseph made him throw it away because it was poisonous and later I heard the servants exclaiming with horror in the kitchen, because it was a dangerous green mamba and we could have been killed. But it liked my brother Ronnie, while he had it, and lay curling itself around his arm and neck when he played with it. But we all hated the cockroaches which crawled around everywhere. Ronnie and I hunted and killed them. They were mainly in the kitchen, although disinfectant was put down nearly every other day – I think they were immune to it.

The only times I remember Ronnie being still was when he was lying under the avocado tree doing his homework, or asleep in his bed on the stoep.

Frequently he would go into Dad's garage and open the petrol cap of the green Dodge and sniff the petrol. I wanted to as well but he wouldn't let me near it.

'You're too young,' he said, 'you're never to do this.'

'Why?'

'Shut up. Because I said so. Never.'

And I never did. And I always think that may have been why, in the end, he got so sick.

· 3 ·

'It'll be just like a vacation . . .' my mother said.

I paled. My heart thumped. I started to shake with fear. 'No, *please, Mommie, no!*' I began to cry. Five rounded blades in a circle turning into my arm, the blood and the pain of a vaccination were something I could not bear to go through again.

My mother smiled proudly and looked at Auntie Thel. 'This child has always been sensitive, you know. She takes these things to heart. When I told Joan and Ronnie, they seemed hardly surprised. Well, I suppose she's younger. She can't be happy about leaving her father – although God knows there's little enough he does about *that*.'

I watched them, alerted. What did vaccination have to do with my father? As a fearful child, I often misheard.

'Please, Mom,' I said, 'I'm *scared*.'

'No need to be,' she said. 'It'll be like a holiday. I'll go up to Johannesburg this week with little Markie, and then you and Joan and Ronnie will come up in the train in a few days' time. I'll be married to Uncle Oscar then and you'll go to a new school and we'll all live in a big house in Saxonwold with your stepsister and your two stepbrothers. It'll be a new life. It'll be just like a vacation.'

I felt a moment of relief. I had misunderstood. I was not to be vaccinated. I was to go on holiday.

The only holiday I remembered was when Nurse McGrath took me on the *Cape Town Castle* to visit her friend at Seapoint when I was two. I had cried till my throat was dry before we left. I didn't want to go with McGrath and I thought all my family were going to have a lovely time without me. My memories of that voyage were sharp and painful. I had thought the children in the playroom knew one another and that I was the only stranger, so I wandered out, down a long corridor, and got lost. I began to cry. A man stopped and asked what I was looking for.

'I want my room and I want my nanny,' I told him.

'Which is your room?'

'It's got a blue door,' I said.

We both surveyed the rows of blue doors. He took me up lots of steps and down lots of corridors, into lounges and bars. His hands were sweaty and I could feel his panic. Nurse McGrath was very angry when she found me.

'You want chaining up, you naughty girl,' she said. 'Wandering off like that on your own. Dear Jesus!'

That feeling of being lost amid doors that all look like my door has often been with me.

I looked up at my mother. Her face was flushed and excited. I had been called out of class because she had come to see me during school time. I was at Maris Stella convent and had been there as a weekly boarder on and off since I was four, when my brother Mangelwurzel was born. I was now eight years old. We lived about ten houses down from the convent at 417 Essenwood Road. I don't know why my family wanted me reared in a Catholic convent. Although we were not brought up in a religious way, our family followed the Jewish traditions. At the time when I was beginning to fall in love with gentle Jesus and had determined that I would be a nun, my family was *kleibing nachas* because my uncle Alf, my mother's eldest brother, became a founder member of the Orthodox shul. I tried to explain what it was all about to my Catholic friends and when I started getting cold responses because 'the Jews killed Jesus', I applied to Sister Eugenius (whom my father called Sister U-strike-us because she used to hit me across my knuckles with a ruler) to let me go to confession and try and repent for Uncle Alf. But Jews weren't allowed into confession.

Having sent me to the convent, my mother must have had certain misgivings because she then arranged for me to attend Talmud Torah – the equivalent of Sunday school for Jews – on Sunday mornings. I was frightened by the foreignness of the other

34

kids. They sang in a funny language about things I couldn't understand and pretended they were trying as hard as they could to get to Israel because it said in the Bible they should. It wasn't surprising that I found it somewhat confusing. My father used to hum 'Palestine for the Palestinians' to himself in the car to melodies of Italian operas or Beethoven symphonies even though he was a Saturday synagogue-going Jew.

After a couple of months at Talmud Torah, I gave up religion and I never took to it again.

My mother was frightened of nuns so she wouldn't come inside the convent, and we were standing on the grass verge in front of the car. The car door was open and there was a sense of urgency, as if my mother was already in flight.

So everything *was* coming to an end.

'Are we taking Phineas and the others?' I asked her.

'*Darling!*' my mother said. 'Don't be silly. At Uncle Oscar's house there are *lots* of servants.'

Thelma, my mother's third sister, said: 'And they tell me they are a lot better trained up in Johburg than the Durban ones. All you get here are Zulus.'

I began to cry. My mother kneeled down and put her arms around me.

'Don't cry, Normie. You'll see. It's going to be wonderful. And when Daddy wants to see you he can always send for you. You can have holidays in Durban.'

'What about Nurse McGrath?' I asked.

'Nurse McGrath is so lucky,' my mother said. 'She has found a wonderful position looking after lots of babies – at the Coloured Child Welfare near Mitchell Park. Uncle Oscar is going to be a real father to Markie and all of you, so we won't need a nanny any more. And Sarah can go home and look after all those children of hers, and Edith, well, Edith is too old to work now.'

Everything had been arranged. I had felt for a long time that everything was ending but when had it all been planned? No one in the kitchen had said a word to me. Did they know?

'I don't like Uncle Oscar,' I said.

35

'Don't be silly,' my mother said. 'You've never even met him.'

Some years later my mother told me about Oscar.

I met him long ago (my mother said) in Johannesburg. Anne, our cousin, was celebrating her twenty-first birthday and I was invited. Only me. I was the eldest. I was eighteen years old and it was my first real party. My sisters were so jealous! I went with Mommy and my second brother, Walter, who was only little. Daddy gave us his new car and the chauffeur drove us up to Johburg. It wasn't like now. There were no tarred roads and it took three days.

The party was marvellous. They had a huge house in Park-town, with a sweeping staircase. There was dancing downstairs, and outside there was a marquee for food and games. And of course there was a band. Anne's parents did everything they could for her. But what could they do? She had those huge feet and she was over five foot five. But despite all that, she was a lovely person. Her figure was like an ironing board. I felt so sorry for her. Mind you, eventually she married Louis – he was quite a catch – a dentist. I'll never know what he saw in her. She was a real plain Jane.

As soon as I arrived, I went up to the bathroom and on my way down the stairs I looked at the dancing. I saw the most hand-some boy I'd ever seen in my life dancing with Mavis Gevisser – she was a nothing if ever I saw one! I couldn't take my eyes off him. I danced with lots of the boys but I kept looking to see where he was. I asked Auntie Rose who he was and she said, 'Oh! That's Oscar Goldberg. He's a polite enough boy – a stud-ent of chemistry.' In the marquee at dinner, imagine my surprise when he came up to me. He'd been asking everyone who *I* was! He asked me to dance and we danced together the whole of that evening. I was so in love.

The next day he came back to the house and proposed to me! He did it properly like you read in the books. And he brought some flowers for Mommy.

I didn't know what to say but immediately knew I wanted to

marry him. I'd never seen anyone so handsome – like a film star. I couldn't say yes. I had to ask Daddy. My mother didn't have any say in things like that in our family and anyway I could never talk to her about anything. I mean, we all loved her a lot but she was so awful.

She was from the East End of London – Spitalfields, would you believe it – and my father was ashamed of her. She ate whatever she felt like, she didn't care about her figure and she had absolutely no taste at all. She made friends with just anyone – even Greeks. Her clothes were simply *awful* and she would just as soon wear glass as diamonds. She never knew what colour lipstick to wear and although we had lots of servants she used to want to do the cooking herself. We hated that. Daddy used always to tell her to get out of the kitchen – that's what the cook's there for. But she was stubborn in her own way and she defied him and made him unhappy. She had no breeding. We all knew it. We learned absolutely nothing from her. Daddy even showed us how to buff our nails. Honestly, I didn't want to introduce her to my friends, I was so ashamed of her.

Daddy was from Poland – from the Polish aristocracy. He had an uncle who was the mayor of Lodz, as you know. Well, we'd tell people that Grannie was from Plymouth and then she used to go around telling everyone she grew up in Whitechapel. It was awful.

I adored Daddy but as the oldest of six of his daughters and three sons, I never got enough from him. They were always scrambling for his attention and love. I was Daddy's favourite child. I'm sure I was. Daddy was very strict and when he hit us we knew it was for our own good. He hated punishing us and he said so, but we benefited from it. We all thank him for it now. He wouldn't let us buy clothes from shops. Mommy had to make them and she couldn't sew for toffee. But Daddy said it would help us not to grow up proud and would make us appreciate things when we were older. And it's true, we did. We weren't allowed to play with other children because, of course, most of the children had no manners. And also there were all sorts of diseases you could get from them. We owe everything to Daddy.

Anyway, when Oscar proposed, I told him I would talk to Daddy when I got home and then he could come down to the house in Durban. Daddy had built a great big house in Ridge Road overlooking the whole of Durban. Everything was specially fitted – it had copper pipes, the first copper pipes ever fitted to a house anywhere in the world, I think he said. And everything was tasteful and beautiful. Daddy chose everything. There were rose-coloured carpets and there was gold around all the skirtings – oh, it was beautiful. He couldn't leave it to Mommy because she had such terribly bad taste. Even the plates, he chose.

When I got home I rushed into Daddy's study and told him all about Oscar. He nodded his head. He was always so wise and comforting.

'So little Millie has fallen in love,' he said. 'Well, we'll have to find out all about this Mr Oscar Goldberg.'

A few weeks later Daddy told me he had invited Oscar down to Durban. I was in a state of such excitement waiting for the weekend. I remember rushing over to Cissie – she was much thinner then, and she lent me a beautiful white crepe-de-Chine dress. I couldn't borrow her shoes because my feet were so small but I had some white pumps.

Well, the day eventually came and Oscar arrived. He was even better-looking than I had remembered.

We weren't allowed to talk at the table, though when we had a guest, Daddy would make conversation with him. He didn't say anything to Oscar and I thought it was because he was so young – we were the same age. After lunch Daddy went to his study and Mommy, Oscar and I went into the lounge. The rest of my brothers and sisters had to go to the playroom. I felt very important and also very nervous.

Eventually Daddy sent a servant to call us into the study. Daddy said he had absolutely no objection to our getting married, we could do so as soon as I could get my bottom drawer together. 'But,' he said, 'not a penny from me. She'll have to live on whatever you can earn.'

I didn't understand that. I didn't see what money had to do

with it and I didn't understand why Daddy was being so hard on Oscar. I mean, it was quite the usual thing for a young man to be set up. Fathers or fathers-in-law were always buying them businesses or taking them into the business or something.

But Oscar left for Johannesburg the next day, and he hardly spoke to me. I hadn't realised that he had to have help to buy a chemist's shop, otherwise his degree wouldn't mean anything. Daddy told me later that Oscar didn't come from good stock. He had emigrated with his brothers from Kovno Gubernia in Russia, where his family was apparently so poor that he had to sleep on a stove to keep warm.

I was brokenhearted. I couldn't understand why everything had suddenly gone wrong. All the girls thought he was the handsomest boy they had ever seen. He got married soon after. He married a rich girl – I heard her father was a millionaire. I thought he married her because he had to have money or his whole life would have been ruined.

I nearly died. Apart from everything else – and I was so desperately in love with him – there was the shame of it. I had told everybody we were in love and that we were going to get married and then the next thing he was married to somebody else.

Daddy sometimes had evenings at home and he entertained all the leading Durban people. Even the mayor came. Bill was invited often. I don't know why Daddy liked him so much – but he did. He said Bill was one of the only real intellectuals in Durban. Daddy told me that Bill was in love with me. So I started looking at him in a different way. He was much older than me and he wasn't very handsome. He had your sort of thin face, you know. Anyway, one thing led to another – I don't remember very much about it all that long while ago now, but after we had been to a Sunday afternoon concert at the City Hall – your father always liked that boring Bach stuff – Bill proposed. I said I'd tell him the following week.

I sort of tried it out on everyone. I said to Cissie, 'What would you say if I told you Bill and I might get married?' and she said, 'Oh, Millie, what a catch! He's *wonderful* – a *real* man – and so mature.' Everyone said things like that and I began to look at

39

him in a different light. Everyone thought he was marvellous.

Bill and I got married and when I had Doreen – my first baby, who died – Oscar's wife, Miriam, had a son. When I had Joan, Miriam had a daughter. Then I had Ronnie. Two weeks before I had you, Miriam had another son. That's when she died in childbirth. I thought God would punish me for not being sad about it – but suddenly Oscar was free and I felt sure he would come and get me.

You were born at the Clarabell Nursing Home in Durban and I couldn't wait to get out of there. My milk dried up a couple of weeks after you were born. I tried to go up to Johburg but then I heard from Anne that Oscar was taking out that dreadful Sally Greenstein. I got terribly ill and that's when the doctor said I had to go away on a long trip to get better. I went on a world cruise. It was wonderful. I won the fancy-dress contest on board. The boys made a big box and I dressed up as a doll and they carried me in the box. Everyone said I was a sensation. It was terrible for me leaving you when you were only a couple of months old but the doctor made me go. The doctor said he wouldn't be responsible for my health if I didn't have a complete break. Anyway, I left you with Nurse McGrath – she was a wonderful nurse. If anything, Joan was the one I felt worried about. Ronnie was always so independent, but Joanie was a very deep little thing. She was five then and she could get very solemn about things. She was always advising me about you, Ronnie and Markie. She worried about you, you know. She was such a funny quaint little thing. Just like somebody's granny! She'd say, 'Mom, have you cuddled Norma today? Have you seen Mangelwurzel?'

I'd say, 'I haven't seen her. I've been so busy all day and Nurse McGrath says she's playing happily in the garden. I saw Markie a few minutes ago.'

And then she'd ask, 'Shall I call her in to see you?' And she'd have a stubborn tone in her voice.

Sometimes, if I said, 'No, don't bother her if she's happy,' she'd snap at me and say funny things. She was my little conscience!

But TG, you were all fine when I got back.

You kids complain that you had a miserable childhood, but let me tell you, you were known by everyone in Durban as the Sunshine Kids because you were all so happy and adorable and came from such a good home. But I suppose mothers can never do right, can they?

When I got back, I heard that Oscar was probably going to get remarried. But he didn't. After Miriam died, Oscar started writing to me. They were wonderful, passionate letters and I have kept them all. He said he could not break up what was a good marriage and no matter how many letters I wrote to him explaining what things between Bill and me were like, he just said he couldn't do it. I could never have left Bill on my own.

Three years passed and they were agony. Bill and I hardly spoke to each other. He went sailing in his rotten yacht every weekend and I played more and more poker. Everyone in Durban thought we were madly happy, and I let them – I didn't want them to feel sorry for me.

Then Oscar wrote that he was coming to Durban. At last I felt we were going to get together after all that time. Just as I was beginning to feel better about life, I found I was pregnant again. I was always getting pregnant. Mommy said Bill just had to look at me and I got in the family way. I was devastated. I went to see the doctor who did abortions for the family and he said that he couldn't do me again because it was too close to the last one. He said it could damage my insides and that I would have to have the baby. I didn't know what to do. He said the same when I was pregnant with you. I don't know how *you* happened. I never slept with your father in much more than the nine months before you were born. I must have caught you off the lavatory seat! With all you children, people didn't think your father was a homosexual, but it seemed every time I did get him to make love to me, I got pregnant. Your father hated contraceptives and I didn't know what to do. My sister Bea used to say I just had to sit on a warm chair to fall pregnant. She made me sound like a farmer's wife. But I read that nature selects the very best for breeding. I think she was jealous. She only had Eleanor and

41

then, years later when she remarried, she had Peter. But I had had five of you! My sisters only had two or three kids.

Your father was pleased when I got pregnant with Markie. He used to drive you kids around in his green Dodge and let you play with any other kids and do anything. It's because of him that you were all so wild.

But of course I adored Markie. He was so sweet – he still is. When he was four, Oscar came down to Durban to stay. My sister Beatrice had just got a divorce. She'd married Stashik Stiller – our first cousin. I didn't even think that sort of thing was legal. Can you imagine what I felt like when Oscar started taking Bea out? I think she only did it to spite me. I know my sisters have always been jealous of me – I'm the oldest, you know – but I never thought one of my own sisters would do that to me. I felt broken. I didn't want to go on any more. I couldn't see the sense in life.

And then there came that wonderful day. Oscar telephoned me one afternoon when I was having my rest. He wanted us to meet. I couldn't drive myself – I was too nervous. I got Philemon, the driver, to take me to Durban North, where he was staying with a relative of his. It was a dreadful house in Burman Drive. In those days they hadn't cleared up the swamps and that area was full of mosquitoes. I don't know how people lived out there. I always thought it was for poor whites. Some Sundays your father would take us for a drive in that area and, apart from the mosquitoes, it was overrun with monkeys. They jumped on the car and you kids used to feed them bananas. But imagine living there! Oscar said he wanted us to marry, that he'd always loved me and that he couldn't wait for me a moment longer. He said all the children would be his adored children as well and that I should start divorce proceedings against Bill.

We met for three months like that. I couldn't do anything. I didn't know how to. My brother Alfred was a lawyer and I did sort of mention it to him in a roundabout way but he was absolutely horrified. The family put up a terrible fuss, as usual. They never liked Oscar. They were always prejudiced against him.

Then poor darling Daddy died. I've never got over his death. He was young, but he had a heart attack. He had worked so hard for us and he loved us all so much that he got taken. TG, he had a wonderful life.

My life has never been the same without Daddy. He used to advise me in everything. You children laugh because I have his photograph hanging in so many rooms, but I need to feel him close to me. I was always his little girl, even when I was married. If I was ill or sad, he'd come and make everything better. Even though he always liked Bill and made him an executor of his estate instead of his own sons, he knew how hard my life was with him.

Our divorce was horrible. It was really hard to get a divorce in those days – you had to prove that your husband had done really dreadful things to you. The main one was if he slept with another woman. But you had to bring photographs of it into court. There were special people who did that work but of course Bill wasn't sleeping with anyone else. He didn't even sleep with men until after I divorced him. Bill didn't want a divorce. He was quite happy for me to be miserable. He didn't understand. He said it was because he didn't trust Oscar but I knew it was only because he wanted to keep me like a butterfly imprisoned in a cage. That's how he treated me. Like a jewel that should never be touched or something.

I had to tell the court he was a homosexual. I know it affected him – homosexuality is illegal and all that, you know, but what could I do? He didn't want a divorce. He was so gloomy about it all. He just didn't understand. They gave me a divorce but they said I hadn't proved anything against Bill with other men, and his telling me he was homosexual wasn't evidence.

We decided not to have any of that custody business. We didn't want to fight over you kids. I couldn't take responsibility for all of you anyway. Bill was the guardian, of course, but he never cared what happened to you children. When it was all over I went to Johannesburg, to the house in Saxonwold where Oscar had lived with Miriam.

I found out then that he'd loved her and he was besotted with his three kids. The house was full of her paintings and he wouldn't let me take them down. Everyone always said I could have been a famous painter, like Rembrandt – I think he's the one that painted all those dark pictures, and they called those cigarettes after him because he was so famous. I liked painting flowers and pretty things, but Daddy wouldn't let me study it. He couldn't stand bohemians and people like that. I always felt I'd missed a big chance in life.

After I lost Doreen and the doctors said I had to have another baby or they would not be responsible for my health, I had Joan, and then I thought about taking up painting but there was so much to do. Everyone in Durban was throwing parties and we often used to go up to Johburg. I couldn't have done anything regularly because I never knew what was going to come up and I didn't want to miss anything. I was very musical as well, you know. I love music. Not the kind your father likes – that Pop-popieff character and those heavy bands. But I loved the dancing music and all the boys used to say I was so light on my feet.

When we got to Johburg I was so disappointed in the house. It was gloomy – awful décor – and Oscar wouldn't let me change a thing. I wanted to do one of the rooms in a new beautiful peach shade and I just got my head snapped off. But it was a big house and it was in a very posh street.

The servants were uppity – they resented doing *anything* for you – and Oscar didn't like me having breakfast in bed and he wouldn't let me wear slacks, and Johburg was so *cold*. And he was so strict with you all – especially little Markie. He was jealous of the poor kid, you know. Well, you know men!

I did *everything* to get close to his kids but they just went their own way. Most of the time they treated me as an intruder and they always had their noses in books. I felt sorry for the motherless little things but they were cold to me and I could never get through to them about the finer things of life. They had an auntie Annie – their mother's sister – and they treated her as their mother. It was terribly hurtful for me. I had sacrificed my own children for those motherless kids, and they were just stiff-necked towards me.

44

We were married in a registry office. I had the most marvellous hat you ever saw. It sort of sloped over my face. It had a wide, floppy brim – very flattering, darling, if you were to wear something like it, with your big nose – and I wore a cream sheath dress. I got quite a shock when we were walking down the path afterwards and Oscar gripped my arm and turned me to face him. I thought he was going to kiss me but he said, 'Well, when I wanted to marry you, I wasn't good enough for your family. Your father wouldn't help me. I can't afford your extravagances – you can live on the Stiller millions.' I looked into his eyes and I could see then how hurt he still was by that meeting in poor darling Daddy's study. Of course I didn't believe him – I mean, in those days husbands always supported their wives. It was a disgrace if you worked – you poor girl.

When I married your father he was stubborn and he wouldn't take a penny from my family. I don't know what he was thinking of. How could we have lived on his salary? He earned nothing! He was a chemist! That's why Daddy bought us the house for a wedding present and gave me my own money – an allowance, it was called. I got it every month and Daddy opened a bank account for me in my married name and if ever I ran out of money, Daddy gave me more. Your father used to say I was extravagant but I wasn't raised to know the cost of things. When we were little, we weren't even allowed in shops. Daddy brought us everything. Daddy always looked after me, until he died.

When I was with your father, I used that money to make life better. It was my pin money. Your father paid all the bills. He was good about those things. But when I married Oscar, it felt as if I had to pay for everything – even your birthday presents.

His household wasn't well run. There wasn't enough help and I had to get a maid. Daddy had paid for Nurse McGrath and now I had to do without her. I never realised that dreadful woman had done so much around the house. All of a sudden everyone was asking me everything and I had never anticipated a life of drudgery, creeping around linen cupboards and worrying about what kind of hunk of meat we were going to eat. The servants in Durban were like friends, always wanting to please. In Johburg it was hard to get proper servants – all the natives wanted to work in shops and factories. And if they didn't fancy you, they'd just hand in their notice! The servants there were so spoiled and they were bloody cheeky. I tell you, going to Johburg was a terrible shock for me. And they knew absolutely nothing about living standards up there.

Oscar had told me that we would live as one big happy family and I believed him. I was very shocked when he wrote to me at the last minute and said there wasn't room for Joan and Ronnie in the house and I'd have to send them to boarding school before I left Durban. Then, shortly after we arrived – I had you and Markie with me – you had to go to boarding school as well. There really wasn't enough room. His kids had their bedrooms and we had ours and there was a tiny room for Markie, and that was that. I had to have you for the holidays and we put a little bed in the girl's room for you. But there was no room for Joanie at all. Of course I explained it to Joan and she understood. She had had a mother all her life but Oscar's daughter, who was almost exactly her age, had lost her mother when she was five years old.

But when I got that letter, I couldn't believe it. For years Oscar had written about how you would be his adored children! But it made sense. The house would never have held us all anyway. And the schools he picked were so good – the very best in South Africa. Of course Bill didn't want to pay. He said he couldn't afford it. But he did. He was always moaning about money.

That's when you went to Redhill. I fell in love with the uniform. The other schools made girls wear those awful dark gyms, but you wore red-and-white spotted blouses with Peter Pan collars, grey tunics, proper silk stockings, navy coats and eighteenth-century straw bashers. The headmistress believed in fashion for girls. It was the most expensive girls' school in South Africa. Even Elizabeth Karageorge, Princess of Yugoslavia, went there – and millionaire's daughters like Jean Erleigh. Oh, there were lots of famous people's children there. I checked that out before we sent you! We didn't know they had such a poor exam rate, and that you would have to spend years in tents while they built the bloody school. Anyway, an education is often a drawback for a girl. And you were always too bookish. Men don't like that. How was I supposed to know you were really unhappy there? Everyone told me that kids always say that when they go to boarding school. Every time I came to see you, you got itchy bumps or a sore throat or something so I thought you'd do better on your own. In any case, Oscar decided we'd have to go and live in Bloemfontein. That's why I had to leave you in Johburg so soon after we arrived. But you were fine. You had your friends – that nice little girl Adele Abel you were always talking about, whose father was a doctor and who came from Matubatuba! What an odd little thing you were – 'little ugly mug' I used to call you. And you had such quaint ideas.

Ronnie was very uncooperative. He kept running away from boarding school and he went to live with your father. He was always a wild boy – until after his first marriage. Then he settled down.

Joanie was a terrible problem. She lost a lot of weight and I thought she was too thin. I took her out of school and then she did her matriculation exams anyway and insisted on going to university, so she came down to Bloemfontein and stayed with us. Boys were always phoning and calling for her and Oscar always thought they had come for me. Once I went to the door and there was this pimply-faced boy asking for Joan, and Oscar barged up to him, grabbed him by the neck and accused him of coming to see me. We never saw that poor fellow again! Oscar was so jealous! It's a disease, you know. Anyway, when Oscar and I had rows, Joanie was always interfering and shouting at him and accusing him of being cruel to Markie or you, and eventually he wouldn't have her in the house, so she went back to Durban.

I think Oscar always knew I'd have to live in Durban. He didn't want to and the family never liked him. But I couldn't bear to be separated from my family and all my real friends. I hated Johburg. We had a few good years in Bloemfontein, and the house was absolutely wonderful – I put a lot of money into that house. But our neighbours were Afrikaners – honestly, there was hardly anyone worth mixing with. The Jewish community there were mostly Russians and they were hoity-toity with us even though Oscar was a Russian Jew. They called us Polacks and Galitzianas – dreadfully rude people. They give Jews a bad name.

I always loved Oscar – through everything. We used to have the most terrible rows and upsets, though. He never understood me and he always thought I was too extravagant. He had no idea of how to live a good life and he was always moaning about the bloody chemist's shop. Sometimes I couldn't bear all the rows – I left him quite a few times and went back to my family in Durban. Eventually Oscar got the message and sold up his chemist's shop in Bloem and we went back home.

So that's how I finally got back to Durban. That's where we belong, you know, darling.

I shifted uneasily after my mother's long story, comparing her memories with mine, marvelling at her ability to make the disasters sound like triumphs; making everything right, even if she had to turn some things upside down to put them the right way up for the picture she wanted to create. Her life had been so enclosed, so limited that anything that was not already familiar threatened and frightened her. Living in South Africa had poisoned her, had made her unable to take care of herself or of her children – had made her as dependent as a baby. And then she made a virtue of dependence! She was part of a poisoned generation that could never envisage change of any kind.

Dad, Joan, me and Ronnie.　　　　Mom in fancy dress as a doll.

Me.

The divorce picture: me, Joan, Mom, Ronnie, Mangelwurzel.

· 4 ·

Joan and Ronnie sometimes had terrible fights – screaming, yelling and hitting each other – which used to fill me with terror. But despite this, they were very close. Often I would see them walking or sitting in the garden, engaged in deep conversation. Three years separated them and they were a united front against McGrath and other grown-ups. Sometimes when I came upon them they would break off or shoo me away. And I accepted this special relationship as I accepted my parents'. I was excluded and it hurt but in some way it gave me a sense of security.

Ronnie and my father had an uneasy relationship. They were joky with each other and my father used to get exasperated with the complaints about Ronnie – which seemed to come from all quarters. He mostly turned a blind eye to everyone. I sometimes wonder if Ronnie was trying, with his madcap life, to get our father's attention. But he never really did. I suppose my father was selfish. Certainly he did not include Ronnie in his yachting or other activities but Ronnie became an adept sailor, chess and bridge player, learning from other people. And my father never participated in any of my brother's activities – football, fishing and games – as some fathers did.

But when our family was breaking up, things got worse between my brother and my father. Ronnie tried to persuade Dad not to let him be sent to boarding school and said he wanted to stay in Durban with him. My father shrugged his shoulders and said, 'Your mother wants you to.' And Ronnie, who was eleven then, shouted at Dad and was bitter and nasty.

'I hate parents,' he said. 'They don't understand anything.'
'What?'

49

'Anything! They're not responsible – the bastards! And it's not only us. They don't care about Phineas or Edith or Joseph or Philemon or Sarah or Sixpence, and what's going to happen to all of them? What about us, too? How are you going to grow up properly? What about Mangelwurzel? Mommie can't look after him and Nurse McGrath is leaving – thank God! And I've got to go to boarding school. And what about Dort Rex – and everything?'

'What are you going to do? What shall we do?' I asked.

'I'm never going to speak to them again,' Ronnie said.

Phineas and I went together to the tennis court. He got a big spade and dug up a corner of the court and we buried all my dolls together. He made a very deep hole and covered it carefully so it did not look like mole mounds. 'They'll be very safe now, Miss Norma,' he said. 'And one day you come home and you can get them all up and you'll have your family again.' And he got his guitar from his room and played me 'Tula, Tula', a Zulu lullaby, which was my favourite song.

'Oh, Phineas,' I said. 'I don't want to go.' He looked at me sadly and shook his head and lifted me onto his lap.

'You grow up right, Miss Norma, like Master Ronnie says. You be a strong girl.' And when we left, he ran down the driveway after the car, waving and shouting, *'Hamba gahle! Hamba gahle!* [Take care!]'

Edith didn't stop crying. During those last couple of days before we left for Johannesburg, she walked around the kitchen mopping her face with a man's handkerchief, and every now and then she would break into great sobbing gasps and throw her apron over her head. She was going into the absolute poverty of enforced retirement.

Sarah's face was very hard and bitter and she smacked the pots down and banged the broom on the kitchen floor. Sarah had no job to go to so she was going back to Zululand, with no income for her family.

'You people!' she kept saying. 'How am I going to feed my children? Eh?' She would bang the pot on the stove. 'You all running away, leaving me with no job? Haai!' Bang went the tin mug on the draining board. 'You people! You don't think about other people, you people! Haai!' And something else would bang down somewhere. She went on repeating, 'That madam! Haai! That madam! Hau!' as if no words could describe her anguish.

But she was very gentle with Joan. She washed her hair and sat in the garden combing it bit by bit so it wouldn't hurt, talking to Joan, telling her secrets. How that woman loved my sister Joan!

Philemon just laughed – he was going to be Auntie Ettie's driver. He looked at everything going on around him as if it was quite usual and every now and then would give a great bellow of a laugh – as when McGrath got the gold watch. He thought that was a tremendous joke and he doubled up with laughter. When we went to see him in the kitchen before we left, he said, 'You white people make so much destruction you even do it to yourselves!' And he laughed and went out of the kitchen, shaking his head and swinging his legs.

Joseph sat on the back step outside the kitchen and put Ronnie and me on each of his knees. 'It's too heavy, Master Ronnie,' he said. 'You must look after your sisters. You must respect your parents – heh, yes, even your new father. What will happen to your baby brother? Haai!' He wiped his brow in some confusion. '*Nkos pezulu!* [Lord above!]' he said, 'I don't know what is happening to this family! Who will cook for Miss Millie, eh? Who will look after the master, eh?' Tears came into his eyes and he turned away and walked to his tin room behind the tennis court, scratching his scalp with his fishbone.

My mother, always marking special occasions, called in a photographer the day before we left and there we were – recorded for all time – the unhappiest group of people you could imagine. She made a curl in Mangelwurzel's blonde hair specially for the photo. As soon as I heard the word 'photographer' I rushed into the bathroom and wet my hair and poured a bottle of Dad's Vitalis over it. It didn't lie flat but at least it wasn't a frizzy bush. Joan was overwhelmed with sorrow and just stood there in deep misery. And my mother, dressed in

51

white, looked polished and glamorous as usual.

I felt no sense of excitement about starting a new life, only a numbing dread. I didn't even think about not living with my father, I must have assumed he was coming with us – even though I had been told he wasn't. He just disappeared a few days before we left.

Ronnie and I went to his tree house for the last time and he said, 'You're allowed to talk in here today, OK?'

'What about?'

'About anything.'

'I don't want to go away,' I said.

'Well, neither do I, so what about it?'

'Nothing,' I said. 'Well, let's hide all the tins and comics for when we come back.'

'We'll never come back. I've given the tins of food to Phineas, and I've sent the comics to Sixpence with Sarah. We won't be to-gether any more, you know,' Ronnie said.

'Why?'

'Don't always say "Why", it sounds ignorant. The point is, you won't have anyone to look after you.'

'I'll be with Mom,' I said.

Ronnie sat quietly. Then he said, 'I don't want you to forget some things. Remember all Dad's stories, they're important. Don't ever think clothes are important – they're not. Always try and work out for yourself what's fair.'

'OK,' I said.

Ronnie sighed. 'You have to fight hard to do what you think is right.'

'OK.'

We sat there a little while and when we got down, Ronnie took a hammer and used the back of it to prise off the nails of the ladder so that no one could ever climb up to the tree house again. Then we went to the banana-tree buddha and prayed to Allah and Ronnie said we had to put our heads on the ground seven-teen times. Then he got his new penknife and stuck it into the buddha's heart and left it there.

For the last few nights before we left, Joan put me in her bed and cuddled me to make things better. She cried a lot, her eyes were red and she was very sniffy. Joan had always been like my real mother. She used to ask me, 'Have you brushed your teeth?' and things like that. And when I was sick she used to sit with me and read me stories. She looked after me and she used to tell me that I was beautiful. She said, 'You are beautiful inside and out. Believe me. Look in the mirror. You have to grow up liking yourself, otherwise you'll never be able to like other people.' She had frizzy hair like me and, though I knew she hated it as much as I did, she said we ought to be proud of it even if Mom was always trying to make it flat. Joan tried to shelter me from the pain of life. She put plasters on my cuts and drew funny faces on them and she defended me to everyone.

For those few days left in Durban, she mothered me even more. She packed my things and put some of her chocolates in between my clothes.

'Will you write me lots of letters?'

'You'll be living with us, won't you?'

Joan remained silent and wiped tears from her eyes with her hand. 'Well, anyway, Vroomie, I'm going to miss you like anything,' she said.

I went and sat on her big lap and she put her arms around me and we both cried. 'Don't let Mom know we're unhappy,' she said. 'She only wants a chance to live a happy life.'

'OK,' I said.

'Remember it's hard for her too.'

'Why?'

'It's hard for women to be happy, isn't it? And look at me. I'm so fat, I'll never be happy.'

'Ronnie says you can get thin whenever you want,' I said. 'And he said you shouldn't practise film stars. You should be yourself.'

'It's very hard for me,' Joan said.

'Well, don't eat chocolates any more then,' I said.

I did not know then that Joan was never to come to the Johannesburg house – she was going straight to boarding school.

I'll never forget how happy my mother was when she told me it was going to be just like a vacation I don't think she gave much thought to the fact that we would be leaving our lives – our father, Phineas and all of them, our dog, our friends and each other. She thought only of Oscar – that wonderful man – and how happy we were all going to be. But the next five years of my life *were* like a vaccination. The five blades didn't stop turning – but they turned in my heart. And it was also just like a vacation – I felt completely lost.

At boarding school I began to realise that it was the system that was wrong. It actually made people evil – sometimes without their knowledge. I became opposed to privilege for whites because I learned it led to brutality to black people.

I was a boarder at Redhill School in Johannesburg for five years. These years were the start of a conscious fight. I didn't know what I was fighting against, I just took each issue as it came. We were about fifty girls, mostly from divorced homes or from rich overseas families. It was a school for turning us into young ladies. I didn't want to be a young lady. My brother Ronnie had been adamant that boys and girls should act the same.

I was assigned to Livingstone House: the other houses were Smuts and Rhodes. I fought tooth and nail against Rhodes, and everyone who was in it. I thought Smuts House was bad, but Rhodes! My father had told me a bedtime story about Rhodes. To stop English people from fighting a war against their rulers because they were poor, Rhodes had decided to make English people better off by robbing Africa. When I came face to face with Rhodes House at Redhill School and saw how they were making this dreadful monster into a hero, I was aghast at the sheer evil of it. I denounced Rhodes in a history essay and failed the course that term.

The academic standard at the school was low. There were only a few names on the matriculation board. We were there to learn to be rich, married 'madams' of large houses with lots of servants, to ride horses and hunt them, to play tennis and to debate.

54

From the start I thought the school was a fraud. It was run by a Mrs Hill from England. One evening a week she donned a red sequinned evening dress and played renditions of 'In a Monastery Garden'. That was our musical education. In Musical Appreciation I lauded Bach – whose work she disliked – and accused Mrs Hill of being musically backward. I got gated that term.

We were taken to see *Hamlet* in Afrikaans and when I heard, *Omelet, Omelet! Ek is jou pappie se spoek,* I laughed out loud and was sent to sit in the school bus.

For three years we lived in tents and got drenched every day when it rained because the school was in the process of being built. The donation to the school of a hockey pitch or tennis court by a parent meant prefecture and other honours for the daughter. Unfortunately Mitzi Newman's father donated an ex-race horse, Balator, to the school. Mitzi wasn't a good rider and she was killed falling off it.

I had two special friends at school, Adele Abel and Doreen Field, and in the dorm at night I used to tell them stories – my father's stories. Sometimes we would rouse the other girls to go night-swimming naked in the school pool. The postmaster used to gawp at us through binoculars and, whenever she saw him, Lee Goudvis used to do a duck-dive to show him her bum. When Mrs Hill caught Lee, I got gated for being the ringleader.

Our headmistress was having an affair with one of the fathers and they used to meet in the vegetable hut. We peeped through the brick vent holes to watch them. In Ethics, when we were learning about the sanctity of marriage, I asked Mrs Hill what one should do if a man gets you in a vegetable hut and tries to pull your broeks off. I got gated for that.

In geography I was taught that Bartholomeu Diaz, Vasco da Gama and, later, Jan van Riebeeck had discovered the Cape. My father had already told me they hadn't – there had been lots of people already living in the Cape. I told the class that when van Riebeeck arrived he dispossessed the KhoiKhoi of their land and they fought wars against him.

Our English teacher was dotty about the *Rubaiyat* of Omar

Khayyám, and we had to learn it off by heart. When it was my turn to recite a verse I said:

'Oh thou who didst with forethought and intent
On all the blacks your awful rage to vent.
Thou shalt with sure predestination round
  get punished
And nothing will your bloody deaths prevent.'

Miss Thompson did not hear what I said, but the girls giggled and I had to repeat it. I was sent to Mrs Hill, refused to apologise, gave her an argument, and was gated till the end of term.

We were not allowed to talk to the black staff who roved the school rolling pitches, painting tennis lines, cleaning, mowing, emptying, serving at table, cleaning floors, polishing windows – like a team of robots. I made friends with some of them and this caused anxiety among the teaching staff. Mrs Hill wrote letters to my father, complaining about my behaviour. But as I always passed my end-of-year examinations, my father never responded to Mrs Hill's letters. He used to show them to me and laugh.

During the long holidays I went to Mom and Oscar, who were living in Bloemfontein. Jim was our houseboy. He was tall, thin, and he was dumb. My family said he was stupid. The other servants interpreted for him and interceded for him. My mother tolerated him because, in addition to cleaning and polishing all the wooden floors and windows of the huge house, Jim also did the gardening, looked after the tennis court and cleaned the swimming pool. Usually he could be seen crouching almost motionless over a bush or shrub, balancing on the balls of his feet, knees bent, head down, as if studying a leaf or an insect.

Jim was obedient. He would listen carefully and do exactly as asked with a slow studied attention. But he *was* odd. He didn't behave like the other servants, and he never seemed to finish a job the way we expected.

Children are intolerant of the handicapped and my brother Mangelwurzel and his friend Tarby Brown, who was spending his holiday with us, were no exception. But Jim did not respond to their taunts. They would give him their shoes to clean and he would squat outside the kitchen door, polish, brushes and rags circling him, and rub and brush and polish until the black shoes shone back the gold of the hot sun. Then he would leave them on the kitchen step. The boys would shout and scream at him to 'Bring them upstairs!' and then it seemed as if Jim was not only dumb but deaf as well.

They would rush up to Jim in the garden, wanting him to give them a ride in the wheelbarrow. He would stand, looking to one side, wait till both of them had squeezed into the barrow and then pick up the handles and suddenly heave them over to the ground. No matter how they shouted, yelled or pleaded with him, he would simply walk away. He never even turned his head to them.

Every evening, he put on his white jacket and trousers with red chest riband and white gloves to serve us at the dinner table.

After dinner, the dining room was cleared and cleaned, but every now and then Jim's red waiter's riband and white gloves would be found draped over the sideboard. If one of the servants wasn't quick enough to remove them before my stepfather saw them, there would be a terrible row, Oscar accusing my mother of not being able to keep decent servants, my mother pleading that Jim was backward but he was a good boy, he cleaned properly, he did the garden well, he painted the lines on the tennis court straight, he rolled the court *really* flat, not like the last Jim we had. But often one of them just said to the other wearily, 'Oh, that stupid boy. Ring for Maisie to take the bloody things away.'

In the heavy heat of midday, Jim would go out under the hot sun next to the driveway and run the hosepipe over his head – all over his thick cotton top and shorts (the uniform of houseboys in South Africa). My mother would get very angry. She didn't want anyone to know we employed such a stupid boy. Now and then, when it became too much for her, she would ask Annie, the head maid, to call him:

'Get that stupid boy Jim here. I keep telling him. Ask him to come here.'

Old Annie would shuffle off as quickly as she could, swish-swishing on the carpet in her old red felt slippers, and painfully descend the stairs: hand clinging to the banister, arm leaning against the wooden struts as she lowered first one swollen foot and then the other. A little later, the distant slam of the fly-screen door heralded them coming up the stairs, Annie breathing heavily from the effort but loudly chastising Jim as if she wanted everyone in the house to hear her:

'You know the poor madam she's tired. The madam she told you last time – you don't wash in the drive. Hau! Every day wetting your clothes, you stupid boy. All the madam's visitors see you there they think the madam she's no good! Now the madam she'll give you the sack!'

They would arrive upstairs and stand in the doorway of the day sitting room: Annie with her hands clasped in front of her, head bowed; Jim gazing blankly across my mother's shoulder.

'Jim, I told you last week you can't wash there. Do you want to get the sack?'

Words of translation in an African language would flow in a stream of clicks and gutturals from Annie to Jim. Jim would stand in contained stillness.

'He says he won't do it again, madam, for sure,' Annie would say, nodding to get it over with.

My mother seemed to accept the fact that Annie could mind-read Jim's thoughts.

'Well, tell him if he does, that's the end. Tell him if I have to speak to him one more single time, he can go.'

'Yes, madam, I tell him. Don't you worry.'

My mother would be left in a state of angry frustration, knowing she had achieved nothing.

Jim never looked directly at us. Whenever we spoke to him his eyes slewed somewhere to our right. My mother would ask him to fetch a parcel from the shop, Jim gazing blankly at the emptiness just above her shoulder, and when she had repeated herself in a loud voice he would make a polite about-turn and, barefoot, walk swiftly out. Some time later a parcel would appear on the kitchen step, on top of the fridge or on a table. My mother would be screaming her impatience because he was taking so long, only for Annie or Maisie to discover it lying here or there, Jim having disappeared into the acre-and-a-half of our garden.

Unlike the other servants, Jim never bowed, bobbed or rubbed his hands together. If my stepfather gave him a sixpence tip, Jim just took it and held it till Oscar turned away before putting it in his pocket. He never placed his two hands to his head in gratitude as was the custom. My brother Mangelwurzel said he was a cheeky kaffir even if he was dumb.

I was ten years old then. One morning I awoke very early. I tiptoed down to the kitchen and climbed under the table to do my french knitting. After a while, I heard the sound of the servants coming in and, just before the fly-screen door whined open, I heard a clear male voice speaking Zulu. I felt frightened and squeezed into the corner under the big table with my back to the fridge. I heard Maisie put on the kettle and Annie getting down the pot for the mealie meal and then, from under the fold of pale green oilcloth that covered the table, I saw Jim's legs, crossed as he sat on the wooden box. He was talking just like a man: conversing, motioning with his arms, explaining, outlining, demonstrating. I sat frozen, terrified of exposure, and waited for them to finish their breakfast.

At last Annie sat down on the kitchen chair and the others left. I came out and Annie gasped and grabbed me by the arm.

'Hau! Miss Norma! Why you not still in bed?'

'I heard Jim speak,' I said.

'Hau! Miss Norma. You forget about Jim. You go back to boarding school next week. You don't tell the madam – nobody – nothing about Jim.'

'Can he speak English?' I asked.

'Please, Miss Norma. You forget about Jim. You forget about Jim, I make you a *big* tin biscuits you take to school. With coconut on – Lamingtons, like you like, Miss Norma.'

'I won't tell,' I said.

I went out into the garden and saw Jim crouched in front of a bush far over on the other side of the tennis court. I squeezed between the wall and the wire of the court and stood a couple of feet away from him and I saw he was crouched over a big book.

'Hey, Jim!' I said.

'Who's Jim?' he said. 'My name is Duma Khumalo.'

'I know you can speak,' I said.

'Oh, yes,' he said. 'I saw you there, under the table.'

He spoke English with a better accent than my stepfather. He sounded like a white man.

'Why do you pretend to us you can't speak?' I asked him.

'Do you really want to know, little girl?'

And he sat down and closed the book and placed it carefully underneath him. 'You see,' he said, 'I need a job. There are no jobs if you're like me. They feel too threatened. I've had lots of jobs. I did filing in an office once, and although I spent most of my time running errands for the secretaries – and cleaning the lavatories – they still threw me out. I used one of the whites' cups instead of an enamel mug and Miemie Pretorius, the office junior, complained. So the boss said that I was a cheeky kaffir and that anyway I knew too much and they just threw me out there and then. One minute's notice and I was standing outside on the pavement. No job.

'Once I had a job as a messenger at the bank – you know, the big bank in town. There was a teller there, Jakey Prinsloo – he couldn't even count properly. His till was always wrong, it never balanced. I went to jail that time. They said only a clever bugger like me would know how to crook a bank.

'Well, I've had a lot of experiences like that. So I have to get a domestic job so I can study for my LLB.'

'Your what?' I asked.

'Listen, little girl,' he said. 'There's big work to be done here in this country. You better know about it before you get poisoned like all the others – well, maybe you already are.'

He stopped speaking and looked down at the grass.

'I'm not poisoned,' I said.

'There's big work for me to do. Our people are suffering, our land taken away. People going to jail because they haven't got a pass, people being sent to work on farms and being beaten

60

because their pass is not in order. Children going without food. People always going to jail. We need lawyers, people who can stand up in court and say the truth – tell the whole world the truth. You people, you just drink your education. We have to fight for it. Man, I tell you, I've got big work to do in this world. And if they knew, they'd kill me, man – hey, they'd kill me, never mind give me a job!'

So many times in my short life I had heard the words 'I'll kill the cheeky kaffir', about so many people, in so many different contexts. Only the day before, Mr Botha from next door boasted to my father how he beat up his cheeky kaffir. 'I gave him one helluva crack, man. I showed him once and for all. If you can't get respect one way, you just got to get it another. They call me "Block of Ice" but by hell they damn well respect me.'

I don't know what happened to Duma Khumalo. I left for school a week later and I never saw him again. When my brother and his friend shouted, 'You so *stupid*, Jim,' I closed my eyes tightly and hoped he wouldn't be found out and think it was my fault.

And that week, Duma Khumalo looked into my eyes. If he'd ever done that to my mother or my stepfather they'd have known.

Twenty-two years later, in 1964, I did hear that someone called Duma Khumalo had been detained under the 90-Day Law. But the name is a very common one in South Africa. There must be hundreds of Duma Khumalos.

My brother Ronnie had been sent off to boarding school in Johannesburg with a case full of labelled clothes and he had to leave the whole of his life behind.

At the school, as part of the initiation of Jewish boys, he had to measure the rugby pitch with his nose on the ground. He did it, and ran away back to Durban with his nose skinned almost to the bone. By then Dort Rex and our house had been disposed of and Dad had moved to a flat on the eleventh floor of Ottawa Court in Gillespie Street near the South Beach.

Every time he was sent off to a new school, Ronnie ran away back to Durban. He stayed in different places – sometimes with Dad at the flat but mostly with friends. I saw little of him but he wrote me a few short letters:

Dear Vroom-Vroom, Been staying at the Geek Club with Rob and Josie. Very nice – you should hear how Steve Gale blows his trumpet now – just like Bix! Uncle Jim Cranko gave me a job at the OK Bazaars in the glass department. Lousy. All I get is my hands full of glass chips. Don't take all that girls' boarding school stuff lying down. Put up a fight, Vroomie! He who never fights, never wins. Teachers are the enemy. Are you doing maths? I've got a book and Rob is teaching me. One day I'll be a captain and you can come on my ship. If you don't know maths you can do the laundry but if you learn a lot you can be first mate. Cheerio my deario – RJC.

Dear Banana-girl [the name for Natalians], I hear you do not like school. You are not supposed to. Out of school isn't so hot either. Your brother – RJC.

Sometimes I spent my school holidays at Dad's flat in Durban. Once my visit there coincided with Ronnie's presence, when I was thirteen and he was fifteen.

After our parents' divorce, our father retreated into his own world. He had nothing to say to us and if my mother was mentioned he became agitated and pale and walked away, so we never spoke of her in front of him. Dad breakfasted at 7 am and if we were not at the table, he ate without us. He forgot to cater for us and often bought only one piece of fish for his dinner – although when he registered that we were at home, he would sometimes take us downstairs to the Ottawa Café for viennas and mash.

He left for work at SA Druggists every morning at 7.30 and came home at 5.30 for his supper. Then he went to the yacht club. On weekends he went sailing in his yacht and we hardly saw him.

I persuaded Ronnie to give up his job. My uncle Jim Cranko was a director of OK Bazaars and he had told our dad that he wanted Ronnie to work his way up from the bottom. I was furious that this meant Ronnie had to ruin his hands cutting glass

– and, anyway, Ronnie was never interested in getting to the top of that organisation. I detested my mean, arthritic uncle Jim after that.

Ronnie's hands were a terrible mess – red and lumpy, full of glass chips and in some places infected. I spent much of our holiday sitting with a tweezer and dabbing his hands with disinfectant, while Ronnie, typically, ignored what I was doing and never flinched with the pain it must have caused him.

At fifteen, Ronnie was different from the little boy – the big brother – I had known. In some way we had changed places, and he often looked to me for advice and approval. It was not only his hands that were wounded, it was as if he had suffered a great wound inside himself. He was often solemn and sometimes remote – like our father. Gone were his chatter and his lectures.

Sometimes we stayed away from home for two or three days but no one noticed. Our big powerful Durban family acted as if we did not exist when we were with our father. All that was to change when my mother returned to live in Durban with Oscar a year later. Then I was once again subjected to the restrictive family code. But my brother Ronnie never went to their houses and they forgot about him.

After that holiday, Ronnie got a job as galley boy on a whaling ship bound for the Antarctic. He spent six months a year for the next three years whaling and he brought me back lots of whale's teeth.

We did not know that Ronnie was studying on his own to be a sea captain.

When he was eighteen Ronnie was conscripted into the Royal Durban Light Infantry. There was no war then – it was all drilling and shining your Sam Browne belt and your shoes. He hated the army and said that the discipline was senseless and cruel. He took up weightlifting and became the Durban champion bantamweight. He was very pleased when the army let him go.

He became the manager of the Geek Club and a promoter of Durban jazz musicians. The club was near the docks, a bare basement with round wooden tables. It was home for out-of-work musicians and working musicians would finish their jobs and then arrive at one or two o'clock in the morning for a session at the Geek.

One night, Ronnie was trying to evict a drunk sailor who was picking a fight with an equally drunk drummer. A crowd gathered round and the sailor suddenly whipped out a knife. Ronnie grabbed him and in the melee the knife slashed Ronnie's arm. A young woman, who had been sitting at a table on her own, helped get his jacket off, ripped her petticoat and bound his arm. That's how Ronnie fell in love with Jean. His letter to me explained:

Dear Vroomie, I've met this terrific woman, Jean. She's a bit older than me. All hell's broken loose. She's not Jewish! Mom says I haven't tried and she doesn't like her. She says people should never marry their first girlfriends. What do you think? I'll try and explain. She's quite poor. You should see their house! It's on the Bluff, but very comfortable. She wears the same clothes in the day and the evening. She's so exciting. Ever since I met her we have been having a great time. We went to Umkomaas and then I took her to the Moonsamys' at Umhlanga Rocks and when we went camping at Amanzimtoti *she* put up the tent!

Anyway, this is to let you know we're getting married next week. Dad doesn't mind. I got a telegram from Joan saying 'Congratulations to you and Jean – present follows'. I hope she hasn't become like all the rest and sends us a butter dish.

Anyway, Normie, what do you think? Love from your brother, Ronnie.

Of course I approved. I approved of everything Ronnie did. They had no money and lived in a shack on the beach somewhere on the south coast. My family were appalled.

Ronnie became skipper of Collins's diamond yacht which dredged diamonds off the Namibian coast. He was away from Jean for long periods and about a year after they met and married he returned home from one of his trips and found her gone. He was devastated. He searched for her everywhere. He gave up his captaincy and returned to the Geek Club, where he sat despondently day after day.

Our father, on the advice of Uncle Alf, my mother's brother, bought a 'farm' at Paddock on the Natal south coast and asked Ronnie to manage it. So he spent a lonely year trying to make a go of the 'farm'. But nothing would grow on the land and it was too small for cattle. I went to visit Ronnie there in that bleak place. The ground was wet and clayey and it was impossible to know what to do with it. Ronnie had a calf for a pet. The animal used to follow him around the land and come into the house with him and lie down beside his bed. After Dort Rex, he never owned another dog.

Mom was then living in a house on the Berea with Oscar and our half-sister Clarice, and Ronnie persuaded Dad to sell the 'farm' and moved in with Mom and Oscar.

He turned half his bedroom and the spare garage into a photographic studio and worked hard to become a photographer. But most of his photographs came out red.

Mom was keen for him to remarry and she set out to make plans. She had a friend, Dolly Cohen, whose daughter Cheryl, the story went, had had an unhappy love affair. Cheryl had to have an excuse for being twenty-four years old and still not married. A broken heart was the only acceptable reason. Dolly took to bringing Cheryl over to the house. Mom tried to persuade Ronnie of the benefits of such a match.

'She's *Jewish*, darling. She comes from a good home – wonderful people. Her father's a *doctor*. You haven't even got a proper job – and they've got *pots* of money. You should just see Cheryl's bottom drawer.'

'Who wants her bloody lobola?' Ronnie asked.

Ronnie wanted nothing to do with Cheryl. Mom would urge him to 'come down for tea' and he would emerge from his dark room into the Louis XIV lounge where the two mothers would sit telling them how wonderful they both were.

'What a marvellous cook Cheryl is,' her mother would say. 'I had a party the other night and Cheryl cooked a five-course meal – perfect!' She looked at Ronnie for approval and he nodded, silent.

'Ronnie is so good with his hands,' my mother said. 'He can

mend anything. I've always said he should have been an engineer. But his father's a yachtsman and he gave Ronnie this crazy idea of going to sea. Well, that's all over now, isn't it, darling? All Ronnie wants to do is find a nice girl and settle down.'

One day my mother bought a diamond ring for Ronnie to give Cheryl.

'I'm not giving it to her,' he said. 'What for?'

'*Darling*,' Mom said, 'she's a *lovely* girl. She comes from such a good family. It's an *engagement* ring.'

'Well, you give it to her, then,' Ronnie said.

And my mother did – on Ronnie's behalf!

After that, teatime in the lounge had the three women sewing and Ronnie was being asked to admire tablecloths and embroidered sheets. Suddenly, one day, he realised that unless he did something quickly, he was going to be married to Cheryl.

'I don't want to marry her, Mom,' he said.

'Oh, you can't disgrace the family *now*,' my mom said.

'Why? How's that a disgrace?' Ronnie asked.

'Well, it's been in all the papers – yesterday – the engagement!'

The next day Ronnie broke our mother's heart and left for Johannesburg. We never heard anything more about Cheryl and I don't think my mom stayed friends with her mom.

Ronnie became a grain merchant in Johannesburg. I was in Durban at Dad's flat when Ronnie telephoned me.

'Listen, Normie, I'm coming down to Durban to see you.'

'OK,' I said.

'Don't tell anyone I'm coming down. I'll drive straight through and meet you at the Cooey in about eight hours. I have to talk to you.'

He arrived, looking older.

'I'm thinking of getting married again,' he said.

'Who to?'

'Her name's Marlene.'

'Do you love her?' I asked neatly.

Ronnie looked at me with something like contempt. 'She's a

really wonderful person,' he said.

'Ja,' I said. 'But either you do or you don't.'

'Of course I do, but I don't know whether I'm going to ever get over Jean, you know,' he said.

'Well, you can't have Jean. She's divorced you. She's gone.'

'I don't know what to do,' he said. 'Marlene's terrific! Honestly, you should meet her.'

Ronnie and Marlene got married. He seemed to forget Jean and the sea. They lived in a little flat in Johannesburg's Berea – a far cry from the affluent Berea in Durban. And Ronnie became a pipesmoker and he seemed happy.

Then they had their first son – and they named him Basil! When Ronnie told me, he gave me a quizzical look. I was on the point of exploding into laughter – because I thought he was joking – when he gave me a stern look. I checked myself. He never said anything. I never asked, and of course we didn't giggle. There was suddenly a great barrier – a gulf between us. After that I never knew what to say to my brother.

In 1966 I left for England. A few years later, when Basil was three and Cedric two, Ronnie died of cancer.

· 5 ·

When I was fourteen, my mother decided I had had enough school and I was very pleased to leave Redhill. But no one had any idea where I should live. I spent some months at my dad's flat near the beach, reading and swimming. I discovered his library. Dad's books were carefully stamped on the inside covers with a decorated oval border and the words 'W. Cranko – Private Library'. I read more and more avidly as I came face to face with the politics of South Africa. I discovered that my father's bedtime stories were about the black history of South Africa and the history of Ireland and the Soviet Union. His shelves contained first editions of Marx, Engels and Lenin – many of which I found too difficult to read. There were piles of old newspapers – some in Zulu and other African languages – rows of journals and articles on South Africa.

I became excitedly aware that there had always been people who resisted the system we lived under in South Africa. There were accounts of many battles and wars of resistance, as well as articles about the conditions and laws. I read about the 1913 Land Act which had deprived black people all over South Africa of the right to their own land. Although they made up 87 per cent of the population, they could only occupy 13 per cent of the land. I found out that black people could not vote because in 1936 the Representation of Natives Act was passed, and that the Masters and Servants Laws kept them as virtual slaves to white employers. There were articles on the formation of the African National Congress in 1912 and of representations made to British royalty to alleviate the situation of black people.

My father's library was packed with information and every now and then I would come across pages containing notes written in his firm script, marking particular passages.

In the evenings, when he was home for brief periods, I would try to engage him in conversation about this material, asking when and why he had got it, but he wouldn't be drawn. He said, 'The real history of South Africa is in those shelves. You should read it all,' or, 'When you've read through that lot, you won't accept what's in the history textbooks.' And he would smile and go to his club or disappear into his bedroom.

I became friendly with the girl next door, Memory de Vos, and her mother, Gladiole, who worked as a shop assistant and drank ginger squares. She was a kind, motherly woman who sewed me a green full-circle cotton skirt. Memory was a student at the Durban Business College so I enrolled as well. My mother was appalled when she found me in such unsuitable company and decided I should have to live with her, Oscar and Clarice in the house they had bought in Currie Road. I was happy where I was and did not want to leave. My mother never visited my father's flat. She had claustrophobia and could not go in lifts and Dad was on the eleventh floor. But in any event my parents took care not to meet or attend the same functions. My mother sent my two youngest uncles, Wally and Stanley, to fetch me and they would brook no arguments. I packed my case while they waited for me and they drove me to my mother's house.

I was back in my tight, restrictive Stiller family environment. This meant dressing up to go shopping with my mother and two or three of her sisters or her friend Cissie each morning, having tea at Payne Brothers, and then, while they slept or played cards in the hot afternoons, I would swim in one of the family pools with any of my cousins who were around, and servants would bring us afternoon tea in the shade near the pool. Then home for dinner. My brother Mangelwurzel had been left up in Bloemfontein as a boarder at Grey College. My half-sister Clarice was still a baby. When she was a little older, she became a savage little thing, used as a ping-pong ball in the continual erotic fights between Mom and Oscar. These fights usually ended up with them going to their bedroom. When Clarice grew up and married Ricky, she became a sensitive, pleasant young woman, who managed to combine my mother's good taste and Oscar's practicality.

In the evenings Mom and Oscar played cards, and I read in my room or sat in the kitchen talking to the servants.

I tried to befriend my cousins, Wendy (Auntie Ettie's daughter, who was two years older than I) and Eleanor (Auntie Bea's daughter, two years younger), but they were for ever going to the hairdresser, the dressmaker or the elocutionist – you weren't supposed to speak like a South African, you had to try to sound English – and spent their evenings either attending or planning parties. They also did courses in Pelmanism, Entertaining in Your Home, and Home Furnishing – though Eleanor later escaped to England and studied orthoptics. My cousin Margaret (Auntie Thelma's daughter) and I were like fish out of water. I never accepted the few dates that boys invited me to, and Margaret, who was very beautiful, hated boys and was a 'social disaster'. But her father insisted that Margaret should date. After she had dutifully been out with a boy and was taken to the front door, he would say, 'Will you go out with me next Saturday night?'

'What for?' Margaret would ask.

'To see a film.'

'But I've been out with you already!' Margaret seemed genuinely puzzled when she explained to me, 'I don't know what the hell they want. I go out with them and all they want is for me to go out with them *again*.' Margaret's father kept her tied to Durban until she was in her late twenties. Then she ran away to Australia, where she could remain unmarried. Our other cousins were much younger.

Every Friday night the whole family gathered at Grandma's house in Ridge Road. We all dressed up. The men had new haircuts, wore silk handstitched suits and glossy ties. The women had their hair set; I had to have a comb dragged through my frizzy hair and then have it pulled with a hot iron to get it to lie straight. We wore crepe or taffeta dresses and wedgies and I was always being told off by one or other of my aunts because I didn't paint my nails. My auntie Bea, who fancied herself as the cultured member of the family, always spoke of my 'naked hands' as if I was running around with no broeks on. It was bad enough if you painted them the wrong colour, but if you didn't paint them at all you were 'just like a shiksa' – a real outsider.

The men and boys would come home from shul – the women and girls seldom went except on high feast days – and the long ritual meal would follow. Uncle Alf said Kiddush, the heavy sweet wine was blessed and drunk and the *kitke* bread blessed and broken. Dishes of home-pickled cucumbers, green olives, chopped liver decorated in the shape of a Magen David made from the separately chopped white and yellow of egg, chopped herring, and rolled butter in special dishes to keep the pats cold, were spread out on the table. We had chicken soup with *kneidel* or *matzokleis* followed by three kinds of fish: gefilte, lemon and fried '74' or *kingklip*. The meat was usually an overdone roast, with vegetables and an array of salads. There was a choice of four or five puddings, including Auntie Ettie's niggerheads – as our Durban family called profiteroles. Never hungry, I would play with the food on my plate while Auntie Bea, who usually managed to sit next to me, taunted me with one thing or another. Once she jogged my elbow and said loudly, rolling her r's and clipping her vowels in the way South Africans do, 'Eat your carrots! Carrots are good for you, you know, Norma darling – they make you see in the dark.'

My young cousins, alerted to the exchange that was certain to follow, paused, their mouths full, listening. The servants standing at the ready around the room in their white suits with red or blue sashes, begloved in white so that their black hands would never touch our food or any vessel that contained it, hid their mouths for the giggle that was sure to come.

'Yes,' I said, with the advantage of having read some of my father's chemistry books, 'carrots contain vitamin A. A deficiency in vitamin A means the retina cannot synthesise visual purple – and so one develops night blindness, which eating carrots can correct. But for those of us with a normal diet, eating carrots would have no effect whatsoever.'

Everyone was now listening. Uncle Wally said, 'Where d'you

learn thet, Norm?'

Auntie Bea said, 'Ja, darling. But they've got carotene in as well!'

'Auntie Bea,' I said, 'carotene is just the layman's term for vitamin A.'

'Well, you eat some anyway,' she said. 'They good for you. They'll make your hair curl.'

There were screams of laughter, and my aunties wiped their variegated shadowed eyes with their white hand-laced, initialled hankies.

'That's quite true,' I said loudly. 'They *can* make your hair curl.'

Auntie Bea moved a large mouthful of carrot to the other side of her mouth. 'Make your hair curl? *Reelly?*'

'Yes,' I said. 'If you use them as hair curlers.'

There was a burst of laughter. One of the youngsters choked and spat his food onto the embroidered tablecloth and a forest of hands hit him on the back. There was a sudden exodus of servants through the swing doors to the kitchen. Auntie Bea went red, jabbed at a pickled cucumber, turned her back on me with one shoulder hunched up and started a studied conversation with her daughter Eleanor sitting on her other side. My mother said, 'Oh, Normie!' in a disappointed way. The men tittered briefly and got back to their talk of business and labour. Margaret looked at me sympathetically. Wendy glanced vaguely around – she didn't follow conversation very well. Grannie was busy eating and was always too worried about getting a frown from one of her daughters if she spilled anything on the cloth. But my aunts were looking at me reproachfully, except my mother's youngest sister, Auntie Ruby, who came and put an arm around me. I bit back tears.

On Friday nights Uncle Cyril, Auntie Ettie's husband, who became the head of the family after my grandfather died, would choose whom to see. Anyone who wanted to get engaged, start a business or buy a house would have to speak with him. The men would sit together in the 'den' and the women and children in the lounge.

72

My family believed that if girls were educated, it would be hard for them to get husbands – so we all left school when we were about fourteen. We were supposed to take a course or two in cooking or domestic science or even interior decorating but I had done a short typing and shorthand course at the Durban Business College.

Life was predictable. I was expected to hold a job of some sort for a couple of years and try to have a date every Saturday night, and when a boy with the right parents (and a good bank balance) came along, then – ideally at about the age of eighteen – I would get married and have three or four children. To have any more was considered coarse: if I had fewer than three, people would say there was something wrong with my 'tubes'.

I began to dread my future.

My sister Joan had married a dentist and they had been allowed to leave Durban to go to Odendaalsrus, a town in the Orange Free State. Gold had recently been discovered and there was a sudden influx of people into the tiny town and plenty of work for a dentist.

I decided to run away to Odendaalsrus to be near my sister.

So one Friday night, after the endless courses of food, when the women had gone into the lounge and the men to the rumpus room with its billiard table and fish-tank walls, I asked Uncle Benny to tell Uncle Cyril I wanted to speak with him. Uncle Benny was Auntie Ruby's husband. He owned the Revelation suitcase factory and other businesses.

'What you want?' Uncle Benny asked. 'You can tell me. He won't speak to you unless it's important. You only fifteen. Why don't you ask Auntie Ettie?'

'Uncle Ben,' I said, 'I want to go to OD and stay with Joan.'

Uncle Benny laughed. 'Fat chance. Hey, Cyril,' he said, interrupting everyone. 'Listen to this! *She*' (pointing his finger at my head) 'wants to leave Durban.'

Uncle Cyril laughed. 'You go in the lounge with the girls, darling,' he said. And Uncle Benny gave me a fond smack on the bum, dismissing me.

I had to run away. They wouldn't even listen. With some

money saved up from my wages I bought a train ticket to Odendaalsrus and spent the next couple of weeks hinting broadly that I wanted to leave Durban. But no one took me seriously. So I went to Dad's flat and left a note propped on his dresser, another on my mother's bedside table, and I told everyone in the kitchen I was going to Joan in Odendaalsrus.

'Hau! Miss Norma,' said Uriah the cook.

It was a depressing thing to hear. It expressed the total horror of what I was about to do – the impossibility of it all.

I think I was waiting, wanting someone to persuade me to stay. Leaving home was too serious to work out properly. I only knew that I had to break free – free from the pettiness of the life they led, the awful family sayings, the prejudices, the make-up, the wedgie shoes, the quarrels about nothing, the denigration of everyone who wasn't in our family. But I was even more frightened when I tried to imagine what it would be like to leave. Facing nothing – everything – alone. Thinking about it like that, there were times when all the restrictions, restraints and stupidities seemed preferable – not at all negative, just comfortable boundaries encompassing the familiar.

As I entered the lounge where the women were, I heard the crack of laughter and the shrillness of their voices. Rosenthal cups were held high, little fingers crooked (by the book), perfect nails – painted, hair all set in the same style, occasional tables loaded with knickknacks, gleaming stinkwood sideboards and whatnots, Royal Doulton figurines of beggars and British royalty, cherry chocolates in fluted china bowls – china always fussy and fluted, flower arrangements standing on end, orange juice in Venetian goblets. The women in our family do not drink alcohol.

It almost looked like an upper-class gathering – like the real thing. But the garish floral sleeveless dresses, the vivid eye make-up, the perfectly shaped cupid lips on powdered faces, the harsh laughter trying to be a ladylike tinkle, and the strident accents betrayed the tastelessness of the 'noovo reetch' – the thing they all hated the most. They talked to each other, confidentially, about people who 'laughed coarsely', perhaps to remind one another to tinkle. And about people who were not bred into refinement as they were.

'Let's face it,' I once said to my mother, 'we come from *shit!*'

My mother had paled and then reddened with terrible anger. Suddenly her beautiful hand lashed out and she hit me across the face. 'Our family,' she spat, 'is the most highly bred, refined family in this country. Your grandfather, poor darling Daddy, was an aristocrat from Poland. One of his uncles was the mayor of Lodz!'

'Grandpa made his money getting Jews out of Poland during the war,' I shouted. 'That's a terrible thing to do – to make the families pay to save people's lives from the Nazis. And who did he know who could *let* the Jews out? Only Germans. He must have had a lot of Nazi friends. And what about the Jews who couldn't pay people like Grandpa? They all went to the gas chambers, I suppose!'

My mother sat back in horror. 'I don't know who's been telling you these dreadful stories,' she said. 'Probably people who are jealous of us. Your grandfather was a *jeweller*. And he used to *help* people.'

'So how come,' I had asked, letting all the pain of the gossip I had heard about the family spill out, 'so how come an immigrant *jeweller* with *nine* children could retire a multimillionaire at the age of forty? And how come he could build such a huge house in Ridge Road – *with* the copper pipes you are always boasting about? And a huge farm at Roodekop? And *how come,*' I asked, 'the families that he is supposed to have helped don't talk to our family – loathe us all? And where do the Stiller millions come from?'

'Don't you dare use that word,' my mother had said.

'What – what word?'

'Don't you dare call poor darling Grandpa an immigrant.'

I felt everything sliding away from me.

My mother checked herself and looked down sadly at her hands, slowly sliding her rings around her fingers to face the front. She fingered her gold and platinum bracelets. 'I don't understand you,' she said. 'I really don't. Well,' she said, with a sigh of resignation, 'you always did take after your father, and God knows he came from nothing. I'm only paying the price for my own mistakes.'

I thought about that as I was standing at the lounge door looking in on that rich Durban tapestry, knowing that I was soon to leave them all. But I felt that without them I would have no identity. I was just a name with frizzy hair and school shoes.

As I entered, my mother was in full flow on a familiar theme.

'Well, they *are* getting yellowy, Ettie. You've probably sprayed them with your perfume. Girls! *Never* allow perfume to touch your pearls. It makes them porous,' she said loudly to everyone who regularly heard this advice – insisting on her role of the knowledgeable eldest sister.

She gripped my arm as I passed, her fingernails digging into me. 'Where you going, darling? Come here, your bow is untied again. You look a mess. I can put *anything* on Joan, you know,' she said to everyone, 'a mealie sack, and she looks beautiful. But this one – you can spend a hundred pounds and she still looks like nothing. Don't you, darling?' I smiled my wide smile and cocked my head to one side. Inside my heart was a stone.

My mother, the expert at all things decorative and a know-nothing at life! She used her gifts and energy to make life look right and whenever the picture skewed, she was always able somehow to prop it back up again.

Yet, all the hurts, all the things that destroyed me seemed somehow warm and comforting, now that I was leaving.

The following day I wired Joan and, a couple of nights later, I took a small overnight case and walked to Durban station. I caught the night train. I had an uncomfortable journey, wondering if the police would haul me off at the next station or if irate junior uncles, speeding in Oldsmobiles and Jags, would arrive to fetch me home. But I arrived without incident and Joan gave me a warm and wonderful welcome. Durban was behind me. The arguments, the objections, the tears and entreaties were all to be dealt with from a distance and from Joan's protective custody.

My sister was wide-eyed and excited that I had struck out on my own and defied the family. She and Rolf were living in a small room behind the surgery, so I would have to find a place to stay – and get a job. The gold mine was the only possibility.

They were shaft-sinking at Freddies South and I applied for the position of secretary to the Study Department. At my interview I was asked whether I could type a stencil and read a graph, whether I could work a switchboard and a duplicator. I said yes to everything. If I admitted there was anything I could not do, I felt sure I wouldn't get the job. I was taken on.

I arrived at the mine office with my face covered in Leichner make-up, hair slicked down, wearing wedgie shoes, hoping to look as old as eighteen. But it didn't matter. There were few women to fill the many office jobs and I was welcomed and asked to relieve the mine switchboard at lunchtime. The switchboard was in a tiny room banked by three metal walls containing numerous small black squares. Each square had a hole, like a hooded eye, and convex grey discs with numbers flicked up and down over them, each making its own clicking noise. In some of the holes were strange-looking plugs with thick black cords which crisscrossed each other and made a mess of the whole panorama of technology. As soon as I entered the room, the operator, Yvette, indicated a notepad with a list of names, grabbed her bag and left, saying, 'See you!'

I sat down with three walls of grey discs clicking at me and a row of things buzzing in front of me. I decided to start from the beginning. I had to stop all the clicks and buzzes so I could concentrate and work the thing out. I opened my arms wide and gathered the cords in both hands and, sweeping them into a holdable mass, yanked them out of the holes. The clicks became more insistent and people began tapping on the glass door of the switchboard room. I got up and opened the door a fraction. 'What you want?' I was trembling and nearly sobbing.

'I was cut off.'

' I was talking to the underground manager of Freddies North and I was cut off.'

'Something went wrong with my phone. Can you get that call

back right now?'

I said to everyone, 'The switchboard's out of order and the engineer is busy fixing it now. I'll get your call back as soon as he's through.'

I went on saying things like that through the lunch hour. When Yvette came back she took one look at the board – all the silver plug heads neatly in their front slots, cords out of sight, the board silent except for a few clicks here and there – and she said, 'You've never used a switchboard in your life, have you?'

'Well, no. Not one like this,' I said.

She laughed and stayed with me for a few days during her lunch hours until I learned.

The mine was new and my office was luxurious, with a large desk, Remington typewriter, couch and easy chairs, wall cabinets and bookshelves and a pile carpet. I went through the drawers of the desk and, among the rubbers, paper clips and Biros, discovered three bottles of red nail polish which I threw in the bin.

The Remington typewriter was new to me. Babette, in Geology, taught me how to switch the machine to stencil to disengage the ribbon and enable the type bars to cut through the wax. These were terrifying days for typists, before Tipp-Ex, and I found that if I made a typing error on a stencil there was no way to rub it out. You had to have *perfect* typing. It sometimes took me eight stencils to get a perfect original.

On the Thursday of my second week at the job, I returned from my relief stint on the switchboard, and my boss, a very polite Swiss, Mr Sahli, called me into his office.

'I see you've requisitioned another box of stencils, Miss Cranko,' he said.

'Yes. We do use an awful lot of them.'

'I've noticed,' he said. 'But we had a three-month supply in, you know.'

A couple of days later he came into my office with an armful of stencils he had extracted from my wastepaper basket. 'Haven't you heard of correcting fluid, Miss Cranko?'

Oh, the terror of those days!

I immediately requisitioned correcting fluid from Stationery and the next day there arrived on my desk three bottles of the red stuff I had thought was nail polish.

Twice a week I went down the mine with my boss and representatives from all the departments that were responsible to Study. It was a frightening journey in a mary ann – a bucket – that swayed and bumped its way down two terrifying miles. Freddies South is one of the deepest mines in the world and of course there are no lifts during shaft-sinking.

For eighteen months I shared a small tin mine house with Francine, one of the mine secretaries. After work each day we would go swimming at the Odendaalsrus pool or I would go horse riding. The mayor of the town, Oom (Uncle) Sijs Odendaal – whom we called Oom Shiess (Shit) – used to ride his horse importantly through the town each day – a big fat man in a Boer hat. He was pleased that I could ride and lent me a horse whenever I wanted one.

The town hall was the venue for all occasions, and I went there with Joan's Jewish friends to celebrate the high feast days when it was used as a synagogue, with Afrikaans friends to receptions when they got married, to beetle-drives for local charities, to Burns night when Scots got together, to Anglican services and to plays performed by the local dramatic society.

Joan and I kept in very close touch – I popped in to see her at the dental surgery most days. But her friends were reminiscent of my Durban family, a high-society set of young Jewish couples – a doctor, an accountant, shop owners, a chemist – and I did not want to enter their world. My friends were young Afrikaners who worked on the mine, and an elderly woman, Sarie van Wyk, whose son was a bookkeeper at Freddies. She told stories of the great Boer trek to get away from the domination of the invading Britons – of the hardships and the concentration camps set up by the British where Boer women and children died like flies. Her Boer heroes hung on the walls of her little house, faded sepia prints in thin wooden frames. I arranged to eat at her little mine house each evening and she cooked very tasty Afrikaans meals – the very best food I have ever eaten.

Odendaalsrus is situated in a completely flat stretch of country. At night the sky seems so low and the stars so bright that, walking along a road, with the faint swishing of the grasses and the stridulating crickets, I felt at perfect peace with the world.

A small hillock, Koppie Alleen (hill on its own), was the only landmark for miles, a little bump among scores of windmills. The land was arid and riddled with dongas, steep gullies made by soil erosion.

On weekends about fifteen of us would drive in cars to the wild open country to camp, swimming in rock pools, making fires to cook our food, and the baboons high on the rocks above would pelt us with stones.

These were happy days. The Afrikaners I met were friendly and hospitable. Their families welcomed me in the dorps surrounding Odendaalsrus. We enjoyed life – and if there was racism all around me, and if the black maids and miners were visibly suffering, I did not want to see it. I didn't want anything to disturb the contentment that being with this wonderful group of healthy people gave me.

Eventually the mine house was needed for a married couple and I found a small room in a house in the married quarters with a young Afrikaans couple, Maria and Frans van Rensburg. Frans was a shift boss at Freddies. He had a magnetic personality and they were both very popular. There were lots of visitors to their home and Maria provided endless relays of tea, beer and *koeksusters* – the syrupy biscuits so loved by Afrikaners.

Frans would tell fantastic tales: of underground, of the dangers of working two miles from the surface, of heat exhaustion and the hazard of methane gas, of the shortage of labour and the mine recruitment programmes for black workers. He also told us stories of camping out in the veld, of dangerous animals and no water, of getting lost and finally, without food, finding the way home again. He told us the story of how they first arrived in Odendaalsrus when there was no accommodation in the town at all and they had had to live in their Nash car. 'Kitchen in the bloody boot, bedroom in the back. Radio, the lot. Man, I used to shave with the radiator water, but it was worth it. Talk about rags to riches! That's the understatement of the bloody millennium. It was unreal, you know. There's nothing so marvellous as shaft-sinking money with added danger money and shift pay and, on top of all that, overtime. Out o' sight, man!'

I loved listening to Frans's stories, always told with explosive enthusiasm. Everyone would agree with Frans's opinions, however outlandish they were. 'I think they should boot out all the bloody foreigners off the mines. They just polluting us Afrikaners. They got crazy ideas about everything, and they no good at keeping the kaffirs in order.' The assembled company would agree, with shouts of *Vrystaat!* (Free State!), the brotherhood cry of the Afrikaner nationalist.

I would sit enjoying it all but feeling uncomfortable, thinking about our black servants in Durban, people who had cushioned my childhood and made it bearable.

I tried to tell them not to use the word 'kaffir' but Frans would laugh. 'You Durbanite Natalians with your fancy ideas! You not even South Africans. You all English. Go back to England, man! A kaffir's a kaffir no matter what you call him. Jesus! Listen to this:

'There's this guy, van der Merwe, comes into a pub, sitting there, talking to himself, shaking his head sadly. His friend comes up to him.

' "Hey Van, *wat mekeer jou?* [what's the matter with you?]"

' "Oh, no, man," says van der Merwe. "I don't know what's what any more. And what's more, I don't know who's who. I was up last week in Rhodesia and I had a car accident and now I'm just completely lost."

' "Ag, no, Van. Did you get injured then, or what?"

' "No. No injuries, man. I had to go to court."

' "What happened, Van?"

' "The magistrate asked me to tell him in my own words what had occurred. I told him. I said, I was driving down this road, slowly and with due care and caution, obeying all the rules of the road. Suddenly, this kaffir jumps out in front of my car and I run him over."

'Van der Merwe took a sip of his beer and sat back shaking his head.

'"So?" asked his friend. "So what happened?"

'"The magistrate stopped me. He said, 'Mr van der Merwe, in *this* country, we do not refer to people as kaffirs. We refer to them as Africans. Fined twenty pounds.'"

'Van shook his head again, took another *sluk* of beer and said, "Man, I could of *swore* it was a kaffir."'

They laughed.

There were always stories about the 'foreigners' – the Swiss, English, Scots and German mining engineers, who formed a quite separate social group. 'He might well be a bloody good engineer but he knows nothing about kaffirs and *boerewors* [sausage],' I remember Jannie van Wyk saying once. 'He speaks to kaffirs as if they was white but he treats them worse than shit and he says *boerewors* makes him vomit! *God, man, hy's 'n rerige bliksemse rooinek* [God, man, he's a real English git]!'

I was embarrassed when the Jews were the subject of their swearing, but they seemed not to notice my presence. *'Bliksemse Jode!* It's a pity Hitler didn't finish the whole bloody lot off, man. They own all the bloody shops and they make everything so expensive a person can't live properly.'

One Sunday about twenty of the van Rensburgs' friends came to a *braaivleis*. We sat in the garden – a new patch of bare red earth – on striped beach chairs. The beer flowed and the marinated steak and *boerewors* sizzled on the *braai*. And Frans told a story that changed my life.

The white miners were given lectures on the dangers of smoking underground because of the presence of methane gas. It was clear that these talks made little impression on the white shift bosses. But the black miners, who had to do the most dangerous jobs, were shown horror films of the results of naked flames. These were terrifying pictures of explosions, with bodies blown apart and blood and guts spattered on the rocks underground. The dangers were very real. There were accidents – explosions and fatalities – every day during shaft-sinking at Freddies. No black miner could have escaped seeing a colleague killed or injured by a rockfall, and losing a limb was a daily hazard. Black workers who became crippled were sent home to starve without a pension. Everyone wore Edison Safety Cap lamps underground to detect methane and the black miners, who were constantly being warned, were highly conscious of the danger of a naked flame.

Amid the roasting *braai* and salads, the hot sun and friendly people, the iced beer and the warm peaches, Frans was sitting shirtless and tanned in his khaki shorts, the blonde hairs on his legs winking in the sunlight. He leaned forward in his seat, telling this story:

'I was down there. It was about three hours after the shift began and I was dying for a smoke. So I left the boys to get on with it and took myself off up by the rocks and lit up. Bugger me if the boss boy, that Sam, doesn't come up to me.

'"Basie," he says to me. [Basie is a grovelling diminutive for boss.] "Basie, the gang asked me to come and have a word with you, please, baas."

'"Don't stand there looking half-cocked," I said. "What you want?" He was rubbing his hands and I could see he was damn scared.

"Please, basie, don't smoke down here. It's too dangerous. They sent me to ask you – the others. Please, baas. There's methane here."

'I looked at him. I tell you I was bloody angry. I was fokin' annoyed.

'"Bloody kaffir! Who are you to tell me what to do? OK, OK, you say it's all the boys. OK, you boys, now who else thinks that he can tell me what to do, hey? Who else feels he wants to criticise me as if I don't know what I'm doing? Ja, just you come forward, man."

'Three of the buggers steps up to me.

'And then,' Frans said to us, enjoying the denouement of his story and the exercise of his power, 'and then I said, "OK, you boys. Each of you take the end of a vent pipe now, and take it up to Level Two and back here again, OK?" '

He made the four men carry two heavy ventilation pipes up and down from level to level until they collapsed from fatigue and heat exhaustion. Then they were sent to the surface where an ambulance took them off to hospital.

'I was so bloody angry, I can tell you. I was so fokin' annoyed, I didn't give them their salt tablets. But one thing's for sure. I won't have that lot breathing down my neck again. That'll teach the buggers to question my authority, isn't it? I'll tell you I won't have no more trouble out of that bloody gang. Jesus, man! They'll just have to get me another boss boy. If you get a bad one on your team, you've had it, you know.'

To a chorus of 'Cheeky bloody kaffirs!' and 'Jesus, man! You should have given him a bladdy good hiding first,' I quietly left the garden and went to my room.

I sat on my bed brushing away angry, impotent tears. I had lived with this cruelty all my life. In Odendaalsrus it was cruder, more obvious. Racism was more openly accepted – even applauded. At home in Durban it had been implied, and was subtle through traditions. But everywhere, black life was cheap. The daily accidents underground, the maiming of hundreds of black miners in the course of their dangerous work was not enough. These people, who were mainly immigrants from surrounding countries in Africa, had to live in single-sex concrete barracks without their families, contracted to work for one-year terms, and were subjected to the dangerous whims and fancies of racists like Frans.

I felt overwhelmed by the injustices. I could stay in OD no longer. Somewhere I had to find people who thought as I did. Johannesburg was the largest city in South Africa – perhaps there I would find an organisation I could join to fight the system. I hurriedly packed my case, left a note for Maria with two weeks' rent and went to Joan to say goodbye. I told her that I had left the van Rensbergs' house, and what I had heard that afternoon.

Joan took me in her arms. 'Don't be so upset about things like that, Norm. Those Afrikaners are just ignorant. Johburg will be awful on your own. Where will you stay? What will you do? There's nothing *we* can do. The natives have to sort out their own problems. You don't have to take it on your shoulders. Can't you just make the best of life? You've got a good job here.'

'But it is my business,' I said. 'And it does upset me. You've got no idea what it's like working on the mine. These miners are so unprotected, so dependent on the tiny income from their jobs to support their starving families at home. They're not allowed to form trade unions, and if they get injured they're just sent back to their homes to starve. They're subject to the pass laws and summary arrest – more than half the black population has been arrested for pass offences. And you want me to sit around thinking everything's fine because those laws, that racism, don't apply to me personally? I can't go on pretending that if I don't see it, it doesn't exist, even if I contribute to it.'

'But what can you do?' Joan asked. 'I mean, even if you don't like what's going on, how can you change it? You've got your whole life in front of you. It shouldn't be your worry, really.'

'But it affects us, doesn't it? Just look at our family in Durban. They're nice people, kind and loving in their way. But look how this whole system has poisoned them. They have maids who've worked in their houses, sometimes for fifteen years and more. They don't even know their real names. They pretend it's not there – starvation and disease and the whole grinding condition of poverty. That dehumanises everyone. It's dehumanised all of us. Unless we're concerned about everyone, we all suffer.'

'Well, how would you want things? How would you make it fair?'

'I don't know,' I said. 'I really don't. It's all so big and we take everything for granted. Suddenly I don't want to take anything for granted any more and say that's the way it always has been, so that's the way it's got to be. I suppose I can be happy as long as I keep my eyes closed. But they keep opening!'

'It's just a phase you're going through, Norm. Growing up is very hard.'

'Please don't patronise me,' I said. 'In one way or another I've *always* felt this. From our earliest days we've seen what goes on.

85

Every white person is the boss to them. You've seen it yourself. Even as kids the servants used to ask us to sign their passbooks giving them permission to be out on the streets. They were too scared to ask Mom or McGrath – because often they'd just wave them aside. I don't think Mom even knows what a passbook is. There we were, little kids, with power and authority over black adults. How have we come to accept that any black person passing can be yelled at by a white: "Hey, you! Jim! Carry this, do that, help the madam, push this car! Do this, do that, or you'll get a crack"? Black people have become less than animals to almost the whole white population. Starvation wages, arid land, lousy jobs, laws, guns, whips! Look how housewives order their meat from the butcher: "4 lbs chops, 4 lbs prime steak, 2 chickens, 2 lbs dogs' meat, 2 lbs boys' meat"!'

I sat back, for a moment. Joan looked up sadly. 'That may all be true, Norm. But as I said, what can *you* do about it? Where on earth did you find out about it all, anyway?'

'You know Dad's bedtime stories. I found out they were true histories. You remember he had that story we loved about the Specially Apt Necessary Nation Corporation. It championed the cause of the people. It had multiple branches and representatives. They wore different-coloured armbands and tried to solve the different problems of the green people, the grey people, the blue people. You remember?'

'Yes, of course,' Joan said. 'I thought Dad's stories were wonderful fantasies, but I found out at school that one of them was a history of the French Revolution, and there was one about the October Revolution in the Soviet Union. And lots of them were about Irish people. He had a real thing about the Irish question.'

'Yes,' I said. 'But most of them were about South Africa. And this one was about the history of resistance in this country. You remember! The Specially Apt Necessary Nation Corporation – which was Dad's name for the South African Native National Congress – discovered that all the different people actually had the same problems and they all had two legs, two arms, one head, so it wasn't necessary for them to be separately represented. So they changed themselves into the Apt Nation

Corporation so that they could solve their problems as one group. And then, because that didn't solve them, the Clever Young Lions challenged the policies of the older organisation and they won the day. The Apt Nation Corporation then adopted stronger, more direct, up-to-date policies. Do you know what that was really about?'

Joan looked at me quizzically.

'It was the story of beginnings of the resistance to apartheid. It was about the formation of the African National Congress. The ANC's idea was to draw the black tribes into one nation to fight the injustices they were all suffering. The Clever Young Lions – as Dad called them – were the Congress Youth League, which had brilliant young students heading it, like Anton Lambede, Nelson Mandela, Walter Sisulu, Oliver Tambo and Govan Mbeki. The Congress Youth League brought militant policies into the African National Congress.

'I discovered Dad's library when I stayed at the flat. It was like finding a gold mine! He had histories – books, articles, newspapers and pamphlets going back years, relating to struggles for liberation all over the world. I found out about people like Marx and Lenin. Lenin was a great humanist, both a thinker and an activist. I found his writing quite easy to understand. He explained society – how the motivation in our society is profit and how this means most people will live in poverty. He showed how to change this for the benefit of the majority. He explained that real power is concentrated with those who control finance. It was fascinating. We didn't hear about him at school. I suppose his writings are suppressed in this country. Lenin gives the recipe for people to get rid of injustice and the government must be terrified that ordinary people will read his books.

'I found articles written by black people in South Africa – by Sol Plaatje, Dr Dube and an amazing man called Pixley ka Isaka Seme. They were leaders of the ANC. They wrote about the suffering of the black people and they petitioned Britain for justice. But they never got anything from the British. When the Union of South Africa was created, Britain handed the power over to the whites – they caused the beginnings of legal racism in this country. Dad's library is a real eye-opener.'

'I've never heard of any of these things,' Joan said. 'I've never even met a black person who could read properly! But why do you have to go to Johburg?'

'There's obviously no resistance in Odendaalsrus. I want to get in touch with an organisation – there must be one that I can join in Johburg.'

'Why don't you ask Dad?'

'Oh, you know. It's impossible to talk to Dad these days. He's changed so much. He doesn't seem to be interested anymore. I did ask him once and he said something like, "If you stick your neck out too far, it'll get snapped off." Something really off-putting like that. I couldn't connect what he said then with the man who told us all those wonderful stories. He's shut down – monosyllabic.'

'When we were last in Durban,' Joan said, 'we made arrange-ments to see him one night. Went all the way there and he'd forgotten. He was just going out. Then he complains that we never see him.'

'I did once ask him, what about all his talk when I was little about fighting for what's right? He looked at me – a funny sort of look – and he said, "Well, Vroomie, you might just get your elbows knocked off!" I couldn't make sense of that either so I dropped it. Poor Dad, he is such a *good* man. I suppose he feels life has trampled on him.'

'Well, he *is* right,' Joan said. 'If you go around promoting ideas that black people should be like us, you're going to get into trouble. But if you want to go to Johburg now, I'll drive you to the station. I'll always help you, you know, even though I really don't understand what bee you've got in your bonnet. First, though, let's try to get you fixed up with somewhere to stay.'

Joan phoned around her friends and came up with a family in Johannesburg that took in lodgers, so it was arranged that I would stay with the Blechers.

And so I left Odendaalsrus and took the train to Johannes-burg.

Also lodging at the Blechers' was Helen Navid, who worked at the Entokozweni Health Clinic at Alexandra Township – a dormitory town for black people who serviced the needs of white Johannesburg. Helen was helpful and suggested I should join the Discussion Club. 'That's where progressives go,' she said. She would take me with her when next she went and introduce me to everyone. Meetings were held weekly, but she would have to get permission to bring me along.

Sitting at the Blecher table at dinner, I heard about the campaign that was about to be launched by the ANC – the Defiance Against Unjust Laws. The campaign was to be led by Nelson Mandela – he was the volunteer-in-chief. He was to be arrested first. The plan was that everyone would break the laws and go to jail – the jails would be so full that the authorities would not be able to process all the people who were arrested. Black people would get on white buses and trains, sit on white benches, go through doors marked WHITES ONLY. Whites were to do the reverse. This would bring to the attention of the world the growing number of draconian laws used to oppress the black people.

On the following day, 26 June 1952, I prepared myself to go to jail. I dressed carefully and put an extra pair of broeks in my handbag and sewed the button on my skirt waistband. One of my mother's oft-repeated warnings was never to wear a safety pin – you don't know when you'll be in an accident and then they'll find out how untidy you are. Well, going to jail was nearly the same. I didn't know where to go – and I hadn't asked. I made my way to the Joubert Park, where I sat alone on a bench marked NIE BLANKES – NON-WHITES. And there I awaited arrest.

There were not many people around, but my heart pounded and I was very frightened. I should have found out the details. There was not a policeman in sight yet and I didn't know then that some police wore plain clothes. I sat on that bench, waiting for a hand on my shoulder. My fear increased, but I also felt a sense of great satisfaction: I was protesting against the unjust laws. It seemed a miracle that the day I arrived in Johannesburg,

I had met people who knew something about what was going on in the resistance.

Two black nannies with their white charges looked at me askance and sat on the grass nearby. I waited another hour and at half past four I went home.

Over 8000 people were arrested in that campaign.

I got a job working for an electrical contracting company and I made contact with some of my old school friends. They thought I was crazy. There was very little support among white people for the liberation struggle in the fifties. I thought that the minute I informed them about the things I knew, about the injustices and the laws, they would be sure to join in. But they looked at me blankly. They didn't want to know.

I became a regular weekly attender of the Discussion Club and met people who were to become heroes and, in some cases, martyrs of the liberation struggle – people like Nelson Mandela, Walter and Albertina Sisulu, Moses Kotane, Ahmed Kathrada (Kathy), Babla Salojee, Duma Nokwe, Farid Adam, Robbie Resha, Betty du Toit, Yusuf and Amina Cachalia, Mosie Moolla, Barbara Peltu, Cecil Williams and many others.

The Discussion Club was a forum for progressive education. We learned about the real South Africa – not the version in the white press or the white history books.

I'll never forget attending a meeting addressed by Walter Sisulu. He was then secretary-general of the ANC and he had been a Congress Youth Leaguer with Nelson Mandela in the 1940s, so I had read about him in my father's papers. He was about forty years old, a warm friendly man, full of confidence, and he exuded a quiet energy. He had a wonderful warm smile and a keen sense of humour. He spoke to us about the need for all who opposed apartheid to act together. He was clear and direct, unlike some of the speakers, who spoke jargon and if you didn't understand it, you missed the point. Walter Sisulu told us that he would fight all his life for the abolition of discriminatory laws and for the freedom of all South Africans, irrespective of colour or creed. He was to be one of those instrumental in setting up a white wing of Congress – the Congress of

Democrats. Until the formation of COD, the Communist Party was the only organisation whites who opposed racism could join.

In the discussion that followed Mr Sisulu's talk, three young whites argued that if black people had the vote it would lead to havoc and war because the majority of whites would not accept it. Feeling very scared, wobbling, I rose to my feet and made my first public contribution. Right now, I said, violence, havoc and degradation were being perpetrated against more than 18 million black people. Three million whites, to keep their material advantage and privilege, subjected the black people to conditions worse than slavery. If we did not all have equal political rights, then total havoc and violence on a massive scale were inevitable. To base resistance on the omnipotence of white power as they did was racist. All whites in South Africa – ourselves included – were tainted with racism, and should learn to serve black people instead of perpetuating an artificial superiority even in the progressive movement.

I halted and then stopped talking. My hands felt sweaty and I was so nervous that my words seemed disconnected. But I felt proud that I had made a sensible statement and was surprised and rather terrified to notice that my opinion was not well received by some of those present. A statement followed to the effect that discriminating against white progressives was racist, and I wondered whether I had expressed myself badly and should speak again. But I was too nervous to say anything more. Little did I understand then that by taking the position that whites should serve the liberation movement, I was challenging the most dearly held concepts of some of the white so-called Communists.

Although the Communist Party was recruiting members from the Discussion Club, I was not invited to join and soon noticed that I was excluded from the inner sanctum – the club within the Club – that the Communist Party members formed.

But at that meeting, Walter Sisulu looked at me with approval, nodded and smiled.

In December 1952, a mass demonstration was called by the

91

ANC on Human Rights Day and Walter Sisulu took my arm and led me to the head of the procession. This kindness by a great man, in the face of the hostility I had engendered among some of my white colleagues, was to remain a lifelong comfort to me. It was encapsulated in a photograph taken that day by Eli Weinberg – a man who photographed many highlights of the struggles of the 1950s.

From what I heard, listening to talk at the Discussion Club and at social evenings, it appeared to me that many white people saw themselves as leaders and interpreters of black people and their struggle. Having been so impressed with my readings of Lenin and my attempts to read Marx, I considered myself a communist, and the arrogance of these white Communist Party members was embarrassing.

There were many black people who felt that 'progressive' whites were trying to dictate to them, demonstrating, often with impatience, their skill in organisation and learning, speech-making and writing articles. Our white education and our privileged upbringing certainly gave us the lead in form. But whatever advantage this form was to the movement, it lacked the content that black people could always give in the struggle for liberation. They were the oppressed. They suffered the sharp edge in every aspect of their lives. We returned after meetings and demonstrations to our comfortable homes and relatively rich lives, they to harassment, poverty, inferior jobs, to the ghettos of apartheid South Africa.

Many black activists felt that the struggle was hampered by rich deft whites. This fact, and disagreements with formulations in the Freedom Charter, led to a group splitting away from the ANC to form the Pan Africanist Congress, whose leader, Robert Mangaliso Sobukwe, said, 'Communism, like Christianity, has been unfortunate in its choice of representatives in South Africa.'

I have always believed that the policies of the African National Congress are correct – all racial groups in South Africa should fight against apartheid and share democratically in a liberated South Africa. It is in our common interest. But equally

Grannie (centre) with her children (Mom fourth from left), 1950.

Me and boyfriend, Mom, Oscar, Joan and Rolf.

From left to right: Yusef Cachalia, Yetta Bahrenblatt,
Walter Sisulu, Norma. Alexandra Township,
Human Rights Day demonstration, December 1952.

Kliptown Congress of the People, adoption of the Freedom Charter, 26
June 1955.

I believe that the domination of whites in the liberation struggle, mainly because of their financial superiority, has always been detrimental to the movement and misleading to the fighting people of South Africa.

In October 1953, the white wing of the Congress movement was formed – the Congress of Democrats, COD, which I joined. Congress had four divisions representing the four major races in South Africa: the African National Congress, for black people; the South African Indian Congress; the Coloured People's Organisation; and the Congress of Democrats. Later, in 1956, came the fifth arm, the South African Congress of Trade Unions. These five arms are often known simply under one title, as the ANC or Congress.

In 1953 the government decided to move the residents of Sophiatown because they wanted the land for white residence. They also wanted to dispossess the black people who owned title deeds to land and property in the area. Congress mounted a campaign to resist the move. As a COD member, I attended meetings, typed documents, daubed hundreds of slogans on walls and gave out reams of leaflets to oppose the removal. Thousands of people became active in the campaign but over 2000 police, with military units and armoured vehicles, went into the area and smashed up Sophiatown, forcing over 6000 people to move. Then they called their new white suburb *Triomf* (Triumph).

I attended COD parties. The Congress movement was the only political organisation that mixed across the races. We met at some rich house in the white suburbs – and a few black people who could get transport to the area would attend. At one of these evenings, at Rosa Woolf's house, I said to Kathy (Ahmed Kathrada) that I felt we should do more – that it was all very well going to meetings and giving out leaflets, but what could I *do*? Kathy smiled.

'You have to learn patience, you know. This is a long, hard struggle.'

'Well, it's bound to be long if we all sit around at socials and meetings,' I said.

Kathy smiled at my naive impatience. He was a man who had fought the system since he was a young boy. 'Come and see me at the Indian Congress office tomorrow,' Kathy said.

The following day we discussed my contribution.

'There's lots you can do,' Kathy said. 'First, you can impart the knowledge you have to others. The Congress Movement is short of typists – you're a typist. How about teaching our people?'

It was decided that I would run typing classes on Saturday mornings. There was one typewriter in the office and I was to try and get another. Congress would put out to our contacts that lessons in typewriting were available.

I went to see my uncle Chips, who owned Cranko Typewriters.

'Your family's not going to like it, you know.'

'You *are* my family,' I said.

'Well, I mean your mother's family. Don't tell them I had anything to do with it. I don't want all those aunts and uncles of yours ranting on at me. They'll raise hell. I'll give you four. They're old ones but good enough to teach on.'

Each week my mother would telephone me from Durban, anxious about my doings. She always asked about my social life and whether I had met any 'nice boys'. When I plucked up courage to explain to her that I was teaching typing at Congress office she was perplexed.

'What do you want to *do* to the natives?' she asked.

'Teach them to type.'

'But nobody would think of employing a native as a typist.'

I could find no answer to that. We always managed to get into these situations of total incomprehension. She made me feel ridiculous. What on earth *was* I doing? There was a long pause while I felt everything beginning to slip away.

'Well, are they *nice* girls?'

'Who?'

'The girls you teach it to.'

'Oh, they aren't only female. There are lots of men as well.'

I could feel my mother faint on the phone. 'You're not to have

94

anything to do with native men,' she said emphatically. She had the firm conviction, in common with most white South Africans, that all black men were rapists, just waiting to get their hands on white girls. I tried to reason with her but she was adamant. 'You don't want to listen, but I want to tell you that one day the black person you trust the most will put a knife in your back.'

'Why?'

'Because. They're not like us, you know. They look at our clothes and our houses and things and they envy us.'

'But that's the point,' I said. 'I don't want to live like we do in Durban, with too much of everything – and people all around literally starving, with no homes, no proper jobs, and not able to be with their families. I want to help change all that – make it fair.'

My mother sighed deeply. 'I don't know what's wrong with you,' she said eventually. 'All I'm scared of is that one of those "boys" is going to take advantage of you. Or you'll be going home and someone will knife you. They all carry knives. You know how dangerous they are.'

It was the old story so familiar to white children. How your old faithful black cook, nanny or gardener would one day become a vicious animal and suddenly stab you in the back. It was part of the mythology that kept black people at a distance.

'Well, if I was them, I'd also feel murderous towards people throwing away their old caviar in the bin, and making me polish sixteen pairs of shoes every day while I was barefoot. Anyway, I've been hearing about black people stabbing me to death since I was born and they've always treated me very well. But I suppose it will be a self-fulfilling prophecy one day. Perhaps they will turn in violence against us one day! But it won't go away if we ignore the situation.

'What do you think has happened to Sixpence? We knew him for years and years.'

'Who?'

'You remember, Sarah's son. Your maid. When I was little.'

'My maid's name was Lenie.'

95

'Well, when I was little, you had a maid called Sarah, and she had a boy of about fourteen. His real name was Zolile but everyone called him Sixpence. He used to come and stay with us for a few weeks now and then to be with his mother.'

'Oh, yes, I remember. She was that cheeky, sullen girl. She was absolutely no good. She was a terrible worker. She was for ever going home because one of her children was ill or her mother had died. She cheated us left, right and centre. She broke a very expensive coffee pot. I think that's the girl.'

'OK, Mom. But she worked for us for years and she had a son we knew. He used to play with Ronnie. Don't you care what became of him? I sometimes think he may have died of starvation in Zululand, or spent years in jail for pass offences. Or maybe he went to work in the mines and his leg got severed in a rock fall. Or maybe he became somebody's Jim and worked in a white garden. That little boy loved us. He was bright and intelligent. He used to shine and polish your car and run to the shops for us. And when anyone spoke to him he had a big wide smile.'

'Well, darling, it's very charitable of you. They all have too many children and then they complain because they can't look after them. But it's got nothing to do with this. Teaching typing to natives is a different matter.'

'No, it isn't. It's a question of caring. I never again want to get close to people and not know or care what happens to them just because they're black. Sarah and Sixpence simply disappeared from our lives.'

My mother changed tack. 'Please, darling! For my sake, don't do it. What can I possibly tell the family? How can I possibly explain to them?'

'You don't have to explain anything about me to anyone.'

'But you know they'll find out. If I just tell them you've become a teacher, that will be all right. But they'll find out. I'm sure they will.'

'Mom, don't be so scared about it. I'm just giving classes once a week. It's no big deal. If you feel you have to, just tell the family I'm teaching typing – that's all.'

'You're putting your life in danger, getting mixed up with the natives – you know you are. You're making me suffer! I'll never understand you.'

And she never did. Her fears were so far from the reality of my life that I could not talk to her for years.

I went to find a good teaching manual and was suddenly struck by the idiocy of what typists had to learn: laying out invoices, statements and agreements – only commerce and law. The people I was teaching wouldn't be able to work in those fields. I decided to adapt a Pitman's manual to a political type-writing one. Armed with the first lesson, I arrived on the chosen Saturday.

Twenty-two people turned up for the first class. I started everyone off learning the home keys by drumming their fingers on their laps, with the first four to arrive using the keyboards. Every week the number of people wanting to learn to type increased. A labourer of eighty came. His fingers were so gnarled and broad that they spanned two keys. Everyone want-ed to learn. In the sixth week over fifty people came. I'd made a register like the one we had at school and recorded reasons for absence: 'Solomon – arrested for pass offence. Agnes – her madam won't let her off every Saturday. Petrus – child ill – has gone home to Transkei. Bertha – in hospital with TB.' There in my little white-girl register-book was written the tragic story of the people of Johannesburg.

The classes grew and Kathy got two more volunteers from the Congress of Democrats, Barbara Peltu and Barbara Cooper, to teach English and shorthand.

Millions of South Africans were voteless, and in 1953 the president of the Cape ANC, Professor Z.K. Matthews, put for-ward the idea of a convention to which all the people of South Africa would send delegates to make known what sort of South Africa they wanted to live in. Chief Albert Lutuli, president of the ANC, then issued a call for volunteers to go and canvass people in every part of the country. Ten thousand volunteers came forward. The Freedom Volunteers, in Congress uni-form – khaki suits, with the black, green and gold Congress colours on their cuffs – then went throughout the country to hear the people's wishes. From schools, colleges, communities, offices, farms and factories came the demands. Some were short, on scraps of paper: 'I want my land back.' 'We want education.' 'I want a job.' 'I want to vote.' There were also sophisticated documents outlining a future South Africa. These demands were sorted into categories and I was called in to help collate and type the drafts of what was to become the Freedom Charter – the programme of Congress.

Nelson Mandela, then deputy president of the African National Congress, was in law practice with Oliver Tambo, then secretary-general, and both were banned by the authorities from holding office and from attending the Congress of the People. Chief Lutuli was restricted to his home in Groutville in Natal.

The white political parties, the United Party, led by General Smuts, which had been in power until 1948, and the Nationalist Party, led by Dr Malan, refused to participate. The government in South Africa has always refused to participate in any national convention.

On 25 and 26 June 1955, the Congress of the People took place at Kliptown near Johannesburg. It was addressed by many leaders and representatives of the people. The logistical problems were enormous: transport, food (including provision for vegetarians), toilet facilities and accommodation for some 2900 delegates had to be arranged.

The air was charged with excitement. For the first time, a democratic representative gathering was taking place to choose a future South Africa. Apart from the delegates, there were many spectators and observers, of whom I was one. The delegations kept arriving and the crowds were gathering. I was walking around with Congress friends, greeting familiar faces, when a policeman came up to me and took my name and address and rudely told me to leave immediately. As I turned contemptuously away from him, I was photographed by his crony, gathering material for police dossiers on those who attended.

It was a boiling hot day and the meeting took place in a huge open square. The police erected roadblocks and tried to prevent people from attending – they arrested over 200 delegates. From all over South Africa – from the remotest parts of the country – the people came. The final tally of attending delegates was 2222 Africans, 320 Indians, 230 Coloureds and 112 whites. They held a forest of placards with the people's demands.

The Special Branch swarmed over the area and encircled the perimeter. They harassed the meeting. They set up a 'registration table' to confuse people; they made arrests and searches and confiscated documents. But the meeting continued. One by one, the demands were voted on. To this day the Freedom Charter is the programme of the African National Congress.

Its preamble states: 'We, the People of South Africa, declare for all our country and the world to know' and then the main headings are:

The people shall govern
All national groups shall have equal rights
The people shall share in the country's wealth
The land shall be shared among those who work it
All shall be equal before the law
All shall enjoy equal human rights
There shall be work and security
The doors of learning and of culture shall be opened
There shall be houses, security and comfort
There shall be peace and friendship

And the document ends:

Let all who love their people and their country now say, as we say here: 'These freedoms we will fight for, side by side, throughout our lives, until we have won our liberty.'

It was just. It was fair. It was democratically decided by millions of South Africans. It was the programme I dedicated my life to.

At 4 am on 5 December 1956, the regime hit back. Police raids took place throughout South Africa. One hundred and fifty-six people were arrested, brought to Johannesburg and imprisoned at the Fort. The trial lasted for four years. The prosecution brought into court, as evidence of communism, signs we had erected for feeding the people: SOUP WITH MEAT,

99

SOUP WITHOUT MEAT. The ridiculous trial dragged on. The regime had creamed off the leaders of the Congress, community leaders and leaders of the trade unions. They hoped, by forcing these people out of activity, to crush the political fervour that had arisen following the adoption of the Freedom Charter. Nelson Mandela, Walter Sisulu and Ahmed Kathrada were, of course, among the accused. Each day people gathered outside the courts holding signs, WE STAND BY OUR LEADERS.

But by then I had left South Africa to go to the Warsaw Youth Festival. This occasion, held in a different country every two years by the World Federation of Democratic Youth, was a forum for progressive young people of all lands to come together to enjoy each other's cultures, participate in meetings and seminars, and exchange ideas. Black South Africans found it impossible to obtain passports or raise the expensive fares. Kathy, Ahmed Kathrada, suggested that it would be useful if I attended as a Congress delegate, and by luck, my uncle Herbert Cranko offered me a free trip to London.

· 6 ·

It had been only a couple of weeks since I'd bumped into my uncle Herbert in Rissik Street in Johannesburg.

'What are you doing with yourself these days?' Uncle Herbert asked.

'Working,' I said.

'Working at what?'

'I'm a secretary at Penman and Jochelson, the electrical contractors.' I did not say that although I was earning my living there I was working all my spare time for the liberation movement.

I did not discuss my political life with my family. It contradicted everything they stood for. They enjoyed the privileges being white gave them.

'Well,' I said. 'I've been studying at night for my matric and I've been saving up to go overseas.' I did not mention that I was trying to find my fares to attend the Warsaw Youth Festival and that so far I had not managed to save a penny.

'Trek Airways owes me a flight,' he said. Uncle Herbert was a director of El Al. 'If you're prepared to leave in a couple of weeks you can have a seat. OK? London will do you good. Just see to it when you're over there that you do something useful.'

The South African delegates were going to form a committee in London in preparation for the Festival. I arrived in London on a bleak day in July 1955. I thought it was freezing. I had thirty pounds to my name and got a room at the Overseas Visitors Club which I shared with a South African girl who worked at the South African embassy. We were not compatible roommates. I got a temporary typing job at Calor Gas in Oxford Street for six pounds a week through Miss Mitchell's

Secretariat, an employment agency in Holborn. Six pounds a week was enough to live on if I didn't eat, so I subsisted on a store of cornflakes and syrup and began to lose weight rapidly.

The Festival in Warsaw was at the end of July and I was to bide my time till then, attending meetings and preparing for the occasion.

One lunch hour I bumped into Rosie – Rosenblatt – a baker trade unionist from Johannesburg. He was an old friend from the Congress of Democrats and the Discussion Club, and he invited me for dinner that evening. That afternoon at work I had more visions than usual of food – of eggs and bacon, steak-and-kidney pies, the chicken we used to have at Sunday lunches at home. By the time I met Rosie I was famished.

Walking down Oxford Street with Rosie, we saw a large man striding purposefully towards us. His right arm was held out, crooked, in front of him and draped over it was a pair of dark-grey trousers. He rushed up to Rosie, full of pleasure and excitement.

'Rosie! What are you doing in London? Oh, man, how wonderful to see you!'

Rosie said, 'Dave, hello there, man! Dave Kitson, this is Norma Cranko.'

David ignored that. 'Where are you two going?' he asked.

'I'm taking her to eat – Freddie Mills, we were thinking of. We're going to have a Chinese meal.'

'Oh, good!' David said. 'I like Chinese.'

My God! I thought. He's just inviting himself along.

At Freddie Mills, David kept Rosie in animated conversation while I ate huge quantities of food. Now and then I looked at David: he gestured continually, almost knocking glasses over, straightening knives and forks as he and Rosie talked about old times and all the friends they had left in South Africa. David chuckled often – an infectious sound which expressed his pleasure rather than the subject of their talk. Their memories were warm and I sat there wishing I had been part of all the people and events they were remembering. The older generation of South African activists sounded as if it had been closer and in some way more more integrated than the young people I had met at the Discussion Club or in COD.

'Remember when Rowley made us become blood donors, during the war,' David said, 'and we all trooped down to the place and queued and most of the guys keeled over at the sight of the needle?'

'Yes,' said Rosie. 'But remember when we pretended an instruction had come through that all comrades had to do a parachute jump and June was about six months pregnant and asked if that was a fair enough excuse not to jump? And you said, "Comrade! Surely you aren't going to plead special privileges for women!"'

They laughed.

David's light-blue eyes, impersonal when he looked at me, were warm looking at Rosie. He was full of intelligence and brimming with energy. Nice brown hair. High forehead. And bloody rude, I thought. How can anyone sit at the table and just ignore me? Obviously he had not studied our family's code of conduct. I remembered my mother's table rules. *If* you talk, and you should only make *polite* conversation at table, then first to the person on your left – a few remarks – then a *different* few remarks on your right and then *right across the table*, so that no one feels left out.

'What are those?' I asked, venturing conversation. I pointed at the fourth chair where he had hung the trousers ever so carefully over the back.

'I just bought them,' he said.

'Well, why were you carrying them like that? Didn't they give you a bag or something?'

'Yes.'

I couldn't think of anything to say. Rosie and he started another 'You remember when . . . '

I was to find out that whenever David bought anything it was a big occasion. He was as excited as a child about it. He wasn't going to hide anything in a bag! We were to stride down many streets flaunting our purchases in our arms.

When they walked me to the tube to go back to Earls Court I

103

felt disappointed. Rosie promised to telephone me and take me out to dinner again. But David just waved goodbye. Most of the men I met at home in South Africa used to go through the motions – ask for my phone number, make some sort of pass I could snub, or say 'See you soon!' or something that meant I wasn't what they called a dog. As I went down the stairs in the underground I glanced up and saw them deep in conversation. I might as well not have existed.

The Festival committee met at the flat of Andra and Gerry Goldman, a South African couple living in London. I took the tube to Swiss Cottage and there, sitting comfortably ensconced in an armchair, was David. He was a senior member of the committee. He had been a delegate to the Berlin and Bucharest festivals so he knew the ropes. The meeting had not yet started and as I entered, David was talking animatedly to the four or five people present.

They were discussing Walter Sisulu's visit to London in 1953 when David had been delegated to escort Walter to meetings. Everyone wanted to know about Mr Sisulu – a man who had been in the South African struggle for fifteen years. He'd been repeatedly arrested and jailed. He had been charged under the Suppression of Communism Act, David said, in 1952 after the Defiance Campaign Against Unjust Laws – when I had sat waiting to be arrested in Joubert Park on my own – then banned and confined to the magisterial district of Johannesburg. Nevertheless he had been on the national action committee which had formed the Congress of Democrats in 1953.

'Despite all the restrictions on him, Walter Sisulu is at the very heart of the liberation movement in South Africa,' David said. 'He has fought on *all* the major issues – tremendously powerful! Everyone goes to him for advice and political discussions and if they are in trouble. When he came over here, he said he was paying a good-will visit on behalf of democratic South Africa. I accompanied him as a sort of guide and guard during his stay in England and everywhere he went, he made a tremendous impression. It was a terrific honour for me. As soon as he got back home, the security police began harassing him again. Last year he was banned from attending meetings and was arrested yet again for attending a gathering to "partake of, or be present whilst others partake of, refreshment (in the nature of tea and/or some such other liquid refreshment, and/or edibles and/or a meal)". The government know full well what they are up against with giants like him, Nelson Mandela and Oliver Tambo. They aren't going to leave them alone, you know. Those guys are really sticking their necks out. But nothing stops them – and their wives are just like them, real fighters. They face hard lives, and they hardly ever see their husbands. They're married to the struggle. People like that ignore the harassment – they just go on like steamrollers, fighting for a just South Africa.'

The audience was spellbound and, when David paused, asked questions until another four or five young white South Africans arrived. The meeting started with the business of organising the delegation. We discussed our uniforms – green skirts with white blouses for the women; the songs we would sing; the gifts we would exchange; and we wondered which of our black comrades would manage to get out of South Africa to attend. We knew that John Motloheloa of Lesotho would be leading the delegation and we were to meet him later. I glanced at David frequently. He had described Walter Sisulu vividly and had expressed such empathy for the wives of the harassed leaders that I was deeply impressed. There was something so attractive about the way he sat, the way he moved and talked. He smiled and chuckled often and was at ease. He had everyone's respect and he made practical suggestions. He was confident and relaxed.

David wasn't at the meeting the following Wednesday and I felt desolate. I had not realised how much I was looking forward to seeing him.

At our third Festival meeting we had a very long agenda. More and more people were arriving to join the delegation. When the meeting broke up I found myself outside the Goldmans' flat saying good night to everybody with David at my side.

105

'Where are *you* going?' he asked.

'To the tube,' I said.

'There's no underground running at this time of night.'

I looked at my watch. It was a quarter to eleven. I turned back, thinking I would ask Andra and Gerry if I could sleep on their floor.

David said, 'You can come to my place, if you like. I have a couch in the bedroom.'

I couldn't find an answer. I continued walking towards the underground. I felt in a turmoil. Was he just being kind? Was it 'Well, we like each other so let's go to bed?' *What* was it? We had hardly spoken a personal word to each other. Perhaps he thought I was a bed-hopper. Maybe he wanted sex and just invited women to his home for it.

'You're going the wrong way,' he said. 'My place is down this road.' I followed him. On the way he was full of chat about the meeting. I felt embarrassed. What if he thought it was quite natural for me to sleep in men's bedrooms? What if he thought it was a sort of deal—I offer you a bed, you give me sex? What would my mother say? I'd show him he'd met his match. I'd refuse even the slightest advance. I'd be quite shocked and superior. Walking with him, talking with him, I determined to show him that I was not to be trifled with.

David had a room in Hornsey, in Fortismere Avenue. He opened the door to his room and said he was going to the bathroom.

'There are some sheets in that box under the couch,' he said. 'You can make it up with them. I've got a spare pillow. You can even have a bath if you like. I'll be back in a minute. I'm just going to brush my teeth.'

I entered the room and stood in the middle of it, looking around in astonishment. It was as bare as a monk's cell. His bed was covered with a threadbare pale-green cotton spread. There was a desk with a clock, a mug filled with pencils and a stack of three filing baskets. One contained shirts, the second vests and underpants and the bottom one carefully twinned socks. The walls were bare, painted white. There was one wooden chair and a shelf of books. Everything was spotlessly clean. No carpet, no heater, no knickknacks. The curtains at the bay window were pale-blue cotton.

I took off my coat and pulled out the box, took out two beautifully ironed sheets and made up the couch. David walked in, holding up a boxed toothbrush. 'Here,' he said. 'You'll need this. The bathroom's just to the right. And here.' He threw me his dressing gown.

Oh, my God! I thought. He even has toothbrushes for the occasion. I decided to have a bath so I could think.

If he comes over to kiss me when I'm on the couch, I'll say, 'I'm not that kind of girl.' No. That sounds precious – and unsophisticated. I'll say, 'I don't kiss every man I meet.' No, that sounds dreadful. I'll say, 'Please don't do that. I hardly know you.' If he says something like, 'Come and have a cuddle,' I'll say, 'Oh, I know all about that.' No, that sounds too coy. I'll say, 'Oh you men! I don't cuddle strangers.' No, that sounds just like Mom. Oh, hell! If my clothes weren't in the bedroom, I'd just walk back to Andra and Gerry.

I emerged from the bathroom very tight-jawed, panicked and sweating. I entered the bedroom.

David was turned on his side and as I got between the sheets on the couch he switched off the light. 'Good night.'

'Good night,' I said. I lay rigid, waiting. Then I heard even, gentle breathing. The bastard's asleep, I said to myself. He isn't going to make a pass at me.

The next morning when I awoke, David's bed was empty. I got up, dressed, and met him on my way to have a wash, jumping up a few stairs.

'My kitchen's in here,' he said. 'I've made us some breakfast.'

The kitchen was bare, yet cosy. A wooden table, no tablecloth, four chairs, a cooker, no fridge, a few shelves. One jar of jam, butter, salt and pepper, a tin of baked beans, a box of eggs, a bottle of milk, one tin of sardines and a wrapped loaf of bread.

David had made bacon, eggs, tomatoes and toast – a real feast. The food was wonderful after the endless bowls of cornflakes and syrup I had been eating. I felt at ease. He was warm and friendly and told me of his days in the army as a sapper. He had been sent to Italy. Out on patrol with two others, David had come upon a German soldier, armed but trying to hide. He captured him, but knew that as his unit was on the move, prisoners would be shot once they returned to base.

'At first he was just another fascist bastard in uniform,' David said. 'But then I looked at his face. I don't think he could have been more than thirteen or fourteen years old. He was standing there quivering. I took his gun off him and, before the others could catch up with me, I pointed some distance away and said to him, "Walk over there to the prisoner-of-war cage." I could speak quite a lot of German by then. The boy stood looking at me terrified. Then he high-tailed it off and away. I don't think I've ever seen anyone run so fast.'

I looked at David in silence.

'It's often worried me,' he said. 'Little fascists grow up to be big fascists, don't they? But he was so *young*. And all the time, you knew you should have been shooting the people at the top. Most of the men in the field were workers like us. If you look at it one way, we were shooting our brothers.' David downed a cup of tea in three gulps, and asked about my family and about the work I had done in South Africa. I began to tell him about my typing classes at the Congress office when he glanced at his watch.

'What time do you start work?'

'Nine o'clock.'

'I'll walk you to the tube.'

We walked the few blocks to the underground. Will he ask to see me again? I thought. Will he ask where I live? Rosie had probably told him.

'I've a room at the Overseas Visitors Club,' I ventured.

'Oh, what's it like?'

'Awful.'

'You should look for somewhere better to stay, then.' Very practical. At the tube he said, 'Goodbye.'

'Goodbye,' I replied.

I couldn't wait for the next Wednesday meeting. It'll be a late one again, I thought. I'm sure it will. There's so much to discuss. Then I panicked in case it might end early enough for me to catch the tube. I'll *make* it late, I thought. For the breakfast. I'm not getting enough to eat. He's poor by Durban standards – but at least he eats well. He's open about everything, trusting, almost vulnerable. He's different. He talks so easily – as if I was an old friend or another man. There isn't that embarrassing barrier that there usually is when you meet someone you're attracted to. But is he attracted to me? I felt that he was, but he had given no indication of it. That week my mind kept dwelling on the things he'd said, the way he looked and all that he'd achieved. He'd been in the liberation movement since he was twenty years old. Now he was thirty-six. We had both known and worked with leading members of the South African struggle. I decided to buy a new black skirt and I also bought some flat black-and-white lattice shoes. More of the £30 went. By the time Wednesday came I had a long list of points to raise at the meeting. And I wore my new clothes.

I arrived early at the Goldmans' flat. Andra and Gerry were still eating supper.

'Where do you know David from?' I asked them.

'He's from Durban, same as you,' Gerry said. 'Why?'

'He doesn't act as if he comes from Durban,' I said.

'What do you mean?' Andra asked.

'Oh, you know. He doesn't seem to be interested in women – hasn't got a clue how to behave.'

They laughed. 'By *Durban*, you mean *your* family, don't you. Everyone from Durban isn't like your family, you know,' Andra said.

'Well, I think he's not at all like the Durban blokes I've met,' I said.

I waited expectantly for him to arrive at the meeting and was very put out when he came in with my friend Barbara Peltu. Barbara had taught shorthand at the Congress office while I taught typing. We sang in a liberation choir together, had joined COD at the same time and had both campaigned during the Western Areas Removal Scheme. Barbara was renowned for her

109

looks – and her beautiful voice. No wonder he's not interested in me, I thought. He's been seeing her. Before the meeting started, I had a chat with Barbara about what she was doing before the Festival.

'I'm going to go with Barney Simon to Europe,' she said. 'I can't bear waiting in London.'

'Are you going out with David?'

'David who?'

'David Kitson.'

'No, why?'

'I just wondered.' I felt greatly relieved.

During the meeting I kept glancing at my watch. By 9.30 we were well into the agenda. Oh, hell, I thought. We're going to finish early. When David said, 'Well, that's decided then, let's move on,' I felt angry and depressed. He's *trying* to get the meeting over with, I thought.

But the meeting went over time. Outside the Goldmans' flat David said:

'Where are *you* going?'

'To the tube.'

'It's too late for the underground now.'

'Oh, hell.'

'You can stay over at my place, if you like.'

This time as we walked to David's room, chatting as we went, I thought, He'll try something this time. He was just being polite. I mean, last time we'd only just sort of met. But I won't simply give in or anything. I don't want him to think I'm easy.

This time we went into his kitchen and he made tea before we went to bed. I declined a bath. I didn't want him falling asleep again.

He went off to wash and then I went to wash. When I entered the bedroom, heart pounding, David was in bed, reading. I made up the couch and climbed between the sheets. David put the light out.

He's going to come over now, I thought, full of excitement. But all he said was 'Good night'.

'Good night,' I said, and in a few minutes I heard that he was asleep.

I lay there seething. Imagine *inviting* a woman into your bedroom, I thought, and then just falling *asleep*. He's all very animated and chatty when there are people around. He even put his arm across my shoulder on the way home. That's a come-on, isn't it? I felt insulted. My mother wouldn't have believed it. She'd often said to me, 'Remember, men only want one thing – they're all the same. And if you give it to them then they want it from someone else.' It was obvious she hadn't met a character like this.

I couldn't sleep. I decided to go to the loo – that would wake him up. As I left the room, I closed the door quite sharply. But when I re-entered the room I realised nothing on earth was going to wake him. Resigned, I fell asleep.

The following morning David made breakfast – sausages, eggs, tomatoes and toast. He told me he had come to England because he was interested in aeronautics. He had qualified as an engineer at Natal University and was a top-notch draughtsman. South Africa was going to need all sorts of skills after liberation, and there was no real industry of that kind at home. He had got a job in aeronautical engineering in Hatfield and become a member of the Hatfield Trades Council. He had won a trade-union scholarship to Ruskin College in Oxford, where, instead of studying for a diploma, which most of the students were encouraged to do, he had opted instead to fulfil the real aims for which Ruskin was established as a working people's college – to have time to read and study, and then return to the factory floor. He deplored the fact that Ruskin managed to turn out personnel managers on the side of the bosses, instead of leaders of the working class. He had loved his two years there, studying politics, economics and Russian. It was a very special time for him. He had made many friends there and he offered to take me up to Oxford to meet the Spooner cousins – the father of one of them gave name to the spoonerism. Later I met these two delightful, very old ladies.

It was wonderful sitting there in that cosy kitchen listening to

111

David talk. He was totally committed to liberation in South Africa. 'I'm only here in England temporarily,' he said. 'It's up to every one of us to fit ourselves to work to build a free South Africa. Black people are doing the main fighting, giving up their lives, and the role of white South Africans is to be prepared to do the same – to assist the struggle wholeheartedly and wherever they can. The benefits will come to us all, and we are all involved.'

David explained that in a free South Africa, everyone would be better off. As things were now, certain people had material privilege but, as human beings, no one benefited. Oh, I agreed with him, with every word. It was exactly what I felt. I thought of my mother's family, doused in money and everything it could buy, discontented, unhappy, constantly visiting doctors, looking for cures for nonexistent physical and mental ills; of all the divorces, the restraints, the unhappiness.

We discovered that there was a time when he and I had lived opposite each other in Durban, in Gillespie Street. David's eyes were warm and animated as we mentioned names of people we both knew from Durban – not a strange phenomenon for South Africans! What was odd was that we had never met at home.

He walked me to the tube and we exchanged polite goodbyes.

I was in a fever of excitement the following Wednesday, but we seemed to be racing through the agenda. The meeting was over before ten o'clock. No couch. No breakfast. No talk with David. The Festival was getting nearer and after Warsaw I would return home to Johburg.

But on the way to the tube, David hurried after me. 'Don't you want to come to my place?' I did.

With the lights out in the bedroom, lying tense in the couch bed between the ironed sheets, with David in the bed with the pale-green cotton cover I found the courage to ask:

'Don't you like me?'

'Oh yes, I do. Very much,' he said.

'Well, don't you think you could show it a little?'

Silence from him.

'Don't you think it's strange that you haven't ever made any

112

move towards me, then?' I asked bravely.

'Oh, well,' he said. 'I'm not falling into any trap like that! If you want me, just come and get me.' He chuckled. 'I'm wary of you Durban girls – one move from me and I'd get some hoity-toity turn off – I'm-not-that-kind-of-girl sort of thing. I'm not playing any of those games.'

'I'm not like that,' I said. 'I'm an honest person.'

'Well,' he said, 'if you want me – I'm here in this big bed. Come and get me.'

I went over to his bed and he lifted up the sheets to welcome me in. My heart was beating in my ears. I snuggled up to him and he held me in his big warm embrace. I did not feel any shyness or shame. All the passion and energy I had sensed in him from the moment he had come striding towards Rosie and me in Oxford Street were there for me. We made love, we talked, we slept and in the morning after we had bathed together and eaten breakfast, David walked me to the tube.

I divided my nights, until I left for the Festival, between David's Fortismere room and the Overseas Visitors Club. On the morning of my departure David caught the bus with me to the station and we stood clinging together until the last minute when I jumped into a carriage – on my way to Poland.

I was lying on the trolley waiting to be wheeled into the operating theatre and I thought for the umpteenth time, Why? Why am I having this abortion? I really want this baby. I was having an abortion so that I could go home. But what could I do there? The role I had played seemed minimal and insignificant, especially now that I had met and fallen in love with David.

After the exciting events of the Warsaw Youth Festival in August, I returned to London and went straight to David's room. Empty! His landlady told me he was in hospital, having had his appendix out. I sped to the hospital, where I found David pale and droopy after his operation.

'I'm back.'

'Let's go home then.'

'You can't. You're sick.'

But David got out of bed, discharged himself and, since friends had taken his clothes, left the hospital clad in his pyjamas and dressing-gown. We got a taxi home.

That was the start of our life together. I moved into David's room and got a job in the geriatric department in the Highgate Wing of the Whittington Hospital. I enrolled for maths and physics courses at North London Poly and I joined the Finsbury Park Branch of the British Communist Party.

David had joined the British Communist Party on his arrival in Britain in 1947. He also belonged to many organisations set up in Britain in solidarity with the South African struggle. He had a busy schedule speaking to trade-union organisations, the United Nations Association and branches of the Workers' Education Association. Both of us were members of the *New Age* Committee, which raised funds for the liberation newspaper in South Africa. The government there regularly banned our progressive newspaper, and whenever it did so, we started another – with a different name, so that in succession our papers were the *Guardian*, *Advance*, *New Age*, *Spark*, *Fighting Talk* and *Liberation*.

Our lives were busy and it was a time of great political growth for me.

In the fifties Britain invited thousands of West Indians into the country, and in Finsbury Park they were packed, sometimes sixteen to a room, in dreadful living conditions. Their working conditions were little better. They did the worst jobs – shift work, hospital work, roads and rail. They joined the Party in droves. One only had to have a discussion about the Communist Manifesto or the local rents issue to find a dozen recruits. But the British Communist Party, I felt, let them down. They never were interested in the most oppressed sections of British society – black people, Irish people, women – who consequently drifted away. But I was ardent, and as fast as they drifted away, I recruited others. I saw clearly the connection between these exploited people and my people in South Africa. We were suffering from the same masters.

All the while I felt I should go back to South Africa but I did not want to leave David. So I decided to learn as much as possible in England – where education was virtually free – to put to use when I was able to go home.

I attended a CP women's school at Hastings and received a grounding in Marxist theory. It all seemed like basic common sense to me and with a naivety I never lost, I could not understand why more English people did not embrace Marxism.

David, who had become Hornsey borough secretary of the Communist Party, had political tasks nearly every night. We both sold the *Daily Worker* at Finsbury Park Underground before going to work every morning. I had college two nights a week, a CP branch meeting once a week and we went to the flicks on Saturday nights – usually the Finsbury Park Astoria. After the ritual Saturday night cinema-going with my Durban family, dressed to kill in organdy, wedgies and fur wraps, with the ritual gift of expensive chocolates by my rich Durban uncles, I found our visits to the local flicks, and our life generally, satisfying. I was living up to my brother Ronnie's injunctions: studying maths and physics. I was working for a wonderful boss – Dr Exton Smith, a geriatrician, dedicated to helping his patients – who had exceptionally high standards of work and research, and who was so polite that if I made a mistake in my typing he was too embarrassed to point it out directly. He would just leave papers containing errors on my desk and I would have to work out what I had done wrong. This made me determined never to make a single error and my typing skill improved enormously. I felt very proud to be the right hand of a man about whom everyone spoke with reverence.

I had never operated in a kitchen. I didn't even realise that water steamed when it boiled – though I had read about it when I studied dialectical materialism. David did it all. He made the beds, cleaned our room, cooked, washed and ironed. I shopped with him once a week, paying little attention. I continued to be an onlooker – as I had been brought up to be in South Africa. We each put three pounds a week in a kitty for our expenses and every few months we would divvy out what was left and then spend it all on a skirt for me, or shoes for me.

Although our days were routine and humdrum in many ways, I found life with David full of fun and excitement. I awoke each morning with a feeling of expectation which was renewed each night when we were going to be together. We exchanged each tiny bit of news. Friends came to stay, on a mattress in the kitchen. Once Harry Bloom stopped over in London en route to a meeting in Portugal to oppose sporting links with South Africa. He spent a couple of days with us. All I could talk about at breakfast was melon-and-ginger jam, which was not obtainable in England. Harry said, 'What's this yen? Are you pregnant?' And on his return to South Africa he sent *100 tins* of melon-and-ginger jam which we had quickly to share out among our friends as we had no place to store it.

The next day at work I fainted and the following morning I

vomited. I ignored this for a few weeks, hoping it would just go away, but there was no question – I was pregnant. I would have to have an abortion. David was in England to add to his engineering experience and he was performing the useful task of gaining solidarity for the South African struggle in Britain, and I did not know for how many years he intended to stay. And I felt I should get back home immediately to my typing class and to do what I could to help Congress.

I had once been to the office of Nelson Mandela and Oliver Tambo, who were in partnership in a law practice, and had done some typing there. People were jammed everywhere, even in the corridor, waiting to see these two men – hoping to get relief from legal problems, coming for political advice. Nelson Mandela was in his shirtsleeves, dynamic, authoritative, efficient, dealing with four or five different matters at once. But he stopped to ask if I had had a cup of tea. Oliver Tambo was quiet, even studious, as he frowned over his work, polite to a point of humility in advising his people. I wondered if they ever went home to sleep. I had never seen people work so hard. That's what this struggle takes, I said to myself: ceaseless work.

Remembering the urgency in that office, and the tirelessness of the leaders I had worked with, made me feel strongly that I should return to do my bit.

And I thought of what my family would say if, unmarried, I had the baby. I had overheard their salacious, stage-whispered gossip about girls who had 'ruined their reputations' and about men who had married 'shopsoiled goods'.

I also found that I was scared of giving birth and then raising a child. I felt I had little qualification for being a mother. Much of my own childhood had been a desperate and unhappy business. On the other hand, I yearned for a baby. When I told David I was pregnant I said I wanted an abortion. He said nothing. His face was dead white as he immediately arranged to take me to a doctor. My pregnancy was confirmed and I was told I would have to be admitted immediately if I was to have an abortion – I was over three months pregnant by then.

117

On the trolley, about to be wheeled into the theatre, I asked myself for the thousandth time: why am I having an abortion? Why was I worrying about what Durban people thought? I really wanted this baby. I wanted to stay with David, even if it meant delaying going home. David had just left me and promised to return that evening. I jumped off the trolley and rushed to the lift. He was standing there, leaning against the wall with his head in his hands.

'Why are we doing this?' I asked him.

'Because you decided.'

'What about you?'

'I don't really count in this. It must be your decision.'

'Why? You must feel *something*.'

'What I feel must not determine what you do now.'

'Well, let's go home then,' I said. 'I'm going to have it.'

David swept me up in his arms and fended off the nurses and housemen who were telling us I was not allowed to discharge myself, issuing warnings and threats.

When we got home David phoned University College Hospital and spoke to the famous obstetrician, Professor Nixon. From then on he behaved as if ours was the only baby ever to be born. He attended all the classes with me, learned deep breathing and panting, read medical obstetric books, took me to the dentist, supervised my eating: only brown bread, lots of milk, no canned food, plenty of fruit and fish.

One Saturday night in the interval at the Finsbury Park Astoria, when I was six months pregnant, David handed me an orange ice lolly and said, 'How about getting married?'

'Why?'

'Because I want to – don't you?'

'Well, yes, I do. But what do you think I'm going to look like? Shall we wait till after the baby?'

'No. Let's tell your mother and everyone and have a wedding while we can still enjoy it. We'll have to move because our place is too small for a baby. I've already had a look and found quite a nice flat in Risboro Close in Muswell Hill.'

We were married on 14 July 1956 at the Wood Green registry

David.

Our wedding, 14 July 1956.

Ronnie.

To darling Dad.

With my fondest

Joan.

Me.

office. My stepsister and her husband, who were living in London, gave us a wedding reception, with caviare and smoked salmon, in their Hampstead flat. Our comrades from the British Communist Party and some of David's aunts and uncles came to celebrate.

John Motloheloa, the black leader from Lesotho who had led our Warsaw delegation, phoned to ask David to do an urgent political job and off he went – in the middle of our nuptials. I had not only married the man, I had married the struggle.

None of my South African family was able to come over for the wedding. I had written glowingly to them about David, and my aunts and uncles sent us cheques and greetings. David's father was Jewish but his mother was not. This meant that, strictly speaking, David was not Jewish. But my mother managed to blur this to the family. She found a young man called Roy Smith who had been to Natal University with David and who recommended him to the family as a studious academic. Roy was a relation of Auntie Rose, who was Uncle Alf's wife. Always one to put the picture right, my mother made David kosher with my family and they remained in awe of his university degree – an education was a rarity in our family.

My brother Ronnie was a poor correspondent. At that time he was trying to farm a stretch of land in Paddock on the Natal south coast with little success, and he was feeling generally isolated. My letters to him did not bring a reply. But he sent us a short congratulatory telegram. I never had any communication with Mangelwurzel. As we had never shared a home, we hadn't got to know each other. He left school before matriculation and went to Rhodesia, where Uncle Mervyn had a clothing factory.

My sister Joan and my mother telephoned often for our news. Joan was longing to meet David and I had to keep describing him to her. She was excited at the prospect of becoming an aunt.

My mother was relieved that I was to be a married woman. She voiced all the fears she must have been nursing for years. 'You've always been so unorthodox, darling, I thought you might become a lesbian or take up with a black man, or something.' And for some reason, when she said that, I was

119

sorry I hadn't done either.

My father was delighted. I was marrying an educated man. He visited us a few months later and took David all over Britain to meet the sailors he had looked after during the war in Durban. He had kept in touch with hundreds of British families. He was disgusted to find that David was a bad sailor. They were invited onto boats of all kinds by yachtsmen up and down Britain and David got seasick even when they were moored. Dad never forgave David that weakness, but otherwise he heartily approved of him. 'Well, he's got his head screwed on the right way,' was the highest praise I ever heard him give anyone. And that's what he said of David.

Hugh Miller, an uncle of David's living in London, recommended 'a nice little place for a honeymoon' in Lewes and we went there, to the White Horse Inn. We found we could only afford one night. After spending it in a four-poster bed and ordering sandwiches and milk at odd intervals through the night, we moved to a pub in Brighton for the rest of the week. An aunt of David's, Countess Natalia de la Fere, David's father's sister, who had married a French nobleman some twenty years her junior – and then a few years later thrown him out for being too old – cycled down from Blackheath to spend our honeymoon with us. We played bingo on the pier, went for walks and bus rides, and it was a very happy week.

On our return to London, I felt I was a failure as a woman. Up till then I had accepted that David would do all the housework, cooking and financial management. Now I was married and going to have a baby, I would have to learn to cook. Three months before, I had enrolled, with my friend Pauline Naidoo, to do a Royal College of Arts Diploma in Typewriting Teaching. Pauline came from Durban and had married the famous H.A. Naidoo, who had organised the sugar workers in Natal. They had had to leave the country because he was Indian and Pauline was white. This was a contravention of the Immorality Act. Pauline came to Risboro Close every Wednesday at lunchtime and I would open a tin of pilchards and Heinz potato salad and put the remains on the kitchen shelf – only rich people had fridges in those days – and then we would go off to college.

One morning, feeling I would have to confront this being-a-woman business, I telephoned my stepsister, a very good cook, and told her I wanted to make David supper. She advised me kindly, 'One of the easiest things is creamed veal with a salad. Buy two pieces of veal, some cream, some onions, lettuce, tomatoes and, for the dressing, some oil and vinegar. Phone me when you get home.'

Heavily pregnant, I legged it up Muswell Hill to the shops, made my purchases and phoned her back.

'All ready,' I said.

'Right. Now brown the onions – two will do – and then phone me back.'

I went into the kitchen, unpacked the goodies and phoned back. 'OK,' I said.

'You can't have browned the onions already.'

'They were brown when I bought them,' I said.

It took the whole day to make the meal – I even made a salad – and I was exhausted but excited waiting for David to come home. He arrived in his usual happy state and while he was telling me the day's news, I led him to the table. He sat down without turning a hair, not hesitating in his flow of words. He ate the meal.

'Do you know what you have just eaten?' I asked him.

He glanced round the kitchen and his eye fell on the tin of pilchards on the shelf. 'Pilchard stew?' he asked.

I was furious. 'It's the first meal I ever cooked – it's *veal*. You are awful . . . I *hate* you!'

'Hey! Hang on a minute,' David said. 'I didn't ever want you for your *cooking*. It's very nice. Really, it was *very* nice. Honestly! It was *wonderful*. It's just that I don't want a fuss about eating. You know, I don't think people should ever make a big thing about food – more than half the world is starving.'

'But if I don't cook,' I said, 'I won't feel like a proper woman and I won't feel like a proper wife.'

David was the second feminist I met. The first was my brother Ronnie. 'Being a woman and a proper wife has nothing

121

to do with cooking,' he said. 'Cook if you want, but remember, eating is just something one does to keep alive.'

I felt hurt, but a load fell off my mind.

We had been given a set of Denby china for a wedding present. One day, while washing up, I cracked a bread plate. I suffered untold guilt – I had *broken one of our wedding plates!* In our house in Durban, breaking crockery was a terrible crime. I remembered the fuss when Sarah had broken a Royal Doulton coffee pot while washing up. She had been screamed at for being a careless, witless creature, and had the cost of it taken from her wages – a very big proportion of her pay, as I remember her complaining. I felt so dreadful about the cracked plate that I hid it at the bottom of the pile of six on the shelf and decided not to mention it to David. But the plates must have circulated. One evening, by mistake, I laid David's place at table with the chipped bread plate. I brought the food to the table – spaghetti, Bolognese sauce and a dish of beetroot. David was explaining to me why Engels had written to Kautsky in 1882, and said, 'You ask me what the English workers think about colonial policy. Well, exactly the same as they think about politics in general: *The same as the bourgeois think.*' All the while his finger was absent-mindedly rubbing over the chip in the plate.

I found myself getting angrier and angrier. Eventually I could bear it no longer. I grabbed the plate and threw it on the floor. 'Haven't you ever seen a bloody cracked plate before?' I shouted.

He looked at me with astonishment. 'Oh, yes, lots,' he said and went on talking.

After the meal he carefully stacked all the plates with the dish of beetroot on top, stood up and said. 'I've seen lots of broken plates in my time – look!' He dropped the lot onto the floor.

I sat transfixed. I didn't know whether to be angry or to laugh. I decided to be angry: I was appalled at the mess, at the waste. All those lovely plates broken! But I had to laugh, it was so funny. We spent most of the evening combing the floor for broken bits of china.

'Why did you do it?' I asked him.

'Don't throw things when you get angry,' he said. 'I can throw things too. Anyway, it's not important. Plates are not important.'

I often got angry but I never threw things around again, and I was so clumsy that when I washed up I often cracked plates and broke glasses and I didn't mind.

Uncle Herbert Cranko came to see me on 5 January 1957 – the day after Steven was born.

'Get your things together,' he said. 'We're going.'

'Uncle Herbert,' I said, 'I have a *baby*. It's a *boy*!'

'I know all about that,' he said. 'That's why I've come to see you. I've never been in one of these places before – not even when my own children were born. My God! This place is *awful*. I arrived in London yesterday and phoned your home number. You've married a lunatic and I've come to take you back home to Johburg. I got you over here in the first place. I feel responsible now for your predicament.'

'Sit down,' I said, pointing to a chair.

'No,' he said, 'I won't sit down at all. Get your clothes on, we're going.'

'I can't go anywhere now,' I said. 'I've just had a baby!'

'Well, give it to its father, and let's go.'

'Whatever is the *matter*?' I asked him.

He was convinced that David was crazy. When he had asked for me on the telephone, David had been in raptures about Steven's birth, which he had attended. He went into minute details of weight, head circumference, and a detailed description of the birth. He told Uncle Herbert how he had taken over from the doctors to deliver the baby. 'I'm an engineer, you know. It's an engineering job really, isn't it?'

'I wouldn't know,' Uncle Herbert had replied icily.

'You wait until the head is crowned and then just tuck your finger . . .'

'I want to speak with my niece.'

'The afterbirth came away so cleanly – they were all amazed! And she didn't have an episiotomy. That's routine now, you know. She's not here.'

'Well, where is she then?'

'I told you, she's in hospital.'

'Young man, *will* you tell me immediately precisely where my niece is?'

From then on Uncle Herbert was too frightened to meet David. He was scared he would be assailed with items of gynaecology, which he could not handle. After I went home from UCH he visited me during the day, first telephoning to make quite sure that David would not be there. David wasn't so keen when Uncle Herbert visited, either – he resented the amount of whisky that Uncle Herbert drank.

Like most rich South Africans, every few years my aunts and uncles travelled 'overseas'. They never liked it, but it was then fashionable to visit Europe. In later years when visiting America became the thing, they liked it a little better.

'Thet South of France is terrible. You can't compare the scenery with the Cape or even the Valley of a Thousand Hills. I don't know why people make such a fuss about it – even the Alps,' my auntie Ettie said. 'And Italy's just dirty.'

My family stayed at the best five-star or de luxe hotels. But Auntie Ettie said, 'The service is terrible and I just order boiled eggs because you can't eat the food. Most of the time they don't even have rice on the menu. Yesterday I asked for some sweet-milk cheese. They didn't even know what I was talking about. They brought me a wooden plate full of bad cheese. Honestly, it stank! I made Cyril complain to the manager and all he could say was it was French cheese and was supposed to smell like that. They must think we fools or something.'

My cousin Wendy was appalled at Germany. 'You know,' she told us, 'they so ignorant there. We met people who can't even speak *English*.'

But they disliked London most – except for Selfridges. 'They need a lot of decent builders here,' Auntie Thel said once. 'The place is all old and horrible.' My aunts thought Selfridges was London. That's where they spent their time when they had to be in London for a couple of days. I once tried to persuade two of

124

my aunts to visit Harrods or Fortnum's, but they didn't have time. They hadn't exhausted Selfridges yet.

My auntie Bea, having divorced her first cousin, Stashik, married David Levy and the family lent him money to set up an ice-cream factory in Rhodesia. It paid off and they duly arrived in London on their 'overseas' trip.

When David went to answer their ring at the door, Auntie Bea, quite famous in Durban as a psychic medium, stepped inside before being introduced, clapped her hands together, and said to David:

'Guess who I was talking to last night.'

'Oh,' said David. 'It must be someone from Durban whom I know.'

'Oh, no,' said Auntie Bea. 'First I spoke to Cecil Rhodes and then to the Tsar of Russia.'

David scratched his head as I came to the door to greet them.

'How come?' he asked.

'I am in touch with the dead,' Auntie Bea said.

'Oh!' said David.

David Levy, fearing she was not believed and disappointed with my David's response, hastened to say:

'It's quite true, you know. Last week she was in touch with Shakespeare.'

'Oh, well,' said my David, 'doesn't she ever speak to any ordinary dead people?'

They thought he was crazy. My David thought they were quite normal.

'Normal!' I said to him. 'There is nothing normal about my auntie Bea. She is supposed to heal warts, illnesses and can even disappear scars. She has a high moral tone and will only mix with people who have dignity.'

'Well, you get that sort of thing in a place like Durban,' David said. 'It's quite normal for that type of society. They can't deal with reality, so there's a sort of hunt for the paranormal. In that way nothing has to be explained scientifically. I wanted to ask her if she'd found out whether Bacon had written Shakespeare but when I saw you look at me I thought I'd better not stir things up.'

He had odd conversations with my Durban uncles too, who, when they were in London, visited us and reported back to the family. My rich uncle George, who had borrowed money from Grandpa to buy a hotel and eventually became the owner of a chain of them – K Hotels – had pulled him aside during one of his visits with my auntie Jeanette. 'Doing all right, then?' he'd asked David.

'Oh, fine!'

'What are you getting, then?'

'D'you mean for my birthday? It's in August.'

'Getting! Salary! Money!'

'Oh!' said David. He thought it a rude question and did not answer.

'What are you getting, then?' persisted my uncle George.

'I'm not that interested in money,' said David, who was earning top rates as an engineering draughtsman.

Then Uncle George, who had been asked by the Durban family to check out David's needs and status, regaled the family back in Durban with the 'facts': David was not interested in setting up a business. He had not even wanted to talk business. David must be extremely rich – so rich that he would not talk about money and had not even touched him for a loan. He was a sort of brilliant academic working in his job for the 'interest of it'. The money was secondary. Even after getting a degree, he had gone to university again, and it seemed he was always studying something. He must have inherited a fortune. 'He is so rich – like Jesus,' Uncle George told my family, meaning Croesus. 'And they live so humbly – they've got nothing, you know. I think it quite likely he's a very religious man.'

David was working in Edmonton. Now that we had Steven, I had to be at home – no baby-minders or nurseries in those days – and we were living on David's wages. We were looking forward to his promotion, which would mean higher pay. But David was called in to the boss one morning and told he would get his promotion if he resigned as staff representative. He came home that night with a long face.

126

'I couldn't do it. I told him so. I told him I would not, not on any condition, resign my shop stewardship.'

'You were quite right,' I said.

'Yes, but how will we manage? I'll have to leave. We've got no money left in the Post Office after this month and we can't come out on my pay.'

'Let's get a couple of lodgers, then.' We had moved into a spacious cheap flat in Albert Mansions in Crouch Hill.

Ada Bloomberg, whom I had met at Congress of Democrat meetings in Johannesburg, was visiting London and needed a room, and Mark Weinberg, my sister Joan's brother-in-law, was working in London for a year. They came to board. I was unhappy with this arrangement although Ada and Mark were ideal lodgers. David and I were never alone and when everyone went to work I was left with Steven, to do the housework, shopping and cooking.

But for a short while this arrangement met our financial problems. Then David, denied promotion, left his job and went into contract draughting, but the market for draughtsmen was diminishing. When the jobs ran out, he decided to train as a salesman for Encyclopaedia Britannica. He was excited at the prospect of doing something completely different and after the training period, he went out on the road.

David was not a bad salesman – in fact he won an award during the course. It was just that after the 'close', when he had convinced some poor working-class couple that their child would not have any chance in the world without a set of *Britannica*, and a deposit had been paid over to him, David's conscience would worry him and he would start talking them out of it and asking them if they could really afford such a big deposit.

I had become friendly with Pixie Benjamin. Her family and David's had been close friends in Cape Town, and David had known Pixie since she was five years old, when she was Pixie Consani. Her father founded Consani's, which became one of the biggest engineering firms in South Africa. In 1952, Pixie had left South Africa and come to England where she got a job as a land girl on a farm. She attended the Bucharest Youth Festival as part of the British delegation and a member of their choir. Pixie had a beautiful singing voice and the South African delegation was too small to give cultural performances at these festivals. In England she met John Benjamin. When they married, John's rich father disowned him. Pixie and John both belonged to FADSAC – For a Democratic South Africa Committee, set up to raise money for a travelling exhibition to inform the world about the suppression of black people in South Africa. Pixie and John rented a flat in Hampstead, where we often visited them. While I talked with Pixie, David would bath Norman, their son.

Like me, Pixie was thinking about returning to South Africa. All activists were needed at home. The Treason Trial, when the leading members of the resistance in South Africa had been arrested after the adoption of the Freedom Charter, was dragging on into its third year. Nelson Mandela, Walter Sisulu and the other leaders were facing possible death sentences. The government thought it could keep resistance down by restraining the top activists. It was time to go home. Everything was pointing us that way.

We wanted to raise Steven as a South African and David's parents kept urging us to bring him home. In South Africa the struggle was hotting up – and the faint-hearted whites were beginning to arrive in London to get out of the firing line. Then Ruth First, a leading member of the liberation movement, urged David to return to South Africa. He was needed at home.

Our respite in London had come to an end. On a cool June day in 1959, with Steven tucked between us, we flew from Heathrow home to Johannesburg.

· *8* ·

David's history of activity against the apartheid regime meant that the South African authorities in London refused to issue him with a passport. He did not want to take British citizenship, to which he was entitled, being adamant that he would remain a South African citizen. So he returned to South Africa with a travel document, an affidavit, signed by his aunt Norah, testifying that she had been present at his birth in Cape Town.

At Jan Smuts airport in Johannesburg we were delayed at customs while they vetted David's unusual entry papers. My sister Joan, having made numerous enquiries, alerted lawyers and friends that we were having trouble entering. By the time we got through the barriers, the other passengers had left the airport and Joan was standing with David's parents waiting anxiously for us. Relieved and excited, we kissed and cuddled. We were very glad to be back home.

Joan had rented a flat for us in Orange Grove, and stocked it with everything we would need. During the first weeks after our arrival David, Steven and I went from house to house, meeting each other's families and friends. I was pleased to have in-laws like Chris and Fred. They were like the normal parents I had missed. They were thrilled to have Steven, their only grand-child, with them in Johannesburg and took him off our hands whenever we would let them. David's brother, Leon, a taciturn and kindly man, two years younger than David, flew down from Namibia to greet us. Joan and Norman invited us to dinner parties to meet their friends. We visited Ronnie and Marlene in their little flat. And of course we went down to Durban to see Mom, Oscar, Dad and all my aunts and uncles.

I was nervous about introducing David to my Durban family

and thought he might be intimidated by them. But they were warm and affectionate. I had worried that David did not know our family rules of behaviour and I could not imagine how he would react to their prejudices and the men's conversations about business, investments and the labour situation. But, as usual, David got on well with everyone. They tried to impress him with their fashionable knowledge and social ways. He watched them quietly and always managed to say something either complimentary or abstruse. He baffled them.

A few weeks after our return from England, with help from David's family, we bought a little tin-roofed house in Victoria, a small suburb of Johannesburg. David got a job as an engineer. Steven was happily settled at nursery school and I became secretary to the managing director at AA Mutual Insurance Limited. We were eating again. We were even getting comfortable. We were thinking of having another baby.

From the first day of our return, David and I were swept up in the liberation struggle. Many of the comrades I had known in Congress in 1954 and 1955 had dispersed – some had been sent into exile, some had left the country because life was getting difficult for activists, and some had merely disappeared to other towns in South Africa.

The Discussion Club no longer existed. Instead, David and I joined the Tennis Club at the Houghton Government School. Here for a couple of hours on Sunday mornings we met Bram Fischer (a leader of the Communist Party who was to die serving a life sentence in Pretoria jail), the Slovos (Joe, who went into exile and became a member of the National Executive Committee of the ANC, and his wife, Ruth First), the Bernsteins (Hilda and Rusty, who went into exile and were members of the Communist Party), Ivan Schermbrucker, a revolutionary giant who served seven years in jail, and others. Here quick conversations were held and information passed. But after a few months we were told to leave – we would blow our cover if we were often seen with people known to be active in the struggle. Since we had recently arrived from England, our leaders in the Communist Party and the Congress Alliance had asked us to operate in secret – under cover. We were members of the underground cell system, known only to three or four other activists.

In the underground, activists were graded according to political exposure. People who were or had been in jail were As, public figures were Bs, those in organisations Cs. Those of us completely undercover – secret members – were Ds.

South Africa was seething with unrest. Black people suffered terrible hardship under the oppressive laws. In particular the pass laws were used as instruments of their suppression.

On 21 March 1960, Sharpeville exploded. The Pan Africanist Congress had called for a demonstration against the pass laws. People had gone peacefully to protest at the police station in the township. They were told to disperse and as they were turning to go, the police opened fire. Sixty-nine were shot dead, mostly in the back. Hundreds were injured.

Unrest continued. There were demonstrations and protests. By 28 March, over 2000 people had been arrested. A state of emergency was declared and the African National Congress and the Pan Africanist Congress were banned. Oliver Tambo, an ANC leader who became president in 1967, and his wife Adelaide were instructed by the ANC to leave South Africa to carry on the work outside the country.

In June 1961, Nelson Mandela, who in the fifties had formed the M-plan – an underground cell system for the ANC in anticipation of its banning – announced that he would remain in hiding inside the country to lead the struggle, and on 16 December 1961, Umkhonto we Sizwe (Spear of the nation), known as MK – the military wing of the African National Congress – was formed.

Mike Harmel, a leading Communist – in disguise – visited me and asked me to join the Communist Party. I was needed, he said, in the technical unit of the underground. I joined. I had not known which areas of the resistance were covered by the Communist Party and which by Congress. Up till then, I had been given tasks to do by well-known activists and I carried them out not knowing which organisation they were representing.

David, an underground member of the Communist Party,

had been attending meetings since our return. The white wing of Congress, the Congress of Democrats, formed when he was in England, so David was not a member of Congress.

He arrived home one evening and said, 'We have to discuss something very important. I've been asked to join MK.'

It was the logical step. We had been discussing the necessity for armed resistance against the violent onslaughts for years.

Since 1912 the Congress movement had fought a peaceful struggle – with no positive result. Chief Albert Lutuli, president of the ANC from 1952 to his death – in highly suspicious circumstances – in 1967, had said, 'For thirty years we have been knocking on a closed door.' Now, in their attempt to wipe out all resistance, the white regime was shooting large numbers of people indiscriminately, not only at Sharpeville, but throughout the country. Nothing they had been able to do had suppressed the struggle for freedom. The Freedom Charter was still the democratically adopted programme people were fighting for.

The Treason Trial had ended. All 156 accused were released back into the struggle. The state had been unable to prove that the Freedom Charter was a document for the violent overthrow of the state or that any actions of the accused were treasonable. But the arrests of leaders continued. Each wave of arrests of leaders led to the emergence of new leaders. The number of ANC supporters was growing by leaps and bounds with every campaign and issue. But the peaceful methods of protest and attempts at negotiation with the white regime had produced nothing but increased brutal oppression. The rulers of South Africa were never prepared to negotiate – negotiations had been sought by the ANC for over half a century.

'What do you think?' I asked David.

'Well, if we want another child, we'll just have to go ahead. The fight in South Africa will go on and any children we have will be part of whatever happens. Think about it,' David said. 'It's a serious move.'

'Yes, but it's the only way from now on,' I said.

'That's right,' David said. 'There was a saying in the French Maquis, *La vie continue.*'

We decided I should get pregnant as soon as possible.

David brought strangers to our home and we visited people I did not know. I never knew whether those we were seeing were social friends or members of the underground resistance. Our cell system meant that each person met only four, five or six members who were involved and the link person who connected with the next cell would know about eight people.

One Sunday David was taking Steven and me to see the Goldreichs who had moved into a new house in Rivonia. They were a couple I had met on and off for a few months. We had recently bought a DKW motor car and I had obtained a driving licence and was driving the car. As we neared the house I slowed the DKW down when I noticed some vegetable sellers on the roadside. This was not unusual – one often saw black people selling beads, pottery, vegetables and fruit. Right outside the gate of the Goldreichs' house I saw a black guy holding up a bunch of carrots.

'Let's buy them,' I said to David. 'He must be in a bad way. Those carrots died a week ago.'

'Drive up,' said David. 'We don't need carrots.'

'It's not a question of *need*,' I said sharply. 'Don't be so bloody mean!' I began fiddling with my bag to find some money. 'He probably hasn't eaten for a week. He's selling *one* bunch of carrots!'

'Just hurry up – drive up quickly,' David said, 'or I'll take the wheel.'

I swung the car up the driveway.

The Goldreichs had certainly gone up in the world, I thought. This was a large property in an expensive outlying suburb of Johannesburg. Arthur was an artist and an architect. But he must have come into a lot of money to be able to buy Lilliesleaf Farm.

As we drove up the long driveway we passed an army of black workers tending the fields. 'He's a bit of a show-off, Arthur, isn't he?' I said to David. 'It looks as though he has a gardener for every weed!'

'Shh,' said David.

We had iced coffee on the stoep, shaded from the hot sun. Nicky and Paul, the Goldreich children, came begging me to play ball with them and we went around the side of the house to play catch. When Paul wanted a drink I took them to the kitchen and then outside to the yard at the back of the house to drink our Cokes. A black worker in blue overalls was sitting on a step in the shade reading a paper. I glanced at him and, with a shock, recognised a face I had seen in the Congress office some five years before. He winked at me. It was then I realised that Lilliesleaf was not what it seemed. It was the headquarters of the underground.

'Arthur,' I said, when I went back to join them, 'I think you had better buy that guard some new carrots.' The vegetable seller was guarding Lilliesleaf Farm. The 'field workers' were bodyguards protecting the leadership of the resistance movement, including Walter Sisulu, Govan Mbeki, Raymond Mhlaba and Ahmed Kathrada, who were in hiding at the back of the house – Nelson Mandela was in jail serving a five-year sentence. Arthur was the technical owner – the front – of the Rivonia house. It belonged to Congress.

For a while Lilliesleaf also became a base of operations for the technical underground. In a studio in the grounds, ostensibly for Arthur's painting, we produced leaflets, documents and posters. There must have been cells set up for distributing these, but the task of passing the material on would be left to our link member. At another base in Johannesburg I typed the first issue of *Freedom Fighter*, the newspaper of MK. The number of our technical bases grew as our workload increased and I would type and duplicate at different venues.

Our daughter Amandla, which means 'power' in Zulu, had been born at the end of July in 1962. During my few months at home with her, I ran typewriting classes for the movement – as I have done on and off through the years. I got to know Ruth First at this time. She came to learn to type. In 1964 she was detained in solitary confinement and wrote a book about her experiences – *117 Days*. On 17 August 1982 she was murdered in

Mozambique, killed by a parcel bomb.

I think our friends must have known that we were working in the liberation movement. We were leading double lives. David would go off to work in the mornings and I never knew when he would return home. Sometimes his 'work' kept him away from home till three or four in the morning – sometimes overnight. Sometimes he would stay home while I typed at one of the safe venues, till the early hours of the morning. Friends who visited us seldom saw us together and our circle of social contacts diminished as our political tasks became more demanding.

On 11 July 1963, the South African special branch raided Lilliesleaf in Rivonia and arrested leaders of Congress. Eleven faced charges in what became known as the Rivonia Trial. They were held under the 90-Day Detention clause of the 1963 General Laws Amendment Act – held without charge or trial, without access to visitors or lawyers. The police said they had 'smashed the underground headquarters of the African National Congress'. Nelson Mandela was brought out of jail to stand trial with the others. He became known as the Black Pimpernel. During his years in hiding, Nelson Mandela travelled all over South Africa, popularising the aims of Congress. He secretly visited Britain and other countries to gain support for the struggle.

The accused in the Rivonia Trial faced possible death sentences under the Sabotage Act. There was an outcry from democrats all over the world. At the trial, in his speech from the dock, Nelson Mandela said:

I and some colleagues came to the conclusion that as violence in this country was inevitable, it would be unrealistic and wrong for African leaders to continue preaching peace and non-violence at a time when the Government met our peaceful demands with force. This conclusion was not easily arrived at. It was only when all else had failed, when all channels of peaceful protest had been barred to us, that the decision was made to embark on violent forms of political struggle, and to form Umkhonto we Sizwe. We did so not because we desired such a course, but solely because the Government had left us with no other choice. In the *Manifesto of Umkhonto*, published on 16 December 1961, which is Exhibit AD, we said:

'The time comes in the life of any nation where there remain only two choices – submit or fight. That time has now come to South Africa. We shall not submit and we have no choice but to hit back by all means in our power in defence of our people, our future, and our freedom.'

And he ended his detailed key speech – his last chance to address the people – by saying:

During my lifetime I have dedicated myself to this struggle of the African people. I have fought against white domination, and I have fought against black domination. I have cherished the ideal of a democratic and free society in which all persons live together in harmony and with equal opportunities. It is an ideal which I hope to live for and to achieve. But if needs be, it is an ideal for which I am prepared to die.

With horror in our hearts we awaited the results of the trial. The lives of those who represented our greatest hopes for a victorious outcome to the freedom struggle were at risk. They were our leaders and our teachers, our friends and colleagues. On 11 June 1964 eight accused – Nelson Mandela, Walter Sisulu, Govan Mbeki, Raymond Mhlaba, Elias Motsoaledi, Andrew Mlangeni, Ahmed Kathrada and Denis Goldberg – were sentenced to life imprisonment.

Chief Albert Lutuli issued a statement appealing to the world, the following day:

...They represent the highest in morality and ethics in the South African political struggle; this morality and ethics has been sentenced to an imprisonment it may never survive. Their policies are in accordance with the deepest international principles of brotherhood and humanity; without their leadership, brotherhood and humanity may be blasted out of existence in South Africa for long decades to come. They believe profoundly in justice and reason; when they are locked away, justice and reason will have departed from the South African scene.

An era had ended.

Although the leadership of the Congress Alliance (ANC, South African Indian Congress, Coloured People's Organisation and

Congress of Democrats) and MK had been creamed off, the membership was still intact. A new leadership had to be found.

Immediately after the arrests had taken place, David was put on the four-man National High Command of Umkhonto we Sizwe. He was keenly aware now that his performance had to match none other than Nelson Mandela's – the leader of MK. Directions had to be given to the units in the field. Those in possession of lists of names, archives, caches and other sensitive information had to be vetted for security and, where necessary, they had to be got out of the country.

Much of our work in the underground was attending meetings to discuss aspects of the struggle. Most of my work on the technical committee was typing. But we were also called upon to do some unusual tasks.

One night David was given the job of locating a high-risk person – S – who had memorised the names of the D (undercover) activists. The underground wanted him out of the country because it was feared that if he were captured, he might, under pressure, divulge the names of these secret members to the security police.

We drove to his house to find that S had gone to the cinema with his wife. We waited around the corner in the car and as soon as the cinema audience came out we jumped out and joined the crowd. When we saw S and his wife, we waited to see if anyone else approached him – the police could not be far behind. Then David went up to him, irritated with relief and anxiety.

'How can you go to the *cinema* at a time like this?' he asked S.

S hushed David up – his wife knew nothing of his activities – and the two of them went off in S's car to our home. I took her to their home, parked a block away and told her she would not hear from her husband for a few months. She looked at me, shocked.

'What's going on? What do you mean?'

'Everything is all right, really,' I said. 'He's just going to be busy away from home. The police will probably call around here soon, and it's better if you know nothing. S will be in touch with you the moment he can.'

She was terribly alarmed and begged me to tell her what was going on.

'Please don't ask any more questions,' I said. 'And don't tell the police you've seen me because it may lead them to him.'

I did my best to allay her fears – but what could I do? She was understandably frightened and every time I told her things would be all right I had a sinking feeling that perhaps they would not be.

At home, David told S how to disguise himself and to be prepared to leave the country immediately. Until that was accomplished, we would all be on tenterhooks.

We hid S at our home for a couple of days – David had dug underneath our house and made a hideaway room – and then passed him to the Escape Committee. He got out safely and his wife and three kids joined him in London.

Later I helped to get people secretly out of South Africa.

I kept away from my family as much as possible at this time. I did not want to implicate Joan, Ronnie or Clarice and I knew that if the police captured David or me, our families would be interrogated or even detained. I know that Joan did not understand this. She thought that, now I was married to David, I did not need the closeness of our relationship and she was hurt by it. For the same reason we seldom visited the family in Durban.

The more involved we became in the day-to-day tasks of the struggle, the more divorced we felt from white South Africans. We heard about the 'key parties' that were then in vogue, when couples went to the homes of the rich in Johannesburg and the wives threw their car or house keys into a pile. The men would each pick up a key and then have sex with its owner – someone else's wife. We also knew that on Saturday nights banned and pornographic films were on view in many Johannesburg houses. Quite a few people had projectors and it was a common weekly entertainment.

White South Africa was sick. Drugs, sex, money and pornography dominated the lives of Johannesburg society. Still, we had a few friends who were not involved in the struggle, and sometimes we turned to them for help.

In times of acute tension and stress, ridiculous and absurd events are occasions for relief. I was given the task of buying two female wigs. Two male comrades were to escape disguised as women. In those days there was no such thing as artificial hair. A wig was specially made from real hair and cost a great deal of money. I was given a wad of notes to pay cash for the transaction.

I could not possibly go alone to a wigmaker for *two* wigs. I needed another woman to help me. I could not take anyone in the movement – it would be wrong to risk two of us and any activist in those days might be under police surveillance. I had a close friend, Marsha, who was not involved in politics but, although we had never discussed the matter, I thought she knew that I was. I went to see her.

'Marshie, I want you to come shopping with me.'

'Where we going?'

'I want to buy a wig – two wigs.'

'You're joking! I know you've got a thing about your frizzy hair – but you can't wear a wig in this heat. And anyway, it's ridiculous – and terribly expensive. You haven't got that sort of money. It's a crazy idea.'

'Nevertheless,' I said, looking at her with hard eyes and compressed lips.

'You mean they not for you?'

'No, I don't mean that.'

'Oh! OK, when?'

'Now – in your car.'

We looked up the address of a wigmaker in the telephone book and drove there in Marsha's Beetle. They had four wigs – samples of colour and style. We persuaded the saleswoman to let us try on all four and took them to the dressing room. Marsha, a tall, dark athletic woman with a shining cap of short black hair, put on an orangey-coloured, shoulder-length, page-boy styled object. I donned an ill-fitting blonde job. We looked at each other and started to giggle. We tried to hush each other up. Our

139

job was to get in and out of there without attracting attention to ourselves. The saleswoman hovered outside the door. We swapped and tried on the other wigs. They were worse. The saleswoman stepped into the room and explained that they would look more attractive if made to the right size. Knowing that we had to leave in a few minutes with two wigs, Marsha and I started complimenting each other on how we looked. She had hers on back to front and the saleswoman yanked it off and turned it round while she was posing in front of the glass saying, 'I think this really suits me, don't you?'

I looked at her from beneath a much too large black nest. 'Really lovely,' I said.

As the saleswoman went out to get a tape measure, Marsha and I collapsed on the floor – she was wetting herself with suppressed laughter and I was wetting myself with the absurdity of it all and with nervousness.

I left Marsha in the dressing room – I did not want her easily recognised – while I went into the reception office with two of the wigs and said, 'We'll take these two.'

Marsha emerged with a scarf covering most of her face. The saleswoman assured us that they were not for sale, we could not buy her samples, and anyway, none of the wigs were our size. I sent Marsha to wait in the car and explained that we needed them for that night – we were having a private party. She went off to call her boss.

A fat little man appeared and told me how impossible it was – I could not take their sample wigs away. In my first attempt at business wheeling and dealing, I said: 'How much? How much to take them now – so that it's worth your while?' And I brought out the wad of notes and flicked them enticingly on the desk.

His eyes glued to the notes, he mentioned an astronomical figure and I counted them off. Then I hightailed it out of there. Marsha went off in her car and I caught a bus and took the wigs to a safe place.

The net was closing in. We clung closer to our children. David was away much of the time but he made a point of reading to Steven whenever he could, and he taught him to read. No matter what time he came home, however tired or worried he was, he would go into Amandla's room, hoping that she would be awake, and when she was, he would sit and talk and play with her.

Sarah, the maid of the family living next door to us, was an elderly woman with whom we became friendly. Unemployment was a problem for black people in Johannesburg and this was compounded by the pass laws. A black person who was unemployed was endorsed out of Johannesburg and packed off to a bantustan. In this way only working black people would remain in the white cities. Sarah asked us if we would employ her daughter, Pumi. She had no papers to be in Johannesburg and we would have to make representations to get her a pass. We employed Pumi, and then her brother, Sisa. We 'employed' quite a few other black people, for some of whom we obtained passes, but many of those we could not help were endorsed out of Johannesburg. Pumi and Sisa became part of our family.

We did not discuss politics with either Pumi or Sisa. We had not wanted to have servants because of the security risk. But they must have known, through observation or through some street grapevine, what David and I were doing because we found that they smoothed our path whenever they could. If we were busy at meetings in the house and an unexpected visitor called, Pumi and Sisa would go to great lengths to see that we were not disturbed and that our visitors did not come in contact with the people attending our meetings. If we were both called away at night, we would return to find Pumi sleeping in Amandla's room.

Steven, who was now seven, had a dangerously high pain threshold. He seldom complained and when he did, it was a medical emergency. One day I got home from work to find him playing in the garden. On the dining-room table was a poem he had just written. It read:

I have a mother whose always sunny
She's sometimes cross
And sometimes funny.

I have an ear rake – Gosh! it's sore!
Aren't I lucky that it doesn't hurt more

I flew outside to the garden, picked him up and took him to the doctor. He was rushed to hospital where an operation was performed on his badly infected, blocked ear.

When he was better and back at school, I tried to spend more time with him. We had had a nasty shock. One day I was at the hairdresser's at the bottom of our road and I suddenly remembered, with my hair under the hose, that he would be arriving home from school. 'Do me a favour,' I said to the young apprentice who was washing my hair, 'please phone my home and ask Steven to come down and meet me here.' She came back giggling.

'A little voice answered "Hello",' she said, 'and I asked, "Is that Mrs Kitson's house?" There was a long silence and then an appalled Steven answered, "*No!* This is Mrs Kitson's *little boy!*"'

Arriving home from work one afternoon, on 22 June 1964, I found the house surrounded with plainclothes security police. I entered our bedroom where I found David, white-faced, standing in the middle of the room while security police were searching our house.

So this was it! They would not tell me where they were taking him – they would not talk with me at all. David hastily scribbled a power of attorney and they left, taking with them some books and handing me a receipt. David clasped my hand reassuringly as he walked past me.

The words 'captured documents' which appear so regularly in the South African press sound evocative. The receipt read, 'One notebook, One copy *Time* March 1964, One pink scribbler, One *Castros Cuba*, One *A Captive in the Caucases*, One *Working Class Wives*, One copy of *Time* Feb 1964 – Signed Lt van Zyl d/Sgt.'

Amandla in my arms, Steven at my heels, we ran to the back of the house to see them put David in their car between two men. Pumi and Sisa stood at the kitchen door, Pumi in tears. The

142

Joan and me, 1960.

Just after David's arrest, 1964.

servants of the houses on either side of us peeped over the fences. I stood woodenly, unbelieving, even though I had been prepared for this for months. And then they drove off. As I turned to go back into the house, the gardener from the house across the road gave me a surreptitious thumbs up and then a clenched fist – the two signs of the African National Congress.

David was gone. But right then I did not feel alone.

When I was about eighteen, my uncle Chips Cranko was dying of lung cancer. I used to visit him every week and he lay there, sometimes barely conscious, with things in his nose to help him breathe, dying for a cigarette. He would wait till his nurse had left us to talk and then in a weak, croaky voice he would say:

'Can you give me a cigarette?' And he would point to the bed-side table, full of covered bowls and silver dishes, among them a box of cigarettes and matches. I was terrified that I would be the one to deal him the last blow but I used to light up one of his Springboks and put it between his shaky fingers. After just one puff he would be seized with a fit of coughing and spitting, hold it out to me and weakly lie back, fighting to recover.

Something impressed me about his total devotion to smoking even in his last gasps of life. For those few remaining months of his life, while I was visiting Uncle Chips, I went from an occasional puffer to a full-time smoker. People are always asking me why I haven't given up smoking – it's so unhealthy, costs so much, it's antisocial. I don't know how to answer, because I've tried and I can't give it up, and I make the excuse that it's because of my uncle Chips Cranko and because of the interrogators Viktor and van der Merwe.

David was detained under the 90-Day Law. It took till the evening of the second day to find out where he had been taken but, with the help of a *Rand Daily Mail* reporter, I learned he was at Marshall Square police station. Detainees are allowed a meal from their families each day, so as soon as I found out where he was I rushed down with a thermos of coffee and cold roast chicken and salad. I had to leave them with the sergeant at the desk.

'I want to see him,' I said.

'Ag, no, Mrs Kitson.' The sergeant laughed. 'There's no visiting detainees. You have to see the colonel about that. Go and see Colonel Klindt.' He laughed again as he took the food basket off the counter and placed it somewhere underneath.

The next morning, 24 June, I joined the queue of anxious relatives at the Grays outside Colonel Klindt's office. Although most of us knew each other, we didn't speak. We just stood silent, waiting. After about two hours I was ushered in to Colonel Klindt.

'I have come to request a visit to my husband, David Kitson,' I said.

'No visits for Kitson.' He did not even look up.

'Look –'

'It's no good being difficult, lady,' he said. 'No visits for Kitson and that's it. If you want to apply again tomorrow, well, that's your affair. You can come back tomorrow. There's no visits for Kitson today. Next!' he shouted, and I was escorted out by a young policeman who was acting as doorman.

I went home to my kids. Amandla was two years old and Steven seven. I had a morning job as a secretary at National Dairy Equipment. Before me stretched six months of rushing off to work, almost daily visits to Colonel Klindt's office, preparing David's meals, delivering them, taking Steven to school and then fetching him and feeding and caring for both the children. Most of our friends stayed away. They were frightened of associating with the relatives of detainees.

But that evening I went to Marshall Square with David's dinner – only to have the first lot returned to me intact. Not a thing had been touched.

'Why?' I asked the sergeant. 'Why didn't he eat anything?'

'How do I know, man?' he said. 'Maybe he's not hungry. You know, a lot of detainees don't get hungry.'

I looked at him in terror at that thought. 'Is he all right?' I asked. 'Is David OK?'

'Look, man,' he said. 'I can't stand here all day answering everybody's questions, you know. I told you, you can bring his supper every night, OK?'

145

I went home and carefully unpacked the untouched basket, hoping to see evidence of David. I unscrewed the top of the thermos and tipped some of the cold coffee into the plastic cup. I took a few sips in the hope of feeling a little closer to him. Then I went to Pumi's room and I asked her if she would stay with me till David came home.

Pumi said, 'Look, don't worry. I'll be here. I'm not going to leave you.'

I did not know then what a lot I was asking of her. Not only would the whole weight of the family fall on her after my own detention, but she was also to be detained and interrogated herself.

But that night we sat down at the kitchen table and discussed my worries.

'Do you think he's on hunger strike?' I asked her.

'No, I don't,' she said. 'The food is your only contact, and David's no fool. You know he would have given you some sign – unwrapped something. I don't think he ever got it.'

The following day I took Steven to school, leaving Amandla with Pumi, and I went to work. Five hours until one o'clock and then a rush to get to Colonel Klindt's office. A two-hour wait and then the inevitable:

'No visits for Kitson. No visits for Kitson allowed today. If you like you can try tomorrow.'

I rushed to the shops to find something nice for David to eat, collected Steven, cooked, then went to Marshall Square and handed in the food. The previous night's food was handed back to me intact again.

'OK, he's not hungry again,' I said. 'Well, I have to do his washing. Where's his dirty clothes?'

'No clothes for Kitson,' the sergeant said.

That night Pumi and I sat around till late thinking whom to phone, whom to write to, what to do.

Just after midnight the telephone rang.

'Is that Mrs Kitson?'

'Yes, who's that?'

'Look, I've seen Dave. He is being interrogated at the Grays –

146

sixth floor. They've kept him standing all the time. They throw water over him. They're giving him a bloody hard time. The bastards are out to crack him.'

'Who's speaking? . . . Hello . . . hello?' The phone was dead.

I did not go to work the next day. Instead, I picked up four tomatoes at the local greengrocer and made straight for the Grays, an old ugly seven-storey building – the security-police interrogation headquarters. At the door I was stopped.

'Look,' I said. 'I'm Mrs van Wyk.' (I picked the commonest Afrikaans name I could think of.) 'My husband has been interrogating those terrorists for days. He hasn't had a decent break or a proper meal. I've brought him something to eat.' I held up the brown paper bag.

To my amazement it worked. They let me in, escorting me politely to the lift. I went up to the sixth floor and opened the first door I came to. There were two desks and a lot of men standing and sitting in the room. Near the window was a black man in the most awful state. He was staggering, wet, and his nose seemed to be bleeding all over his clothes. I closed the door quickly.

I ran down to the door at the very end and opened it. I had a quick glimpse of David standing in front of a window. There were two men with him. His face was very white and he looked drunk. The door was slammed shut as I stood there. Then it opened and one of the men came out and escorted me out of the building.

'You can't come in here, you know, Mrs Kitson.'

I went home. I don't think I've had a proper night's sleep ever since.

Informers had penetrated the underground and BOSS, the Bureau of State Security, determined to smash the resistance. Over 800 people had been arrested by the sixteenth day of David's detention. And then Adelaide Joseph phoned me. Her husband was also a detainee.

'We're going to picket Johannesburg City Hall,' she said. 'It's illegal, but what the hell, we've decided. I'm so worried about

147

Paul. There's quite a few of us and we're taking the kids. We're making placards calling for them to be released or charged.'

That night Pumi and I made three placards and on 8 July, David's eighteenth day in solitary confinement and interrogation, Steven and I, with Amandla in her pushchair, went to demonstrate at the city hall. We joined a thin straggle of defiant men, women and children. The police took our names and addresses and I was threatened with arrest. The white passers-by looked at us in disgust. But we got a thumbs up from most of the black people who saw us.

On 22 July, exactly one month after David was arrested, they came for me. I was taken to Newlands police station and put in the 'Mad Woman's Cell' – one which is kept for women who, they say, 'go suddenly loco'. It had black walls and a broken, stinking loo. After a couple of hours I began vomiting. Later that night I was still vomiting. Suddenly the cell door opened and a very dishevelled and frightened man entered. 'I'm the doctor,' he said, standing at the cell door. 'Now, what's wrong with you? You detainees are always pretending to be ill.'

'I'm not ill,' I said. 'I am reacting to the dreadful smell of shit from that broken lavatory.'

'Well, I can't do anything about smells,' he said. 'But it is terrible in here. Look, I'm going to admit you to the Johannesburg General Hospital as a suspected appendix. Otherwise I can't get you out of here. Just tell them your side hurts, OK? And, listen, don't mention the lavatory. It's got to be something medical, OK?'

And he left.

Hours later an ambulance arrived and I was taken to the General. Two security officers stayed outside the door of the ward and no one came near me till about seven in the morning, when a doctor came to examine me. He discharged me immediately and I was taken in a black maria to the Fort where I spent the twenty-eight days of my detention. For the first three days I was in a cell with Pixie Benjamin, who was on hunger strike.

I was specially put with her to break her strike and was all for doing that. I didn't want to see a good friend starve to death.

As soon as I was locked in the cell, Pixie and I fell into each other's arms. It was wonderful to see a familiar face – to have someone to talk to after the silence and fear of solitary confinement and the impersonal treatment I had received at the hospital. There was so much to say to each other. Pixie had been detained a few weeks before me and wanted to know who had been detained, and whether I had seen John and their children. And she wanted to tell me the jail drill. But we were stopped by the wardress unlocking the door.

'You,' she said, pointing at me, 'Kitson, you godda see the doctor.'

'There's nothing wrong with me,' I said.

'Come on, you. I said come to the doctor.'

Pixie motioned me to go with her eyes.

I joined a queue of five women lined up outside on that cold July winter's day. I heard someone whisper '90-Days' and they all looked at me with curiosity and sympathy.

'OK, you just stand there and wait,' the wardress said, 'and no talking – understood?'

We stood there shivering. I was called first.

'I've told them to bring you here,' the doctor said, 'because your friend is going to die if she doesn't eat. She's a stubborn woman. If you can't get her to have some fruit juice, just get her to take some vitamin pills.'

'I'll do everything I can,' I said.

'You better,' he said. 'You 90-Days are a helluva lot of trouble. OK?'

Back in the cell, after Pixie and I had exchanged news – she had been arrested when a police raid took place at her home and they found a copy of *Fighting Talk!*, our Congress paper – I took a good look at her. She was gaunt, with huge staring eyes. She lay on her back on the thin mattress and occasionally raised a hand when she spoke. But it seemed even that was an effort. She was very, very weak.

'Pixie,' I said. 'You've got to have something to eat. Why are you doing this? It's just stupid. It won't work anyway.'

Pixie struggled to sit up, adjusting a thin pillow and bunching

149

up her jersey to lean her head against the wall. 'You must never, *never* do that,' she said sternly.

'Do what? Pixie, if you go on with this, you're going to *die*!'

'I know all about that,' she said. 'Yesterday the doctor told me my liver would begin to pack up. Every time I see that man he tells me another part of my body is going phut. Apparently in about three days my mind will start to wander – according to them.'

'I just don't understand you,' I said.

'Look, Norma,' Pixie said. 'There are lots of ways of fighting. Not eating is my way and the last thing you should do is play their game and come in here and undermine me.'

'What's the good of fighting if you're certain to die?' I asked.

'I'm not going to die,' she said. 'But what's the good of living if you don't put up the only kind of fight you can? I think I'm going to win. I don't think they can afford to have a white woman die in detention. That's why they're so desperate that they have put you in here with me. We're supposed to be in solitary, you know.'

'Well, how do you expect me to live in here, eat in here and just see you waste away?' I asked her.

'You'll find your own way to get through this,' she said. 'I've found my way. You must be behind me. If we support each other, we'll win, and we'll both feel better. If we oppose each other – and you won't change my mind, whatever you say – we'll be in here feeling rotten about each other.' I looked at her – so brave, so determined.

After the excitement of our meeting, we didn't talk much that afternoon. Pixie was very weak and spent a lot of time dozing – I think she was only half-conscious some of the time. But she taught me to make a pack of cards out of a tissue box. She had been given a stub of pencil which unthinkingly I wore down drawing the cards. Then I sat at the table playing patience.

That evening the cell door clanked open and a basket was held out to me by a wardress. 'This is for Kitson,' she said. I went to the corner of the cell as far away from Pixie as I could and started to undo the food parcels. I need not have worried. Pixie was way beyond wanting to eat. Each item had been lovingly wrapped by my sister Joan – chicken pieces, chocolate biscuits, a thermos of freshly squeezed orange juice, bars of chocolate, tomatoes, oranges – a whole array of food. Pumi must have telephoned Joan soon after my arrest, or Joan had found out when she made her daily telephone call to me. Turning my back on Pixie I ate a little. I did not have much appetite.

That night, as I lay trying to sleep, I could hear her thin wheeze – as if it was an effort for her to breathe. 'I will stand by you,' I whispered in case she was awake. 'Of course I will.'

On the following day there was a lot of coming and going in the cell. In the early morning the doctor arrived, examined Pixie and warned her that she didn't have long to live.

'OK, so now it's your pancreas an' that,' he said. 'I'll give you only a couple more days to live, you know. You stupid, man, jus' stupid. I mean, you got children. You just irresponsible.'

The wardresses kept coming and going, twice bringing others to show them what Pixie looked like.

The wardresses were ignorant, bullying and loud. Most of them came from small towns and were far from home. To qualify for the service, they had to be unmarried and most had got their jobs by having a brother or father who was a prison warder. Life in prison had brutalised them. After all, they lived locked up like the prisoners, and the matron wielded great power over them. They were terrified of her but in their turn they aped her. They were full of enmity for each other and enjoyed seeing one of their colleagues get into trouble. But most of all they liked to gang up on some poor sick prisoner and jeer and jibe. They spoke rudely and were always trying to get possessions off the prisoners – a bath cap, toothpaste, a cake of soap. All day in prison you hear them shouting, laughing, bickering, jeering. Their noise penetrates all the hours until lock-up, when they leave the section.

That afternoon I met a regular weekly visitor to the cells. There was the whirring of keys and a bang as the cell door flew open. A magistrate peered in. 'Any requests or complaints?' and he immediately shut the door. (He was required by law to ask this each week of every 90-Day detainee. But I suppose he was not compelled to listen to the replies.)

Pixie yelled from her bed, 'Hey, you! I have a request. And a complaint!'

There was a pause outside the door and then it opened again. 'Yes?' He stuck his head inside the cell.

'My complaint is that I've been arrested under an interrogation law and I haven't been interrogated. My request is that you should provide us with reading and writing matter – and I want my watch back.'

The door closed as if nothing had been said.

'Pixie!' I yelled. 'You're *crazy*! Imagine complaining that you aren't being interrogated! It's *dreadful*. Someone phoned me when David was first arrested and said he was being tortured under interrogation, that he had to stand for hours and had water poured over him, and I myself saw someone – I think it was Wilton – when I got into the Grays looking for David. He was covered in blood, in an awful state. And you know what happened to Babla – he was thrown out of the window. How can you court interrogation?'

'Oh, well,' Pixie said. 'I might as well try and keep them off the back of someone who has information. I've been out of things since I had the kids – there's nothing I can tell them. And apparently they keep you for hours. I reckon if they interrogated me it would keep them off someone else.'

Just before afternoon lock-up, the matron came, escorted by four wardresses. She was a big, thick, square-looking woman with short straight black hair. She wore a khaki uniform and carried a short sjambok and every now and then she would swish it at the wall of the cell.

'You not getting away with this, Benjamin. You may think you're very smart and very clever. I've had your husband banging at my door all day. He wants to see you. Well, we're not going to allow him to see you until you have something to eat.' The wardresses sniggered at this.

Pixie looked at the matron without expression.

The matron faltered. She was used to prisoners and wardresses deferring to her. But Pixie said nothing.

'Well, Benjamin, you'll see,' and without looking at either of us she pushed one of the wardresses and they all scurried out. The door banged shut.

I was learning from Pixie – learning to square up, learning to treat them with contempt, learning to mask my fear.

We had no incidents the following day. I wasn't taken out of the cell, I washed at the basin. I gave Pixie a good washdown. She was full of pain and her skin was slack and greyish. But she was an inspiration and filled me with strength. She made me feel fearless and full of courage. We spoke a lot about women and what they had to do in the struggle for liberation in South Africa. We discussed the momentous event on 9 August 1956 when 20,000 women marched to the government at Union Buildings in Pretoria to protest against the pass laws. Thousands had been arrested and were crowded into the jails, separated from their families, refusing to pay fines – refusing to let their men pay the fines. We had many examples of our heroic women: Winnie Mandela, Lilian Ngoyi, Adelaide Tambo, Albertina Sisulu, Helen Joseph, Dora Tamana, Annie Salinga. We felt we had to live up to their example, and talking about them bucked us up.

On the third day we were together the cell door opened and a wardress entered. She stood at the door, unconcernedly scratching her bottom.

'Get up, Benjamin. You've got a visitor. Hurry up or you'll miss the visit. Come on, come *on!*'

'She's weak,' I said. 'Don't you bully her.'

'Shut up, Kitson!' she said. 'She made herself weak. Come along, come along, Benjamin.'

I helped Pixie put on her jersey and slippers and led her to the door.

'I don't think she can walk on her own,' I said. 'Someone will have to carry her.' The cell door banged shut while the wardress stood outside and bellowed for help.

Then it opened again and Pixie was carried out like a light parcel by one of the wardresses.

John, her husband, had been applying to visit Pixie. They kept trying to do a deal with him. If he would persuade Pixie to eat, they would let him see her. For weeks, he refused, but eventually he agreed to do what they asked.

When John and Pixie were together in the visiting room, surrounded, of course, by Special Branch policemen, Pixie asked anxiously:

'How are you? How are the children?'

'Ag, don't start that now, man,' one of the policemen said. 'You came here to do a job, Mr Benjamin. Just do it.'

John plucked up his courage and as fast as he could get the words out he said, 'Carry on! They're terrified! Keep up the strike! You're winning!'

Before he could finish, one of the policemen lifted John and flung him against the wall. Then they rushed at him and carted him out of the visiting room.

The next day the matron came to our cell. Pixie was released.

As soon as Pixie had gone, I was transferred to the other side of the jail. This was a tiny cell with barely space for a bed. No chair, no table – just the bed with a dirty grey blanket and a strip of floor. If I stood on the bed I could look through the barred window onto an empty tarred space. I sat on the bed considering. My three days with Pixie had made me strong. And I was strengthened, on being taken to the toilet, to find a pair of Ray Jones's green broeks hanging over the door. I knew they were hers because I had seen them hanging on her washing line once and had remarked on their colour. Ray's broeks gave me heart. They had a casual homey look in that dank place. Back in my cell, I started singing and then did some knee bends and press-ups. I had lost my cards in a cell search. I spent what I thought must be about half an hour brushing my hair and half an hour brushing my teeth. I lay on the bed, banged on the cell door, shouted to see if anyone would answer, and then shouted to go to the lavatory. There was no answer. I could hear distant voices but no one nearby. I sat on the floor, got back on the bed and finally lay quietly on the thin strip of floor hoping I was out of the line of the spyhole.

Later that day there was a babble of voices outside and I jumped up on my bed and looked through the bars. I saw a line of women, two or three deep. I could see the middle section from my window but the beginning and end of the line were hidden from my view. Each woman I could see had a baby slung on her back. Then I heard a yelling and screaming somewhere to my right and, as I watched, I saw a wardress charge up the line swinging her bunch of keys. I saw her flick the keys up by the strap and bring them down on the back of a baby. The child arched and screamed. The mother buckled to her knees, swinging the baby around to her front, lifting her elbow to ward off another blow. But the wardress was walking up the line, swinging her keys at other babies.

I shouted in horror. At my left, beyond my vision, I heard a horrible noise of women and children screaming. I craned and pressed my face to the bars. And then I looked down. There was a small wizened woman standing below, motioning towards her mouth with her five fingers pressed together in an obvious sign: food!

I jumped down off the bed and reached into my food basket and pulled out an orange. I jumped back onto the bed and squeezed it through the bars. She caught the orange and in what seemed like one movement swung her baby around to the front, pressed its mouth open with a fierce movement, and squeezed juice into the baby's mouth. The juice sprayed into the child's face and eyes and it screamed. And then, opening her own mouth, the woman swallowed the orange whole, paused, looked from side to side and then ran back to the queue.

I sat on the bed in shock. I could not believe what I had seen. It was obvious that I was looking at a food queue and that the women and children in the queue were starving. I've never lost that sense of shock.

The following day there was an inspection. Colonel Aucamp came around with the matron and wardresses. The cell door was opened and I had to stand outside the cell. The matron called to one of the black women prisoners and told her to clean my cell out.

When I got back to the cell I sat on the bed and felt a hard lump. I pulled the dirty blanket back and found a book – *The Guns of Navarone*. It made life much easier for me and I kept it for two days before it was taken in a cell search. After that, whenever a black prisoner was sent to clean my cell, I would find things: a pencil, some paper, matches and once even two cigarettes. I learned that ordinary black prisoners always help politicals.

I lost all track of time. No sooner would the morning bread and coffee be delivered than, it seemed, the lunch bread and coffee would come. Or else I would feel I hadn't eaten all day. And then every now and then the cell door would open and I would be taken for interrogation.

My interrogators were Lieutenants Viktor and van der Merwe. In the beginning they were pleasant. Viktor was quite sympathetic. 'We just want you to make a statement, Mrs Kitson,' he'd say. 'This is not a place for people like you. We know you haven't done anything. We just want to know the names of the people who were visiting your husband in the last few months.'

'I'm only prepared to give you my name and address,' I said. 'I have nothing else to say.'

'Like a cigarette, Mrs Kitson?' Viktor would say.

I decided that I would never ever accept their cigarettes. I suppose it was a silly game to play, and there came a time when it was nearly my undoing.

'Have a cigarette, Mrs Kitson?'

'No, thank you.'

Then they would both light up and sit and talk to each other. Van der Merwe was a bit of a clod, but I was impressed with Viktor. He talked to van der Merwe but I knew he was addressing me, impressing me. He discussed the different recordings of the Brandenburg Concertos and their relative merits. He quoted from Byron and from Shakespeare. He was a man of culture and knowledge and I *was* impressed. Although I was terrified of these daily interrogations, as they came to be, I comforted myself that Viktor was a civilised man and that as long as I did not accept their cigarettes I would be strong. I was also frightened of the information I had. I was the one who had bought the wigs. I had helped as a link in an MK action transporting explosive to Cape Town. I had used the typewriters they were looking for. With the technical unit, I had produced the poster announcing the formation of MK in 1961, and had typed the many leaflets, documents and articles for the Communist Party, for Congress and MK. And then there were all the people who came to meetings at our house.

Women are not allowed to smoke in jail. Detainees are supposed to get a thirty-minute exercise period a day during which they may smoke – if they have cigarettes. But for the first few days of my detention I did not have any exercise period. I was craving a cigarette.

The interrogations went on.

'Look, Mrs Kitson, I can get you out of here in one hour, if you just make a statement. Everyone else has made statements. We know all the answers. We just want your confirmation. You've got two kids, Mrs Kitson. Do you know they pining for you? I wouldn't do that to my kids. Don't you want to see your kids?'

It got worse. One day I was taken to the interrogation room and they seemed agitated.

'Sit down, Mrs Kitson. I have some bad news for you,' Viktor said. 'Steven has broken his arm. Pumi has been arrested, so your daughter has been placed in a police orphanage. Now if you just answer some questions, you can go. Have a cigarette, Mrs Kitson.'

'No, thank you.'

After a couple of hours I was returned to my cell. I wasn't thinking straight. I knew it was all lies but I was worrying as if it were true. I pictured Steve in pain. My mind tried to shy away from visions of Amandla in a strange hostile atmosphere. The words of my mother kept coming back to me. 'If you want to go in for politics you shouldn't have children.'

I'm all right, I kept telling myself. I can't do anything about the kids. The people outside won't let anything happen to them.

157

I'm all right. As long as I don't smoke their bloody cigarettes and don't get Swanepoel, I'm all right. Major Swanepoel was known as the Beast. When my friend Babla Saloojee was interrogated on the top floor of the Grays, Swanepoel said he had hurled him out of the window. There is a photograph of Swanepoel, hands on hips, grinning over Babla's broken body.

At my next interrogation, van der Merwe came up to me. 'Are you going to make a statement or not?' he asked impatiently. 'We've wasted enough time on you,' and he gave me a sudden swipe across the face. My head snapped back with the force of his blow and my nose began to bleed. Immediately Viktor came to my side, offering me his handkerchief.

'Come on, Van!' he said. 'There's no need to get rough with Mrs Kitson.' Patting me on the shoulder, he said, 'That chap is terrible, you know. Sometimes I can't control him. I'm sorry, Mrs Kitson. It won't happen again. Have a cigarette, Mrs Kitson.'

'No, thank you.'

It didn't stop van der Merwe having a swipe at me now and then whenever he felt like it.

I would go back to my cell and sit on the bed and worry. I was desperately worried about David, about the kids, about Violet. There was no news from the outside and I was allowed no visitors.

One day I was taken to the interrogation room and van der Merwe walked straight up as if to hit me. Viktor sprang at him. 'No, man, this time it's my turn.'

He lunged out at me, one hand grabbing my shoulder and the other slapping me back and forth in the face. 'You bloody Jewish Red muck,' he screamed. 'You filth, you're all the same – traitors.' He pulled my head back, yanking at my hair, and hit me with his fist in my midriff.

Van der Merwe smiled. 'Do you want a cigarette, Mrs Kitson?'

'No, thank you.'

Many times during the days I would tense, expecting the babble of voices and the food queue to form. When it did come, the women would create a diversion either to my left or right; a great screaming would come from the women; crying from the babies, shouting from the wardresses; and then someone would run beneath my barred window. I would be standing there on tiptoe, waiting for the right moment to throw out all my food, so lovingly sent by my sister Joan – chicken legs, biscuits, chocolates, tomatoes, boiled eggs – whatever I had. What was not immediately eaten was hidden in clothes. I stopped eating altogether. I just threw it all out of the window. At times I must have passed out without knowing it because I once surfaced on the floor with the broken glass of a thermos flask around me.

My days were spent trying to plan what I would do at the next interrogation, shouting and waiting to go to the lavatory, throwing my food out of the window, exercising, keeping away from the spyhole, listening for where the wardresses were, hearing their coarse shouting and laughter. I was always worrying about Steven and Amandla (I did not know where they were or who was looking after them) and about David. A Bible was the only book provided, and I found it depressing to read. All the begetting and the casting out of lepers was horrible. I lost my sense of time. I would be taken to the doctor, taken to the lavatory, taken for a shower, taken to the exercise yard for a few minutes. The wardresses pinched most of the things I was allowed – my toothpaste, face cream, face cloth.

I knew when it was Sunday because then there was singing all day. It came from somewhere in front of my cell but some distance away and sounded as if there was a big hall full of women singing. I expect it was a huge cell. Most of the songs were hymns but I recognised some freedom songs and would join in with them. And Sunday was notable because the food queue never formed.

I could tell when it was about thirty minutes before normal day lock-up by a game the wardresses played with some poor woman who must have had diabetes. I would hear a thin but penetrating wail coming from what I now knew was the 'white hospital' section of the jail where Pixie and I had been.

'Please, can I have my insulin now?'

'Shut up, you stupid,' a wardress would yell.

'Please, please can I have my injection? I'll go into a coma.'

Laughter and shouts from the wardresses. 'Go in a coma then, bladdy fool.'

'Please! Please!'

This would go on and on.

Sometimes she would beg for an egg. 'Please, can I have my egg now? Oh, please! I'll go into a coma.'

'Shut up, you! Shut *up!* The more you call the longer it'll be.'

Silence for a while and then it would all start again.

It was a dreadful game played by mean, power-drunk wardresses. I used to wish that the woman would resist but they were so uncaring that I suppose unless she begged for her medicine, they might have forgotten her.

On the twenty-fifth day of my detention, I was taken to the interrogation room to find Swanepoel with Viktor and van der Merwe. I went blind with terror.

'Now you are going to make a statement, Mrs Kitson,' he said. 'We know all about you.' He picked up a file of papers and started reading from it. 'Joined Congress in 1952. Participated in Defiance Campaign and the Congress of the People. Delegate to Warsaw Youth Festival.' From what he was saying, I gathered he knew little of my more recent activities. I was sweating with fear but I did my best not to show it.

'The sooner you make a statement, the sooner you'll be released,' he said. 'We can keep you here for ever, you know. No one out there really cares. It's everyone for himself now. All the others have decided to save their skins. You see, you'll sing. You'll sing like a bird.'

Silence from me.

'I suppose you think you're doing it for Dave?' he asked. 'Don't bluff yourself. You know how Dave's been telling you he's been attending all those meetings? You know where he really was? He's been having it off with Vera. How's that then? Eh? Do you want to see a picture of them together?' He held up something in front of my face but I closed my eyes.

'He's a terrific man, David is,' I said. 'I never expected a man

160

like him to be satisfied with only one woman.'

It was the first time I had spoken during an interrogation.

Swanepoel hit me across the face with his fist. Then he knocked me off my feet with a side blow to my body. 'Dirty commie,' he shouted. 'You all immoral. You all share your men. You don't know anything about decency, about good Christian family life.'

He was getting very worked up. His bull's head with the thick ridge at the back of the neck was blood red with rage.

'Have a cigarette, Mrs Kitson?' Viktor was at my elbow.

I got up slowly. I was in dreadful pain but I tried not to show it. I sat on the chair and crossed my legs as nonchalantly as I could.

Viktor proffered his pack. I slowly slid a cigarette out and he lit it for me. I felt a sense of relief, of dread, of weakness. I might as well, I told myself, dragging on the cigarette, I might as well just tell them everything. This isn't getting me anywhere. I'll land up being killed. They have all the information they need anyhow. I'm just a tiny cog. I'm only a typist. I don't really know anything of value. I'm not important. They've detained far more important people than me.

The three of them sat there.

Swanepoel turned to Viktor. 'Ag, get her back to her cell, man. The bloody woman's not human.' And to me, 'We'll see you tomorrow, Mrs Kitson, don't you worry about that!'

Back in the cell I argued with myself. Giving in once isn't important. I only took *one* cigarette. But I broke my own pact. No one knows about the pact but me. I'll pretend I never made it. I'm still all right, I told myself. Sore, but in one piece. I haven't ratted on anyone. I might pass myself off as unimportant, but I have vital information that could implicate MK people. If I talked, lives would be at risk. No matter what happens, I will not say a single word. I'm still strong. And I recalled the words of Duma Nokwe, ANC youth leader and a wise friend: 'It's a very hard struggle, this. There comes a time when it isn't only that you face the wrath of the government, the police and all of them; you also face the ignorance of some of the people in this rotten society. No, not only that. There comes a time when you feel alone. And that's just the time when you have to be very strong, very sure, right inside yourself. Because you are never alone. You are one of us. Remember that, won't you?'

Gradually I urged myself back into being strong enough to face the following day. But they didn't come the next day, or the day after that. The following day I was released, after twenty-eight days.

I walked home. I could only think about Steven and Amandla. Pumi telephoned Joan, who had looked after Steven, and she brought him home. He was pale and serious as he hugged me. He thought I had been with David. Micki had taken care of Amandla and she brought her home. The children were all right. I heard Steven say, 'Mommie's sick,' and I must have fainted. Joan took me to hospital. I weighed six stone and had to be fed through a tube in my nose.

The newspapers ignored the hundreds of black people in detention but, probably because I was a white woman, published a photograph of me and said I had a nervous breakdown.

No one ever asks what happened to you in jail, so people hardly ever know. I recently met Joyce Mokhesi, a student at Ruskin College in Oxford who was from Sharpeville and had left after the 1985 uprisings – the same Sharpeville that had risen up in 1960. She was detained and during her interrogation they burned her with cigarettes and with electrodes. She carries the marks on her wrists and breasts. In January 1986 her brother was sentenced to hang with five other young people, including a woman who was so tortured in detention that she came into the courtroom for her trial with a broken arm. Joyce went to a doctor in Oxford and he couldn't take it. He just couldn't believe it. He asked her to go and find a South African doctor! People don't like to ask. They don't want to know.

David came to trial in December 1964, six months after the Rivonia heroes had been sentenced to life imprisonment. He had been in detention and solitary confinement since 22 June. In those months, my world had turned to ashes. After ten days

162

in hospital, where I had to learn to eat again, I got a job working as a secretary to eighteen advocates.

Back home, Steven, Amandla and I were confused and disorientated while I tried to get a routine life going for us again with Pumi's assistance. At night we were constantly disturbed by the security police and my state of mind got worse as David's trial date approached.

He was charged with four others – Wilton Mkwayi (black), Laloo 'Isu' Chiba (Indian), John Matthews (white) and Mac Maharaj (Indian).

The lawyers in the case put it to me that David should plead guilty. I was unhappy about this. Surely to plead guilty would be to admit that he had done something wrong – to renege on our strongly held views that the struggle we were fighting was just and correct. They told me the state would call for the death penalty unless there was a guilty plea. I asked what David's opinion was and they said he had asked them to ask me. I did not believe them. We had dedicated our lives to the struggle for liberation and did not consider ourselves guilty of anything. David would not pull back now. In any event, although David would have wanted me consulted, he made his own decisions. I asked what the sentence would be if he pleaded guilty and they said, 'A couple of years.' I asked what the attitude of the other four wives was and why we could not all meet together. They said that that was unwise and would show conspiracy. I said I did not believe that the wives of the others would agree to a plea of guilty.

I fell out with the lawyers. A new set of lawyers was appointed – I never found out how. Almost immediately I fell out with the brilliant and kind Joel Joffe. I was suspicious by then of what the lawyers would do and in the midst of the turmoil and financial stress of those days I received a letter asking me for R7500 to defend David.

During the Treason Trial, in 1956, Canon John Collins had set up the International Defence and Aid Fund in England to meet the legal costs. I assumed that the lawyers who were acting for our five would try to get their fees from that organisation, or from sympathisers abroad. When they wrote to me, asking for fees, I thought no help was available from any other source.

I was completely broke, having difficulty buying food and petrol. In panic I sent letters off to the United Nations, to friends and to David's union DATA (Draughtsmen's and Allied Technicians Association), now TASS. Jim Mortimer, who was to become Labour Party secretary, was an old friend and editor of *DATA Journal*. He responded immediately and started a collection among his members in England. The 50ps and £5s mounted up and paid for the trial of all five accused.

Once the trial started, and for its duration, we were permitted to write and receive as many letters as we wished and we were permitted to visit our men. They were held in cages underground in the basement of the court. David's first letter read:

Dear Norma,

I know you don't like that. Like your Stiller family, you have always thought it necessary to use stronger terms of endearment. But if I said dearest, it would infer that I had two Norma's, an expensive one and a damned expensive one whereas I have you: one wonderful you. You have taken on the whole state on my behalf – so bravely, so steadfastly. For this I shall always love you. No endearment would adequately express how closely I hold you to my heart. Whatever happens now, remember that. Whatever difficulties you face in the future you will face secure in the knowledge that this humble chap loves you. And you will have problems. When I am not there you will have to face all sorts of things including insult and rumour. People will try to pull you down. They will not manage to do so. That much I know.

I am secure in the knowledge of your capability. I look to you to see to our children and to raise them with the principles we hold dear. Don't lose your effervescence – it represents the fighting stuff you are made of.

Seeing you sitting bravely in court this morning made me feel very happy. I've never seen you in a hat before. I don't pretend to like it.

Having done my bit, I now bow my head to the inevitable, knowing that whatever happens, you are there rooting for me. That is a great comfort.

The comrades ask me to thank you for the wonderful meal you sent down today. Please remember Wilton likes chicken. Can you buy me some stamps? I have received a mass of mail – after the drought it is exciting to hear from people. As soon as I have answered the letters, I will give them to you. You might also like to reply to them.

This letter might seem redundant. We will see each other tomorrow morning before the court proceedings, but letters are private. Who knows when we will be private again. Please write to me. Tell me everything. Dear Norma.

Love, David

The five pleaded not guilty. Most of the proceedings were held in camera. Louis Blom-Cooper came out from England to be an observer and I was told his observation was that the trial was fair – in accordance with the laws of South Africa.

The charges against the five related to the military actions of MK. Informers had caused the arrest of some of MK's supporters and the state kept them in detention as witnesses.

These 'witnesses', held in solitary confinement until the trial, came to the stand, blinking, some disorientated, some showing the effects of torture – and refused to give evidence. The defence would call for an adjournment, during which they would tell the 'witness' to give his testimony. Failure to do so could mean a year's imprisonment for contempt, and none of the defendants wanted their comrades to go back to their brutal jailers. It was with the greatest difficulty that the defence lawyers persuaded these witnesses to give their reluctant evidence – and most of them confined their statements to allegations against 'Witness D'.

In any event, the two main state witnesses, both members of MK, Witness D (Lionel Gay) and Patrick Mtembu, had given full evidence and no testimony from comrades could worsen the situation of the accused five.

Patrick Mtembu had been in solitary confinement in a cell next to Solwandle Looksmart Ngudle, who was brutally tortured in detention and found hanged in his cell. Looksmart was the first person in South Africa to be banned after his death, when a cellmate had insisted on reporting details of his torture. As banned people cannot be quoted, the state thus prevented the facts being known. Patrick Mtembu had been threatened with the same fate as Looksmart Ngudle, and he reluctantly turned state's evidence. He gave minimal replies to all questions and we had a certain sympathy for his situation.

Lionel Gay was another kettle of fish altogether. Standing at the Grays waiting for permission to see David in detention, I had seen Lionel's wife going into Colonel Klindt's office. It was the third day of his arrest. She was carrying a radio, food and books and she had already been in to see her husband. He was to have daily visits! It was obvious that he was being treated differently from the other detainees.

Giving evidence for the state, Gay claimed that the accused had caused the murder of a man named Gangat. It was not MK policy, then, for witnesses to be killed although Gay himself had been in favour of this and had argued for it in his group. The accused knew nothing of the man called Gangat.

Then, further implicating Wilton Mkwayi, the first accused in the trial, Gay claimed that Wilton had carried a gun.

After the trial he got a safe passage to London, where he worked for some time at a London college, and to this day he goes about England unhindered, while Wilton Mkwayi, a magnificent man – trade unionist, ANC leader, freedom fighter – against whom he gave the most damning evidence, remains in jail, in his twenty-second year of a life sentence. And Irene Mkwayi suffers at home. Gay was a member of the Communist Party and managed to persuade the London exiles that he had been a reluctant witness, and his name has appeared on the mailing lists as an ANC supporter. On the London ANC women's committee in the 1980s, I applied for his name to be removed whenever I saw it – but it always reappeared. After David's release, one of the first requests made to him by Sonia Bunting was to meet with Lionel Gay. David was appalled and perplexed at this request. He said he would have nothing to do with Gay while Wilton Mkwayi was still in jail.

There was a celebratory air in court on the first day of the trial. The five wore new shirts and red ties. They looked thin and strained but their spirits were high.

Wilton had been shot before his capture and I heard that during his detention he had been shipped around to sixteen jails.

David was accused number two and had just missed arrest at the Rivonia Trial – he had a meeting scheduled there the night of the raid, but was in bed with flu. The MK headquarters at Rivonia were in the process of being moved to a safe place in Krugersdorp before the raid in 1963, because Rivonia was then considered unsafe – the last meeting was being held at Lilliesleaf Farm when the raid took place.

Isu Chiba was accused number three – a member of the National High Command of MK, he was the link between MK and the Indian community. He was a leader of the South African Indian Congress. He was so tortured during interrogation that he was made permanently deaf in one ear.

Accused number four, Johnny Matthews, had seven children. When he was detained the police searched his house and found a tin of bullets for a .303 rifle. Before the Second World War, Johnny's cousin had left his rifle and the bullets at Johnny's home. Following the instruction, after the war commenced, for everyone to hand in any arms, Johnny had handed in the rifle. He had put the bullets in a tin to prevent his kids getting hold of them. This 'evidence' – that he was in possession of explosives! – was brought into court even though the tin was wrapped intact in a newspaper dated 1941.

Number five accused was Mac Maharaj. He was a member of the central committee of the Communist Party. We knew Mac well. He had been a regular visitor to our Muswell Hill flat in the fifties when he was studying in London.

I had taken both children below the court to see David on the first day of the trial. Pumi waited outside the building to take them home. We held each other's fingers through the wire netting and Steven chatted to David about the Beatles. Amandla, who was two years old, wriggled in my arms trying to get at David, banging on the netting, screaming. David and I looked at each other and hardly spoke that first time. The following day I left the children at home.

These morning visits became very precious. At the cages I met the four wives of the other prisoners, and the ten of us were able to exchange greetings. The boer guards stood close to us

167

and there was no privacy but we held each other's fingers, know-ing that all physical contact would cease at the end of the trial.

I took the children to see David most mornings. It was both important and traumatic for them and for years afterwards they spoke about David in a cage. Steven wrote about his father's wonderful smile and bravery and Amandla asked constantly why she had not been able to cuddle her father when she was with him.

During one of these visits, while David had arranged for the boer's attention to be diverted by his comrades, I smuggled a tiny radio in to him.

At the beginning of the proceedings Mac told the judge that he had been tortured: he had been hit on his penis with a plank of wood which had a nail in it. The judge ignored Mac, saying that that was a matter for another court. The five didn't stand a chance.

That first day in court, I did not listen to the proceedings. I had my eyes on David. I was proud of him. He smiled at friends in the courtroom, and looked sure of himself. I saw him fre-quently raise his hand to pat the back of his head, a gesture of tension I recognised well, but that was the only sign that he was anxious. He looked strong and in command of the situation – as they all did.

During the days that followed we were locked out of most of the trial while evidence was given in camera by state witnesses who were to be protected, and I hung around the court wondering what was going on, fretting.

When we were allowed into the courtroom, and despite the high morale of the accused, I found it difficult to follow the proceedings. My eyes kept wandering from David to Wilton to Mac, Johnny and Isu and then to the ceiling and to the awesome range of lawyers and police.

Part of me believed, or wanted to believe, that at most David would get a couple of years – I suppose I was unconsciously banking on what the first set of lawyers had said. Inside I knew they all faced terrible penalties. At times, looking at them in that

168

dock, I felt married to them all – married to the struggle. I loved every one of them so much as they stood there, always cheerful, always brave. All I and the other wives could do to express these feelings, which we shared, was to send them more and more elaborate and costly lunches. We tried to steel ourselves for the worst.

My family stayed away from the trial. I think Joan's husband wouldn't let her come. David's mother had always supported him and she prevailed upon Fred to attend each day. Oscar kept my mother in Durban. My father had not been in touch with me at all since my detention. Auntie Ettie and Cousin Margaret had sent David books while he was on trial. There was silence from the rest of my Durban family, and silence from my Cranko family in Johannesburg. Some months before David's detention, Ronnie and Marlene had gone to live in the Cape. Ronnie wrote me a letter, which I received three days after David's sentence. They were to return to Johannesburg a few months later.

Dear Vroomie,
    David and you are the best of us. What more can I say? What are you going to do now? You must be short of money. Enclosed R20. Words fail. Marlene and the kids join me in wishing you everything of the best. Keep courage.
Your loving brother, Ronnie.

Marsha and Judy came with me to court nearly every day. My little sister Clarice was there on the day of the sentencing. I did not see her, but there was a photograph of her taking me in her arms outside the court.

After a month on trial they were all found guilty of the same 'crimes' that convicted Nelson Mandela and the other seven heroes of the Rivonia Trial, and sentence was passed: life for Wilton, twenty years for David, eighteen for Isu, fifteen for Johnny and twelve for Mac. I was unprepared for these savage sentences.

With the court in uproar, I stumbled out into the glaring sunshine. Hands and arms supported me everywhere. Out there, the police were ranged around with guns and masses of people shouted slogans and waved their fists. I saw the five being herded into a white police van and watched as they gave the thumbs up, and then I fainted clean away.

The trial was over. The sentence had begun.

· 10 ·

For a long time, going about my everyday life, I was mourning and alienated. Looking back, it seems that I spent that first period in a daze. But then I remember that it was not the daze of paralysis, but rather of overwork – of having too many things to do, of absorbing too many shocks: David's detention, my own, and that of our close friends, the imprisonment of our leaders, the attack on our political organisation, the flight from South Africa of so many friends, and the sudden sole responsibility for Steven and Amandla.

I missed David acutely. He was not only my husband, he was my close friend and comrade. We had been together for eight years. We had discussed everything and made decisions together. He was the chief parent in the family. He had nursed Steven through encephalitis and through his ear operation, had got up at night to Amandla, been home whenever he could for bath-time. He had been the pivot round which our lives turned. Throughout the nineteen years and five months of David's imprisonment, he was there, sometimes in the foreground of my consciousness, mostly just there, somewhere, someone to be taken into account in everything we did – in all the ups and the downs.

At first I felt I was sinking – but often those around me were sinking deeper. You only know women when you are a single mother. Then life descends to the level of household routines, earning a living, school clothes and bills. And all around are other women, suffering in one way or another – from lousy jobs, mean or neglectful husbands, from divorce or separation, from loneliness or just boredom – women who sink into depression and despair, and rise, with a turn of events, to great energy and creativeness. The women of happily married couples don't ask you with two young children to eat in their dining rooms with their husbands and their best crockery. You don't get invited to dinners of boeuf bourguignonne, fresh salmon or roast beef. Instead there are impromptu snacks of baked beans or sardines on toast, and talk – in kitchens – of the children's development, sexual frustration and gratification, women, men, state allowances, work and society. And so my world was peopled in the main with my sister Joan, Marsha, Micki and Judy and the mothers of some of Steven and Amandla's school friends. After the trial, my in-laws drew close and often took Amandla and Steven for weekends.

At first there was the shock of my sudden isolation.

In Johannesburg, after David was imprisoned, there was good cause for those who were involved in the underground to stay away. It would have been pointing the security police at themselves and risking what remained of the organisation to have kept in contact with us.

During David's detention, my mother had been to visit the minister of prisons, Vorster, to insist upon his innocence. She told him she was perfectly certain that her son-in-law had done nothing wrong. After all, she said, he was *her* son-in-law, whereas he only had the word of his police – and everyone knew most of them didn't have a clue! Look at the traffic cops in Durban, she told him, most of them didn't know left from right! Now David, she told him, had been to *university*. Vorster took out a huge dossier on David and explained to my mother that his activities against the government went back to when David was twenty years old. Mimicking his accent, my mother gave me a sample of their conversation.

'Look yer, Mrs Goldberg, even as a *young man* he gave *blood* to Medical Aid for Russia!'

'Well, we were all in that during the war, weren't we?' said my mother. 'I used to send them parcels! They were the Allies – you remember?'

She never knew that Vorster himself had been interned by the Smuts United Party government during the war as a Nazi

172

supporter and member of the *Ossewa Brandwag* (the secret brotherhood of the Afrikaner mafia).

I do think my mother nearly managed to convince the Minister of Prisons (who was to become the Prime Minister of South Africa) that he had arrested the wrong man. My mother held Vorster personally responsible for David's arrest and was quite certain he would find the error of his ways after a few weeks. But when I was detained, she had no more time for him at all.

'It's funny,' she said. 'He looks just like somebody's father, but he's absolutely rotten! How could he imprison *my daughter* and my lovely son-in-law?'

My mother was staunch in her support of us. 'I don't want to know about politics,' she'd say to someone commiserating with her. 'I just know that my Norma and David would *never* do anything wrong.'

My family in Durban were shocked and horrified at the outcome of the trial and they stayed completely away from us. They tried to keep my mother away – telling her that she would be implicated and involve them. But my mother, unbelieving and shocked at David's sentence, managed to make a few trips to Johannesburg after the trial and she brought me great comfort by staying for a few days now and then. She rearranged the bits of furniture in our tiny lounge, sighed over the state of my cupboards and drawers, told me I was 'spoiling the children', railed at Pumi's inefficiency, bought me expensive perfume, and generally brought an aura of her brand of normality – a whiff of my childhood – into my life.

Steven adored his grannie and he won her heart for ever by writing:

I've got a grannie who I adore.
She's covered with kind spirits
From her head to the floor.
She cuddles me until I'm nearly sick,
But when she lets me go again,
I recover very quick.

In my childhood, my father had been the parent who had instilled into me a sense of justice – my mother, it seemed to me then, had played on the periphery of life with nothing more important in her head than playing cards, her clothes and parties. But now that the trial was over she was prepared to take on anyone in support of David and me.

My other ally was my mother-in-law, Chris Kitson. She was a quiet woman, a devout Christian Scientist. From the moment David and I married, I could do no wrong in her eyes. I don't know whether it was her pleasure at gaining a daughter that made her so staunchly in favour of me, but whatever the reason, Chris was always a good friend to me. David's father was very put out when David was convicted. He feared it would interfere with his membership of his Johannesburg golf club and it was a great shame to him. He remained angry and bitter for many years.

After the trial, Joan visited and telephoned me frequently. She was worried about our staying unprotected in the house. She shopped for me and tried to lighten my chores, and we chatted for hours on the telephone even when we had been together an hour before. I had missed her presence at the courtroom but now she protected me wherever she could, drove me to see majors, generals and lawyers to try to get extra visits to see David.

Her husband, Norman, buried his head in the sand, like most white South Africans. He was supportive and kind, but frightened for his family. I visited their house as little as possible because of this, but Joan would beg me to go, and she took Steven and Amandla swimming at their pool most weekends. Their relationship with their cousins, Robbie, Tessa and Lindy became very important for them.

Pumi was my constant loyal support and cheerful companion. We spent many evenings, after the children had gone to bed, chatting about what would happen in South Africa.

The security police didn't leave us alone. They woke the children in the early hours of the morning, throwing stones at the windows of our little house in Victoria, followed my car, parked outside our house – they were never far away. Chris Kitson would take Amandla and Steven to her flat whenever she could to let them get a good night's sleep. One of the acts of the estate agent, when I came to sell our house, was to peel numerous little metal 'bugs' off the walls and furniture, from trees and plants, and even off my Beetle car.

I decided to apply for a passport so that if things got too bad, I would have papers to leave the country.

Steven's life changed the day that David was arrested. The children he had been friendly with suddenly withdrew and instead of going to play at their homes, or having them come to ours after school, he came home alone and played alone. He received no invitations to birthday parties – previously he had been to two or three a week. I transferred him to a private Anglican school, in the hope that it would be a more sympathetic environment than Houghton Government School. It was worse.

One day I arrived home from work to find Steven sitting on the steps of the house, battered, bleeding and angry. He had been beaten up – by the boys and the masters. 'They said I was a commie like Dad,' he explained, 'and I probably am. Mom, what's a commie? I thought Dad was an engineer.' While I bathed his bruises and dressed his cuts, I decided to take my nine-year-old 'communist' out of school.

At the time of David's arrest I was working at National Dairy Equipment doing a morning secretarial job. The police visited my boss and warned him that he was employing 'a criminal's wife'. Embarrassed, he explained to me that as his trade was with the boer dairy farmers, I would have to leave or his business would be ruined. He thought it appalling and offered me R500.

I was terrified at being deprived of my income but, stung with the unfairness of it, I refused the money. He was kind – and patient. 'I owe it to you,' he said. 'You've been a really good secretary. Just look at my position. Please try and understand.'

'Oh, I understand all right,' I said. 'The cops are going to hound me so that I can't earn a living and everybody is going to

175

be full of sweet reason about why they can't employ me. I'm leaving now. That's what you want, isn't it?' He nodded.

'But please let me help you,' he said. 'You must have so many problems. Just take it.'

'No,' I said. And I left.

Problems! Sleep was impossible. During David's detention I had just tried to get through the days: cooking and getting food to the jail, collecting David's washing, keeping a job, and seeing to Steven and Amandla. Detainees got one meal from outside every day. My sister Joan got together with the relatives of the detainees and they started a rota system and, as some of the prisoners were held in Pretoria, a large feeding network got going.

After David was sentenced I worked at a private hospital for about a year doing reception shiftwork, but the night shifts were very difficult. The police chose the nights or early hours of the morning to harass us. They rang the bell and then disappeared, threw stones at the windows and generally disturbed the children's sleep. Pumi was too frightened to stay alone with the children at night – she was frightened of being arrested. I felt I had to be at home with the children at night. After about a year battling with the hospital shifts, I had to leave. I realised that when children lose one parent, they lose both. The remaining parent is out at work or, in the home, too preoccupied with keeping things going to spend much time with the children.

I got a job working on a building site. Here, in the centre of Johannesburg, over a hundred black labourers were employed illegally – for starvation wages. A deal was made by my boss and the Bantu Affairs Office for their stay in Johannesburg. But they were not allowed to leave the site as they had no passes permitting them to be in Johannesburg. They slept in a corrugated iron shed on site and cooked their mealie meal in huge braziers. They were imprisoned within barbed-wire fences. The authorities knew they were there and sometimes police would jibe at the workers through the fence. But South African business was always able to get the labour it wanted, pass laws or not.

I became friendly with one of the black workers, Petrus,

supporting a wife and three children in Pondoland. He asked me for clothes, food and brandy. I smuggled them in. The site manager was a lunatic. He tore across the site, jumping up and down, issuing instructions and threats, picking up bits of iron and sticks and waving them over the workers' heads – and sometimes over mine. He stole bits of machinery and items from the stores and sold them to his friends who visited the site office. He took a dislike to me when he saw me talking with one of the workers.

'Can't you ever stop talking to the bladdy kaffirs?' he asked me once. 'It hasn't done you any bladdy good up to now. I'd 'a thought you was in enough trouble through the fokin' kaffirs as it is. You just a stupid bladdy woman, isn't it?'

Petrus was caught 'drunk', sacked, and sent back to his 'homeland'.

I began to make moves to leave the country. I put my house up for sale to see if it could raise enough money for the trip. My passport applications, submitted every few months, were repeatedly turned down. No reasons were given. I feared rearrest. I heard that the security police were still trying to trace the typewriter used for producing MK leaflets, to find out who had arranged escapes for certain wanted people, where the archives were and who had delivered the parcel to Mr G at the Park Royal Hotel that had led to the arrest of Jack Tarshish – one of my tasks for MK in the underground.

The white prisoners had been jailed in Pretoria, the black prisoners on Robben Island. The prison system had four grades, most privileges being for those graded A. Normally, a reception team interviews and considers a prisoner for six weeks before grading and the most common initial grading is B grade. After six months, the normal practice is for a prisoner to be upgraded to A. The political prisoners went through no reception interview and on their arrival at jails after sentence were immediately graded D – a punishment grading normally used only when a prisoner has committed an offence inside the prison.

During the six-monthly visits we were scarcely permitted to

talk: all subjects were banned except family matters. I was able to tell David little stories about the children but did not want to upset him with the truth: that we were being harassed by the police and that Steven was being victimised at school and that both the children were disturbed and fearful and none of us was sleeping properly. David was not able to discuss anything about the jail. The build-up to the six-monthly visits left me incoherent and palpitating once we were face to face.

We were never in the same room: we spoke through perforated masonite panels and looked at each other through thick glass. We were not able to touch. There were warders on either side of us and a hidden microphone recording our conversation. David once furtively stripped the beading in front of him and found the wires.

David had warned me that life was going to be difficult for us and he urged me to take the children back to London. We had friends there. The morning before the sentences were passed, he suggested I should divorce him. He said he would surely be locked away for many years and I would need to build another life – a normal life – for myself and for the children. After all, nothing could affect our feelings for each other. In the months that followed, during the isolation, with the difficulty I was having getting a job that would pay enough for us to survive, and with the children having increasingly serious problems, this seemed sensible advice. I kept applying for a passport, but if I had to remain in South Africa, a divorce might mean a decent job for me and better treatment for the children. I started divorce proceedings.

One of the things that worried me was David's sweet tooth. We were not able to get any news about jail food but we heard that the sugar allowance was infinitesimal and no sweets were allowed. David was a big sweet eater. I made an appointment to see Colonel Aucamp, the head of security, and requested that David be allowed some sweets.

'Ag, no, man!' he said. 'These people are prisoners, you know!'

'Well, it won't do the state any harm for them to have some sweets,' I said.

'There's no sweets on the allowed list, Mrs Kitson.'

'Well, that doesn't mean they're not allowed. I bet they're not on the forbidden list.'

He shook his head and thought for a while. Then he said, 'Look, if I make an exception, all the prisoners will want sweets.'

'If I can get *all* the prisoners some sweets, will you allow it then?'

'There's a helluva lot of prisoners at Central – and that's part of this jail complex,' he said. 'There's only awaiting trials and your lot in Local. But in Central there's all the long-terms and the awaiting deaths. There's a helluva lot.' Knowing that South Africa has the highest rate of execution in the world and one of the biggest prison populations, I could believe that.

I went round the sweet factories with my sister Joan and my friend Judy and got them to agree to donate large quantities of sweets as a one-off treat for the prisoners at Pretoria Central and Local. Then I went to Aucamp with the news that all was arranged.

'Ag, no, Mrs Kitson,' he said. 'I told you, sweets is not on the allowed list. We can't have sweets in jail, man.' And I couldn't budge him.

At this time I became friendly with Benjy Pogrund, a journalist on the *Rand Daily Mail*. He had done a brilliant piece of investigative journalism exposing the prison farm labour conditions in South Africa, and another opportunity now arose for him when Jock Strachan was released from jail and asked Benjy to publish his experiences.

I went with Benjy to Durban to interview Jock. Jock had been imprisoned for activity in the underground before the Sabotage Act became law. He had served three years. The treatment he had seen meted out to black prisoners was so appalling that Jock wanted it exposed. Jock was a very brave man. He was sentenced to a further eighteen months for these revelations, but the world knew, for the first time, what black prisoners in South African jails routinely suffered: how they were stripped and beaten; how they were made to stand naked with their arms raised and how

179

they were brutally bodysearched; how they were half-starved and, even in winter, had inadequate clothing and no shoes. Jock Strachan's act of telling these facts, knowing that he would go to jail again, knowing that he would be victimised once the regime had him back in jail, was heroic.

Benjy, and Laurence Gandar, editor of the newspaper, were raided by the police. The offices of the *Rand Daily Mail* were searched. Another typewriter went into the Vaal River. But the story was published and caused an uproar.

After two years, my passport application was accepted. I put our little tin-roofed house up for sale and booked our air tickets to London.

The day before we were due to leave I went to Pretoria to say goodbye to David, having been granted a special visit. But when I returned to our house, it was surrounded by plainclothes security policemen. I thought, this is it, they have come for me this time – not to detain me, to charge me. Whenever I feel under threat, I whip up a terrific aggression.

'Get out of my way,' I said to the security policeman as I opened my car door. 'What the hell do you want?' Without waiting for a reply I stormed into the house.

In the kitchen, Pumi was sitting at the table with her head in her hands. A security man thrust a tatty piece of paper into my hand.

'Mrs Kitson! I have come for your new passport.'

I looked at him with hatred, greeted the frightened Pumi warmly and then, as casually as I could, took the letter.

Office of the Regional Representative,
Department of the Interior,
Johannesburg
22nd October, 1966

Mrs N.B. Kitson,
17 Shipston Lane, Victoria,
Johannesburg.

Madam,
Withdrawal of South African Passport

By direction I have to inform you that the Minister of the Interior has in terms of the Conditions of Issue of South African Passports, paragraph I, withdrawn your South African passport issued to you in Johannesburg on the 30th September 1966.

This notice of withdrawal is of immediate effect. The passport is therefore no longer a valid passport for the purposes of section 2 of the Departure from the Union Regulation Act No 34 of 1955.

You are now required in terms of this notice to surrender the passport immediately to the officer serving this notice to you.

Signed (indecipherable)
Regional Representative.

My brand-new passport was confiscated. It had been issued less than a month before, after numerous applications for eighteen months. My only option was to apply for an exit permit and lose my South African citizenship. I had not taken this step before because being a South African was what my life was about and because I wanted to have full rights to enter South Africa to visit David. But now I felt I had to go, whatever the circumstances.

My exit permit was granted without delay and it committed me to leaving South Africa without the right to return. A letter from the Department of the Interior which accompanied the permit contained the words:

2. In terms of section 15(1)(c) of the South African Citizenship Act, No. 44 of 1949, as amended, a South African citizen ceases to be a South African citizen should he, for purposes of admission to the Republic of South Africa become a prohibited person.

3. The exemption from the visa requirements as laid down in section 24(1)(c) of Act No. 22 of 1913, as amended, has also been withdrawn in your case.

4. Should you arrive at a South African port of entry without a visa, you will not be permitted to enter.

My lawyers informed me that if I returned there would be a penalty of two years' imprisonment.

The British consul gave me a British passport because David's father had been born in Islington. Steven had been born in London, but Amandla remained stateless for five years before she qualified for British citizenship.

On the plane I became tearful. Relief at being out of danger and my unhappiness at leaving South Africa overwhelmed me. Tears came and would not stop. I cried from Jan Smuts airport to Nairobi, where the plane stopped briefly. The children jumped about restlessly and charged up and down the aisle, or slept pale-faced, exhausted with the turmoil and emotion of the past few days. After that I had a few hours of uneasy sleep while the plane thrummed ever and ever farther from home.

We arrived in London in October 1966. I was still numb from the events of the past few days – the capture of my new passport and my departure from everyone I loved in South Africa. Steven and Amandla were also suffering. I found a three-bedded room with gas stove and cupboard in Frognal for £16 a week – all we possessed was £100!

The sale of my house in Johannesburg had fallen through. A friend wrote that the sale had not been genuine anyway – a security policeman had pretended to buy it. I could hardly believe this. I was to be persecuted even beyond South Africa. I was always surprised at the personal bitterness of the security police and the energy with which they harassed the wives of political prisoners. They felt threatened by, and could not understand, whites who were politically active. They called us traitors.

My furniture, which I had arranged to have shipped to London, never arrived. I began anxiously hunting to find a permanent place to stay, for schools for the kids, and a job.

Within a week of our arrival, Steven got ill, ran a high temperature, had a sore throat and boils broke out all over his body. I would leave him in bed and go out with Amandla, who was four and wanted to be carried everywhere. I was homesick and scared in that freezing winter, shopping, looking for a nursery school for Amandla, a school for Steven, looking for a place to stay and never knowing where to start. I would go out intending to find a nursery school: get to the corner and change my mind because I did not know where we would be living and I did not want Amandla to be moved around more than absolutely necessary because I felt it would add to her insecurities. So I'd go home, or catch a bus to get out of the cold and look through a blur of tears at bleak London from the top deck. Amandla would sit on my lap, sucking her thumb, contented with the swaying movement, and snuggle into me while I worried about Steven left sick and alone in that dreadful Frognal room. To this day both kids shudder at the very word Frognal.

My cousin Eleanor, who lived in Hendon with her husband and three small children, started putting her considerable energies into helping us get a home. Each evening, I would study for-sale ads in the newspapers, and in the afternoons, after Eleanor had picked up her children from school, she would drive me and the five kids around looking at properties. I got more and more depressed. For the £4000 I had decided we would have to afford – and on which I could hope to repay a mortgage – there seemed to be only damp basements or flats on top floors miles away from buses or tubes.

Eleanor got exasperated. 'Look,' she said, 'I know it's difficult. But you just have to be realistic. I've shown you what's in the price range three-and-a-half to four thousand pounds, now I'm going to show you places that cost more. You'll still think they're awful after anything at home. You just have to find somewhere to stay!'

Housing, even expensive housing, in London horrified me. People would say, passing a Nash terrace, 'Look at *that*! Isn't it *beautiful*?' I would look at the joined-up houses with no gardens and no elbow room and think how depressing to live all on top of one another. I didn't care whether the architecture was praise-worthy or not. It looked dreary to me. I was used to acre-big gardens and roomy detached houses.

One afternoon I decided to go to an employment agency to look for a job. I left Steven in the room in Frognal and took Amandla with me. While walking to the bus stop I was again overcome with the problem of what to do first. I did not know what would happen to the children while I was at work. I would have to find schools for them first. And I could not do that until we had a permanent place to stay – we might live miles from any schools I would find. How would I know whether I would be able to get back from work in time to fetch the children for lunch? I caught the first bus that came to get out of the cold and decided to ride it till the end of the line and then back again.

'Oh, she's sweet!' said a woman sitting next to me.

Amandla was cuddled on my lap. I had been lost in misery, staring out of the window at the grey drizzle of London, feeling cold and hopeless about everything.

'Think yew,' I said with my broad South African accent.

'Where are you from?' the woman asked.

And everything spilled out. How I was looking for a flat, about David being in jail and my being here with two children. All my desperation came out in a rush. That is how I met Terry Macgillivray, who became my good friend and adviser.

'Where are you going?' she asked me. And I told her, 'Nowhere. I just got out of the cold.'

'This bus is going to Kenton,' she said. 'Come home with me. Come and have a cup of tea.'

At her house Terry told me about herself. She was the first of many women I met at that time who was managing on her own in London with children – and Terry was obviously managing very well. Her marriage had broken up when her third child was a baby. She had studied insurance and now ran a very successful business from her beautiful home.

Over a cup of tea at Terry's house, she asked me to go with her to see her bank manager. 'Come and meet him before you take the bus home,' she said. 'I'm sure he'll help you.'

So at a bank in Kenton Park Parade, after a twenty-minute wait during which Terry disappeared, I was shown into the bank manager's office.

'Please sit down,' he said. 'I understand that you have recently arrived from South Africa and you need some bridging.'

'Well,' I said cracking a non-joke in bad taste – as the disadvantaged often do, to keep fear at bay – 'I don't know about bridges but I could sure do with some money.'

The bank manager smiled a pained, tolerant smile. 'Here is a cheque book,' he said. 'Just use it whenever you like.'

I didn't realise that Terry must have arranged to stand guarantor for the loan. I just thought I had met a nice bank manager! I explained to him that the sale of my house in Johannesburg had fallen through, that I didn't have a job, that I had two children and I did not know when I would be able to put any money in my account, but he seemed not to be interested in all that.

'Don't worry,' he said, 'just use the chequebook when you have to.'

Terry was waiting for me outside his office. 'Go and find yourself a flat,' she said. 'That's the important first step. And, when you do, give me a ring – I'll arrange a mortgage for you.'

I had heard that it was almost impossible for women to get mortgages and as for women without jobs – without security! – that was totally impossible. This lately acquired knowledge had been adding to my feelings of despair. Now Terry was offering me hope.

Meeting Terry was like a miracle. Other miracles were to follow.

The following day Eleanor came to fetch me. 'I've found a place I want you to look at,' she said. 'It's too expensive. You can't afford it. I'm taking you because you have to see that any flat you would be prepared to live in is way above your price range. Then we can go back and look at flats that you can afford. I'm taking Sharlene to the doctor,' she said, 'so I'll drop you there – I've made an appointment for 3.30, and I'll take all the kids with me and fetch you later.' I wrapped poor groaning Stevie in a blanket – every time anything touched one of his boils he grimaced with pain – and we went off in Eleanor's car up the Finchley Road. She dropped me outside 2 Hurstwood Court.

My knock at the door was answered by a pretty, drunk, auburn-haired woman. 'My name'sh Shirley,' she said, 'Shirley Arnold. Come in. Wanna drink?'

'No, thank you. I don't drink,' I said primly. I looked at her. She didn't look like my idea of a drunk.

'Where's your husband?' was her first question.

'In jail in South Africa.'

'Good!' the woman said. 'Siddown, siddown here.'

I frowned. I did not want to get into conversation with anyone drunk, any nutter, any neurotic. When I am vulnerable I need healthy people around me. When I'm OK, I feel I can help people with problems. 'Look,' I said. 'I shouldn't really even be here. I can't afford this place – whatever it costs. My cousin insisted on my seeing your flat because everything I've seen for four thousand is so dreadful that I couldn't bear it.'

'Come'n see the flat.' I walked around the lovely three-bedroomed ground-floor flat with two connecting reception rooms and a big kitchen which led off into a communal back garden. 'D'you like it? 'S nice, in't it?'

'It's *lovely*,' I said. 'But . . .'

''Ve you got shildren?'

'Yes, two – a boy and a girl,' I said.

''S nice. I've got three.' She started to weep. ''S yours,' said Shirley. 'You can have it for four thousand.'

'Look, Mrs Arnold,' I said, 'I really can't afford this flat and I don't think you're in a fit state to make a business arrangement.'

She waved the bottle of expensive brandy over her head, wiping tears and snot from her pretty face. 'Thish,' she said, 'ish medicine – doctor's orders. Ish for the pain.'

'Are you in pain, dear?' I feigned concern.

'Yesh,' she said. 'It'sh my heart.' She began crying. I looked about awkwardly. My watch said 3.40 and Eleanor probably wouldn't get back for another hour.

'Excuse me,' I said. 'I have to go to the loo.'

Oh God, I said to myself, wasting time in the loo. Everyone in England is crazy.

When I emerged, Shirley seemed to have sobered up a bit. 'I don't want anyone with a husband to live here.'

'What's the matter?' I finally got around to asking her.

'Last week,' she sniffed, 'the bell rang – that bell right on that front door. The kids and I were waiting for my husband to come home from work. But it wasn't my husband. It was a policeman. He said my husband had been knocked over at Henly's Corner.

He's dead. My sister lives in Canada and all I can think of is to get rid of everything here and go to her. That's why you'll be doing me a favour if you take the flat. Then I can get out, get on a plane and just go.'

Before the contracts were signed, against the advice of both sets of lawyers, we moved into 2 Hurstwood Court and Shirley moved to Canada.

We had little furniture – three beds and a kitchen table. The flat was freezing cold. But now that we had a base, I could get Steven and Amandla into the local school.

I looked about for a job and found one advertised two blocks from the flat as secretary to five doctors, with a West End salary – £1000 a year.

On my first morning at the surgery, during the doctors' eleven o'clock break, I was given a file of letters to reply to. 'Just say the position is filled,' one of the senior doctors said. I spent the afternoon writing, Dear Dr Greenberg/Goldberg/Cohen/Kaplan, The vacancy in this practice has now been filled.

The following day I was asked to put ads in the medical journals for a partner. 'But,' I said, 'I spent the whole of the afternoon typing letters to doctors saying that the position was filled.'

'It is our proud boast,' said the most junior doctor, rising and fingering his tie, 'that we have never, in this practice, had to employ a Jew.'

Standing in the middle of the room with a clutch of files pressed to my chest, I looked around wildly. Then I put the files on the table, clapped my hands together and said, 'Guess what, chaps!'

There was a flutter among the doctors while they ahemmed and aha'ed. 'Well, not secretaries – we don't mind about *secretaries,*' said one of them, 'we mean doctors.'

I wondered whether to make a heroic gesture and stamp out and decided not to. I had to have this job. At least I had made it clear I was Jewish. But I found that our doctors discriminated just as much against anybody who had not been to Cambridge. People from Kent, Boksburg or Jerusalem were all equally repellent. As a South African I have always found London a strange world, where people act in peculiar ways, doing and saying dreadful things – all in the name of civilisation or some noble principle.

The day I took the kids to Child's Way school, I was waiting around with the other new mothers to see the head teacher. We were anxious, the way mothers are on the first day. I was smiling artificially at Steven who was kicking at his shoes, and beaming at Amandla, who was jumping up and down like a terror. A mother next to me said to her child as it was led away, 'Don't you go getting any ideas!' I was appalled. I still am. It was one thing that the school was trying to stamp out Identikit clones – but the mothers seemed to be all for it, too. I thought it was uncivilised. I had to remind myself that this was England – the great democracy! What it really meant for children, as far as I could see, was filing them down and trotting them out all full of law and order and behaviour. I thought of what Gandhi had replied when asked, 'What do you think of Western civilisation?' He said, 'I think it would be a wonderful idea!'

Living in England, I thought that was very appropriate.

My children were never to fit the mould, and they had a hard passage in their English schools.

When Steven went for an interview to gain a scholarship at Haberdasher's Aske's boarding school at Elstree, he stood in front of a a semicircle of begowned masters sitting around a huge table. The head was at the centre. A chair was placed for me at the side – out of the way. Steven, seeing everyone seated, said:

'May I have a chair, please?'

A junior master at the very edge of the semicircle jumped instinctively to the tone of authority and brought out his own chair for Steven. Then he sidled back to his edge and leaned against the table trying to reduce his height. The head growled at him:

'Well, if you've given the boy your chair – *go and get another!*'

The interrogation commenced. Steven was asked a string of unrelated questions – about Brer Rabbit, carbon dioxide,

Macbeth – and to spell a long list of words. The head looked up at Steven. 'You're a very well-read boy!' he exclaimed.

'I wouldn't say that,' Steven said calmly.

'What would you say? It would appear that you have read a great deal?' the headmaster said, keeping his eyes down and swivelling his head.

'Yes,' said Steven.

'That means you are *well-read*,' the head said triumphantly. 'Well-read means you have read a lot.'

'I wouldn't say that,' Steven said.

'Well, dear boy!' he said, getting steamy. 'Then what would you say?'

'I've read a lot of science and a lot of comics – there must be an awful lot in between to be considered *well*-read,' Steven said.

Deciding to smooth his ruffled feathers, the headmaster smiled. I think that was when he decided to like Steven. 'Is the boy correct?' he quizzed a junior master.

There was no reply. The junior master reddened, caught in the frame-up.

'Of *course* he is. He is *quite correct*!' The head glowered around him. There were visible signs of relief around the semicircle. Apparently their reading was that the head was in good humour. Later, he explained to me that Steven was an intelligent boy. He was not a hat-doffer, he was a leader. The school would be proud to have him. But, they said, it would take them about three years to civilise Steven.

'Well, pray you never do,' I said.

He laughed. He thought I was joking.

Amandla never could see the logic of English school rules, and neither could I. I moved her from school to school. In her first year at Henrietta Barnett school in Hampstead Garden Suburb, she subverted all attempts at making her wear the uniform. She did this partly because we could not afford the expensive dresses and jackets and also because she did not think it was right for young people to be uniformed. Once her teacher called out to her in front of the class, 'Amandla! You're wearing one green sock and one red one.'

'Yes,' she replied, 'and I've got another pair just like this at home.'

Amandla got her A levels more through an act of will than schooling.

These first years in London were made more difficult by some of the exiles in the South African Communist Party. I telephoned them on our arrival in London but it was obvious they wanted nothing to do with us. At the time I thought this was because they knew I planned to return to South Africa. Any information about exiles or anti-apartheid activity in London would be useful to the security police if I was arrested and interrogated at home.

Many people that David and I had lived our underground political lives with, people I had helped escape from the country – people whose lives and hopes we had shared – shunned us. Most of them had got out of South Africa with their children and were settled in London. They did not even telephone to enquire about David, much less show any interest in me or his children. I was not invited to any meeting of the South African Communist Party in exile, although I was a member of the Party. I was not approached to join the London ANC. With David in jail, we were to be ignored for ten years.

We did not lack friends. Comrades from our British Communist Party days in the fifties and people we had met in London rallied around. We spent Christmases with, and were welcomed always at the homes of, Alewyn and Joan Birch, Mary and Henry Barnett, Lena and Arthur Prior, Rene Waller, Pauline and H. A. Naidoo and David and Hazel Selbourne. I could not understand why, in London, white South African Communist Party members pretended we did not exist. It was to be years before their distant behaviour turned into bitter hostility. In the early days I just put it out of my mind.

One day at work the senior doctor called me into his office.

'Sit down, Mrs Kitson,' he said. 'I've had a Mr Humphreys on the phone to me from Johannesburg. He told me how he had to dispense with your services when you worked for him – no,

In Trafalgar Square, 1967.

Steven on the Ruskin Kitson Committee march from Oxford
to Trafalgar Square, 1969.

Amandla, me and Steven.

Mom in Trafalgar Square.

Steven.

Amandla, 1978.

wait a minute,' he said as I started to interrupt.

'I know how you feel – he's told me all about it. But look, what I wanted to say is, why don't you bend a little? This chap feels for you and the children. He wants to do something for you. I told him you are now in a flat and could do with some furniture. He's arriving here soon. He wants to see you.'

'No,' I said. 'There's nothing he can do for us. And I don't want his money.'

'But you *do!*' said the doctor. 'And he wants to give it to you. Don't be churlish. Why shouldn't you relieve his conscience – if that's what it is?'

Me churlish?

A week later Mr Humphreys arrived in London and, embarrassed, I met him at Heals. 'Choose whatever you want,' he said. 'Something for the dining room first? A table?'

'That one's fine,' I said, pointing to the nearest table. And we went round different departments of the store, Mr Humphreys making a selection as we went. A few days later, a five-foot round rosewood table with six chairs arrived, a grey settee and two armchairs, a coffee table, wardrobes, drawers, and then the carpet layers came and fitted carpets in the flat.

The miracles happened one after the other, the flat, the job and the furniture. My job was convenient and well paid, but I was getting worried about all the money I owed the bank manager and I went to Kenton Park Parade to see him.

'I'll have to pay you off very slowly,' I said. 'I've got a job now and a home, but no spare money.'

'I never asked to see you,' he said. 'I'm not worried.'

A few months later, the sale of my house in South Africa went through and I paid him off and repaid our debts in South Africa.

I was still worried about how we were going to manage financially. I registered as a freelance typist with Elfrieda Watson at the Hampstead Secretarial Bureau. Thanks to her, I was able to earn extra money typing at nights. After the kids were in bed, I would type away until two or three in the morning. On Saturdays I did two cleaning jobs in Golders Green.

We had a highly organised household. Amandla was the family memory and at breakfast each morning she would run through items for our attention: 'Steven's dentist is at four o'clock and we haven't got any more tea.' 'Mommy, did you write back to Daddy yet? Steven hasn't finished his letter to Grannie.' We kept a jar with spending money on the kitchen shelf and she would keep tabs on it: 'I can't get pies for supper because there's only two bob in the jar and we have to leave some for bus fares.'

Amandla also did the ironing and laid the table. Steven vacuumed the flat, shopped, did a lot of the cooking and washed up. After we had had our supper and watched the television programmes we liked, we would go to the launderette about three times a week. I had white South African standards of hygiene – clean sheets every two days, complete changes of clothing every day, clean tablecloth and cloth napkins each day. I was a wreck trying to keep this up but eventually became human and kept the sheets on the bed for a week and used paper napkins, and then we went to the launderette once a week. I would sit blinking with tiredness while Steven and Amandla folded the hot washing.

Because responsibility was thrust on Steven and Amandla when they were so young, they behaved older than their contemporaries. They did not have time for games and toys. While Samantha Green from next door was playing with a teaset, Amandla was cooking dinner. Both took part in school sports but when Steven's friends were going skating or to cinemas, he was shopping or doing household chores, using his calculator to work out our weekly family budget.

I felt guilty that my children were missing out this stage of growing up which, in Britain, is considered vital to normal development. I consoled myself that for the majority of children in Africa there is no such thing as carefree childhood. That only exists in rich countries.

Steven and Amandla were thrust also into political awareness. At school they took issue with the British colonial education system and were passionate in arguing their views. I had great respect for their judgement. We had weekly family councils when we would each go through any difficulties we were facing, and thrash them out together – sometimes for hours.

Generally they were very good friends, but sometimes they argued furiously. Once, when Steven was about thirteen and Amandla eight years old, he announced to us that Enoch Powell was coming to speak at his school.

'I told them we should have a demonstration,' Steven said.

'What about?' asked Amandla.

'About him coming.'

'You don't want to demonstrate. Just make a human gate. Don't let him in.'

'Don't you believe in freedom of speech, then?' Steven asked, acidly.

'Freedom of speech! *Freedom of speech!*' Amandla shouted. 'You don't let fascists talk. If you want freedom, you don't let fascists talk. Because they'll *never* let *you* talk.'

When she was nine, Amandla wrote a story, 'The New Country', which told of the advantages of socialism. Steven at fifteen wrote an essay for a school project on the discovery of Africa in which he disproved that it had been 'discovered' by any white man; debunked the history books; asserted the land belonged to the black people who had lived on it and quoted Cecil Rhodes on the reasons for imperialist conquest.

From the first week of my arrival in England I tried to get permission to go back to South Africa to visit David.

In December 1967 I was granted an Alien's Temporary Permit to return to the land of my birth, for *five days*. Two of the days included my arrival and departure. By this time David had been upgraded to C, which meant he could have a visit and a letter every three months. But I got special permission to have three visits in the five days of my stay. We were hardly able to talk during these thirty-minute visits. All subjects were banned and every few minutes the warder in charge threatened me that the visit would be terminated if I 'discussed that subject' – whatever it was. I had missed David so much and had waited such a long time to visit him. Of course he asked about our South African friends in London. He believed that the families who had got out of South Africa intact would be looking after us. I did not want to tell him that these people had not even contacted us, and I found these three visits difficult. David and I had always been open and frank and now I was trying to protect him. He was wonderful – cheerful and full of good spirits. The visits put heart into me and I returned to London in a fighting spirit, recharged to campaign for the release of the political prisoners. Two Anti-Apartheid groups had been formed by people who knew David – the Ruskin Kitson Committee and the Hornsey Anti-Apartheid Committee. By highlighting the case of David, they were able to raise the question of all the South African political prisoners.

In July 1968 my sister Joan phoned to tell me that our dad was extremely ill and was asking to see me. She said Dad had something he wanted to tell me. She urged me to apply immediately for a visa to visit him in Durban. She had already been in touch with the authorities, who had agreed that as soon as I went to South Africa House to collect my visa, I could leave immediately.

I went to collect the papers. They said they knew nothing about it. I put my case, made formal application, telephoned every few hours and waited. Each day I telephoned or went down to Trafalgar Square, and each time I drew a blank. They said they were waiting for the authority from South Africa. Each evening I telephoned Joan in Durban to tell her that I had got nowhere. She said, 'I just can't believe it, Norm. Every time I phone Pretoria they say they've given permission. They're just waiting for you to pick up the papers at South Africa House in London. Dad's really *very* ill. Please do whatever you can to come immediately.'

At the beginning of August she phoned me to say that Dad was dying and I would have to come right away. She was taking him up to the Brenthurst Clinic in Johannesburg so that I could come straight off the plane to him.

Whatever it was my father had wanted to say to me so

urgently, I was never to know. We had hardly spoken since I was a child. He had become withdrawn and difficult to communicate with.

Dad died on 6 August. On 7 August I received a telephone call from the South African embassy to say my visa was ready for collection.

In 1969 I obtained a fourteen-day visa to visit South Africa. At Jan Smuts airport I was in the queue to go through customs when two men walked up to me and asked me to go with them. I shouted out to the people in the queue to telephone the British consul. They looked at me blankly as I was hauled off. Without any explanation, I was put in a room and sat there waiting in silence, the two men standing by the door.

After about an hour – or it could have been longer – my sister Joan opened the door. She had seen me get off the plane and had waited anxiously at the barriers. When all the passengers had gone through and still I had not appeared, she had telephoned the British consul and then darted through the gates to look for me. She was ushered out of the room, arguing volubly against this latest harassment. A few minutes later I was released, still without explanation.

1969 was the year when Winnie Mandela was held in detention, in solitary confinement for 491 days, accused of promoting the aims of the ANC. She was kept standing for five days and nights, while relays of interrogators under the Beast of Kompol (Captain Swanepoel) carried out their merciless work. She had a coir mattress on the floor, and two filthy blankets. She was not permitted to bath for 200 days, washing, with her small ration of water, over her sanitary bucket. Her food plate was put on top of this bucket. The food she was given was so poor – mainly porridge and bread – that her health suffered. She urinated blood, swelled up and frequently fainted.

For eleven years she had been harassed, banned and jailed. I always felt a great bond with her, because both our husbands were in jail, we both had two children and the same political aims. Nomzamo, the name she prefers to her 'white' name, is a real people's leader. Whenever I was harassed by the security police in South Africa I thought of the much worse harassment she always suffered.

I stayed with Joan, Norman and their kids. It was good to be back home again. My stepfather, Oscar, had also died in 1968 and now my mother came up to Johannesburg to be with us. Since David's arrest, my mother had been supportive and loyal. She always mourned the death of her beloved Oscar but now she seemed free to give us the love and concern which she had been unable to give when we were children. I think if Steven and Amandla had not been left behind in London, I would have stayed – and faced any consequences.

I felt in a state of suspension between the visits to the jail, waiting to see David again. After every visit, I would go to the head of the prison to apply for another. David was always in control – he had a knack of putting all his visitors at ease. We were still talking through holes in masonite, unable to touch – we could never touch each other or speak face to face while he was in jail.

In 1971 I took Steven and Amandla back with me for the first time. We stayed at Norman's house although Joan had divorced him. A few days after our arrival, on returning from a visit to Pretoria to see David, the maid gave me the message that two men had come to the house looking for me. They had not left their names. The following day, I was sitting in the lounge with Steven and Amandla and their cousins, Tessa, Lindy and Robbie. There was a ring at the door and the maid admitted two men. They walked into the lounge.

'We just want a word with you, Mrs Kitson.'

'What about?'

'Well, we don't think you'd like it if we spoke to you in front of these young people.'

'Go ahead,' I said. 'I haven't got any secrets from them.'

'Think about it, Mrs Kitson,' the tall one said. 'We'll be back again tomorrow.'

The following day when I returned from visiting David, they were waiting for me in the driveway. I made for the house and they stood in my path.

'We want you to come voluntarily, Mrs Kitson. We just want to ask you a few questions.'

'What do you mean, voluntarily? I'm not going anywhere with you *voluntarily.*'

'*Voluntarily*, Mrs Kitson,' said one and I felt something hard pressed into my side.

They hustled me into their car and we drove to Pretoria to Kompol – interrogation headquarters. The days of the Grays in Johannesburg were over. Kompol was a new skyscraper in Pretoria. In the fast lift going up, I felt my strength beginning to ebb away. I had been through this before. Eight years ago I had been strong, but would I be able to take it now? I didn't have anything to tell them. I hadn't been active – except on the issue of campaigning for political prisoners.

I was taken into a well-furnished office – quite different from the brown paint and scratched desks at the Grays. Swanepoel – the Beast of Kompol – was behind the desk and his two henchmen stood on either side of me.

'First, Mrs Kitson,' he said, 'you are going to make a telephone call. You are going to call your brother-in-law at the Brenthurst and tell him that you have come up to Pretoria voluntarily to have a meeting.'

'He wouldn't believe me if I told him that.'

He smiled and dialled the number – he didn't even have to look it up. He passed me the ringing receiver. The receptionist said Norman was out.

'OK,' said the Beast, as if he was one of the family. 'We'll try Stanley.' He began to dial Stanley Goldstein's number. Stanley had been married to my friend Micki and was now married to Lynne.

'I'll just tell him you've arrested me,' I said.

'No, you won't, Mrs Kitson. And I'll tell you why. That's a nice boy you've got there – your son. I heard he was run down at Henly's Corner in London some time ago. I don't know if you thought that was an accident. This time it will be an accident outside Norman's house. No. You'll do just as I've said. Here,

197

we'll see, the phone's ringing.'

I got through to Stanley and hoped he would think it a very strange and impossible thing I was saying: 'I'm up in Pretoria *voluntarily* at Kompol.'

Stanley, probably busy in his office, acknowledged what I said without demur. Swanepoel took the telephone out of my hand and gently placed it back on the hook. 'Now, Mrs Kitson, you are going to make a statement. A few years ago you slipped away from us. Not this time.'

'I haven't got anything to say.'

'Oh, yes you have. We know all about you.'

'I live in London now. I'm not involved in politics at all.'

'Listen to this,' Swanepoel said. And he played me a tape of Pauline visiting our flat in London. Pauline was saying, 'What are we having for supper? Don't touch that, Steven!' and I replied, 'Chicken – can you have a look in the oven and see if it's ready?' It was a meaningless conversation, but it gave me the horrors. At any time I could be listened to, my children could be got at. The South African regime was so powerful, they could do what they liked – even in England. All this was meant to frighten me. I tried to steel myself. If they had let Stanley know I was in Pretoria, surely he would check that I was back in Johannesburg within a few hours.

'I just don't know why you've got me here,' I said, flopping onto a chair and reaching into my handbag for a cigarette. 'Yes, that's Pauline and me in London. So what?'

'We want to know what's going on in London.'

'With who? I'm not active in London.'

'You can join, can't you?'

Silence from me. They wanted me to spy for them.

'I won't do it,' I said.

'What about Steven? *And* you've got a nice little daughter.'

'Well, it looks as though, without my doing anything, you've already tried to get Steven,' I said. 'You've just implied you had my little boy knocked down at Henly's Corner. You people just do whatever you want.'

'Oh, we'll do what we want, Mrs Kitson, don't you worry.

You won't be so self-assured when we've finished with you.' He came around from his side of the desk and motioned to the two men. '*Gaan aan* [Get going], Van,' he said.

I was wrenched out of the chair, one man holding my right arm and leg, the other my left. Quite gently, they leaned far out and dropped me out of the window. Someone was holding my feet. My ankles and knees felt on fire from the sudden strain. Something in my stomach pulled. The blood rushed to my head as I hung out of the window, seemingly miles from the ground below. I might have lost consciousness for a few seconds or minutes while I hung there. I went ice cold. I thought they were going to drop me as they'd dropped Babla. Then I was pulled up and put back into the chair. I sat there, breathing deeply, unable to think, unable to move.

'Well, Mrs Kitson,' Swanepoel said. 'How's it now, eh? We can keep you here for as long as we like, you know. We can give you a few goes like that and you'll never know when we going to drop you, isn't it?'

I did not answer.

'Here,' he said. 'Here's a name and address. You take it. Anything you can get, write to John Smith at this box number. It doesn't matter how small the information is. The first information you give us, you'll get a free trip to visit Dave, OK?' He stuffed a piece of paper in my hand. 'OK, you *kêrels* [chaps], take her back home now. We'll see you again soon, isn't it, Mrs Kitson?' And he laughed.

Driving back in the beautiful purple of a Transvaal evening, I felt sick. They stopped the car and I vomited at the side of the road.

'Shame, Mrs Kitson, you not feeling well, eh?'

They dropped me outside the house and I hung on to the gate for a few minutes before going in. Then I pulled myself together as much as I could. The kids were playing records in the lounge and the maid was nagging them to come to the table and eat. Norman said, 'Hello, Norm. Just in time for supper!' I couldn't believe it. I could not understand the normality of it all. I felt disorientated and my body was sore.

That night I packed our things, and booked a seat on the next British Airways plane. Joan drove me to the airport the following morning and I left her to make excuses for my sudden departure. What would David think? He was expecting me for a final visit. But I had to get the kids out immediately. I was scared, driving to the airport, that we would have an 'accident'. I was scared we would be stopped at the airport. We went through without a hitch but once on the aircraft I heard a kerfuffle near the door, and a hostess came up the aisle and threw a British Airways scarf over my face. The pilot, or someone in charge, was called and I heard him say, 'No, no, you can't see *anyone*. This is British territory. I'm afraid you'll have to disembark.'

Once the plane had taken off, the crew were extra kind to us. They invited Steven and Amandla into the cockpit and the hostesses kept asking if there was anything we wanted. I sat there safe and snug and cuddled the children. But I cried through the long humming night. How could I get home again? Perhaps I could never go home again. Now I was really cut off.

· 11 ·

My friend Judy never had much of a chance, even though she was an elegant, artistic and beautiful woman. She pinned up her glossy black hair, accentuating her fine aquiline features and wide mouth. Her fringe spiked just above a pair of wide, blue, intelligent eyes. And she wore Helen de Leeuw clothes, with their beautiful earthy colours, in styles that showed off her perfect figure and long legs.

I suppose she didn't have much of a chance to have a happy life because she had spent much of her childhood in a Nazi concentration camp and had seen most of her family shot or gassed. When the war ended she was sent to Israel and had to join the Israeli army. Her job was driving military vehicles and years later, when I knew her, she drove her tiny Fiat as if it was a huge truck, with her fine hands firmly gripping the wheel, elbows out for more power, leaning back on the seat, and she would park in the middle of the road – leaving plenty of room for the 'truck' – and alight, slamming the door hard behind her as if she was still dressed in khaki.

She thought she had lost her mother in the Holocaust and as a young girl worshipped her memory and painted fantasies of a fine lady. She searched for her family – as people who had been in those camps did – desperately trying to trace people who would know her, and eventually found a second cousin who had known her grandmother. She was given a piece of pale green ribbon which had tied her mother's hair as a young girl. Even after her fantasies about her mother had been dashed, Judy used the piece of pale green ribbon as a bookmark and carried it with her everywhere – she always carried a book.

But her search for family bore bitter fruit. Her mother fetched up in Israel with a boyfriend and must have been shocked to find she had a beautiful teenage daughter. She didn't like Judy. They were bad-mouthing each other from the word go and on their second meeting she prophesied – in anger – that Judy would end up as a lavatory attendant. For a woman as culturally aspiring and fastidious as Judy, this prophecy was insulting and frightening.

When I met her, in about 1960, Judy was unhappily married to a hairy, sandal-wearing, crass South African, whom she called 'Daddy' – so we all did. (Judy liked smooth, well-shod men.) On Friday afternoons, with our kids playing about us, we gathered in my little garden in Victoria and Judy, in her strange, attractive, somewhere-European accent, would tell Micki, Marsha and me about the same old Thursday afternoon event.

In Johannesburg, Thursday afternoon is traditionally maids' 'off' so Daddy would come home early for a poke. It was an unvarying ritual. The three children had regular Thursday afternoon commitments (like most Johburg kids they had ballet, tap, piano, swimming, deportment or elocution lessons in the afternoons) so they were always out. On Thursdays Judy cooked lunch for Daddy. She was a discerning cook and the dishes she made took time and patience: humus and tahina, slivers of pickled new green cucumber, smoked turkey and beef, tomato and avocado salads, all with their own sauces and dressings; soufflés, caramel custards – decorated and in pretty dishes. Daddy ate voraciously and indiscriminately, piling his plate high, mixing everything – he might just as well have been eating hash: stuffing his mouth as if food was going out of fashion, Judy said. Strict silence over the lunch while Daddy gorged and read, dripping salad dressings and sauces on the newspapers and magazines. Then a bath. And a shave. Meanwhile Judy was expected to change into a négligée. Then Daddy put on his dressing gown, and emerged into the lounge glowering sexily – that was supposed immediately to turn Judy on – the foody kiss that followed was meant to make her swoon and he would lead her to their bed. Her job was to see that he had an erection and she worked at it diligently. If she failed, which she sometimes did, Daddy would get nasty and say she was losing her sex appeal. She laughed as she told us this, to make it bearable for us. But I think she believed him.

Judy hated it all so much that she had to turn to us, her friends, each week, trying to get strength from us – to laugh or get serious about it, so that she could face it all the following Thursday. But she never really could. Making love on Thursdays with Daddy sickened her. Judy never had a paying job. She was dependent on Daddy financially and emotionally and battled to hold her marriage together. She endured the sex and chose music and art as the battlefield – it was safer. While she was poring over art journals and literary magazines or listening to Bach or Mahler, Daddy would be farting in the kitchen or shouting down the telephone about tyres – he was in that line of business.

Her children were like wraiths. They were clever at school and had perfectly shaped heads like Judy and they never wore sandals. Their eyes were so serious when they looked at me that I felt if I said anything I might be taken for a fool. So I didn't ever speak to them except to say hello.

Judy spent her time at art exhibitions and music concerts. She had many *Mittel*-European friends, mostly a lot older than she. To me they were strangers from another world. They ate strange dry cakes and were very polite. In fact they were so polite and elegant that they made me feel gauche. I would bump into them in Judy's beautiful flat sometimes. They were from another world, of culture and concentration camps, and I did not know how to enter it.

Judy opened a world of art and music for me. With her I discovered painters, and I remember sitting over Paul Klee's 'Fishing' for a whole afternoon with her, interpreting many things she saw in that picture. When she discovered the Beatles she told Micki, Marsha and me that a new era of music had come into being with them – that they were very important, and represented the final breakdown of Western civilisation as we knew it. And she introduced me to Bach's Magnificat and to Samuel Beckett.

Judy was always in love. At first we heard about the love of her young life in Israel – Aaron, the artist – and how, long after he had rejected her, she was still loving him. Her fantasy was that her daughter was Aaron's child. But the girl looked like Daddy. Then, because of her horrific experiences as a child, and, I suppose, her dreadful life with Daddy, she had gone to a psychiatrist for treatment, and had fallen in love with him. I think he must have been flattered to find such a beautiful woman in love with him and he wrote her love letters and love poems which led to impotent fumblings on the couch and candlelit poetry readings. It turned out he had Daddy's problem – difficulty getting an erection. So then it was Thursday afternoons with Daddy and Tuesday mornings and Friday evenings with the psychiatrist. But whatever she and he did – and it sounded to me just like what she and Daddy did – was magic, because she was in love with him. In a sea of crude South Africans, it seemed he was intellectual and fastidious. When he tired of her – after very few months – he admitted Judy to hospital where, because she was depressed, she had a series of ECT 'treatments' and was administered a drug which, she said, caused her to have a brain haemorrhage. After that her health was delicate, her memory hazy, and she took sleeping pills.

Her love for her psychiatrist did not lessen. The more he withdrew, the more she loved him. She became too much for the fastidious little man and he suggested she get treatment elsewhere. She got Daddy to plead with him not to give her up as a patient, and for some years she went through the painful experience of loving him while he kept her at arm's length and told her that she had imagined all that had taken place before the ECT. But I had seen the love letters and the love poems. Daddy and the psychiatrist became quite pally – united in their opinion that Judy was 'very sick'.

On one of her stays in hospital she was joined in her ward by another of his discarded amours and they swapped very similar stories, but still Judy's love for her psychiatrist flamed.

When I left South Africa in 1966 one of the saddest wrenches was leaving Judy. I could not imagine being without her friendship. She felt I was rejecting her. 'How can you possibly leave me?' she asked. I tried to explain that I was not leaving her – I was leaving because we were being harassed by the police and I could not get a job – but Judy took it all very personally.

'My best friends live in London,' she said. 'Sidney and Stella Cherfas.' She had spoken about them often. She blamed them for leaving her and was bitter about it.

'Well, you must look them up if you're going to London,' she said. 'They were my very best friends and they did the same as you – they left me. So you'll probably get on with them!'

She and Stella had studied yoga together with the Johburg expert, Manny Finger. Judy had once taken me to one of his classes where we all had to say 'Om' and make rude noises through our noses and I couldn't believe people did that for relaxation. Judy was envious when she heard that Stella was demonstrating yoga on British TV.

'She's just the type to make good,' she said cattily. 'And I was even better at it than she was. But she always got what she wanted, Stella did. She got Sidney. She was married to someone else when she met him, you know. She just left her husband and ran off with Sidney. It was so hard for me – being friends with them.'

'Why?'

'Well, I was in love with Sidney – he's the most exciting man you ever met! And so handsome! You should see him eat a fish! Just like a surgeon. He's so sensitive – someone I could really talk to. It's no fun being in love with your best friend's husband. And I didn't think Stella was in love with him. I'd go there, to their home, just hoping to see him, but he was seldom around. I'll always love Sidney, you know. When you get to London, give him my love.'

I did not contact Sidney when I got to London. The vision of a sensitive man eating fish like a surgeon put me off. But in 1972 we met at one of Pauline's parties in Muswell Hill – that's where I usually met people. We were immediately drawn together by Judy as if both of us had missed speaking about her.

205

'I heard you were very friendly with Judy,' he said.

'Yes, I was.'

We reminisced about Judy and Daddy. 'Imagine what it was like for *him*,' Sidney said as I was railing against Daddy's insensitivities. He leaned back up against Pauline's bookcase.

I looked at him through Judy's eyes – and then with my own. He was tall and good-looking. My heart thumped like a schoolgirl's. His black hair was swept back from his strong face. He was a big man, immaculately dressed, and glowing with intelligence. Plain black leather shoes – expensive. Very expensive. Everything about him was somehow good – tasteful, without being showy or dandyish. I could see what Judy had meant. And he had no knickknacks like Daddy – no rings, gold chains, bracelets, not even a tiepin.

'Do I pass?' he asked while this examination was going on.

'You know,' I said, 'Judy was in love with you and it always worried her because she was friendly with Stella.'

'You're kidding,' Sidney said, laughing. 'Judy was always looking for someone to be in love with. Anyway, Stella and I divorced a couple of years ago.'

I fell silent for a while. I was angry to find him sympathetic to Daddy and passing off Judy's strong feelings for him so lightly.

'Well, didn't you love her, too? How couldn't you?'

'I was very fond of Judy. How can I explain? I took her to a theatre once and when we came out I asked how she'd enjoyed it. She wiped a tear away and went into a paean of praise for the delicacy of the acting. I had thought it was fine, but not so special, and I said so. Judy looked at me as if I'd stabbed her and she said to me, "Oh, Sidney! Where is your *soul*? Have you no *soul*?"

'"Soul! Sole!" I said. "Sole is something I eat with chips on Fridays."

'Judy never forgave me. But she brought that out in me. I could never get to the real woman. There was always that screen of artistic-ness and it came over as pretension. I knew she wasn't pretentious but I couldn't handle it. She made me want to be crude.'

'Oh, she made me feel just the opposite,' I said. 'She made me feel full of potential. She made me feel full of soul. I just don't know how *anyone* can be sympathetic towards Daddy,' I said. 'It's just so *male* to find excuses for him.' I didn't want to see anything from Daddy's point of view. I wasn't interested in justice anyway – it isn't really a part of friendship.

Sidney laughed. 'Is the world all black and white for you?' he asked. 'I suppose it must be. Otherwise you wouldn't be so politically ardent. Don't you know that most of it is grey? Lots of grey, you know.'

'Well, if it is,' I said, 'I'm not interested in those bits. I just want to look at the black and white.'

'What happened to Judy was certainly black and white,' Sidney said.

'I just can't talk about it,' I said. 'I can't help feeling that somehow I let her down. But that's making my friendship with her overimportant. I couldn't have done anything. And yet, and yet, I feel maybe I could have, somehow.'

Daddy had left Judy and had married a younger woman. The psychiatrist dropped her. Judy was all alone. I could not imagine Judy alone – she could not have borne it. In bed one night, she set herself alight – who knows whether accidentally or not – and burned to death.

As if by agreement Sidney and I turned away from each other. The pain of Judy lay between us.

I was leaving the party early to get back to Steven and Amandla, when Sidney stopped me at the door.

'Would you like to have dinner with me?'

'Oh no!' I said. 'I'm not very good at that sort of thing.'

'What sort of thing?'

'Eating.'

Sidney laughed. 'It's not something I thought one had to be good at. Go on, what do you like?'

'Steak.'

'I'll buy you the best steak in London.'

'But I don't like the best steak.'

'You don't? What steak then?'

207

'Steakhouse steak.'

'When?'

'Tomorrow night.'

'What about my kids?'

'Bring them with.'

The following night Sidney came to fetch us in his maroon Jaguar. He apologised for it immediately. 'It's a company car. I'm the sales director – in the rag trade, it's the sort of thing you have to have. I'm always driving clients around, you know.' He turned to face me. 'You weren't serious, were you – about steak-houses, I mean?'

'Yes.'

He was appalled. 'What's your problem?'

'My problem is that I don't think one should make a fuss about food.'

'Food is lovely,' Sidney said. 'What do you want to make a fuss about, then?'

'I don't want to make a fuss about anything,' I said.

'Well,' said Sidney. 'I'm going to make a helluva fuss about you.'

I was to find out in the coming months that food was import-ant to Sidney. He did eat fish like a surgeon. It was fascinating to watch him. There was a whole world of caring and conversation and exchanging that took place over these meals, first, at my insistence, at a steakhouse and then at Mario and Franco's and Pescatore, graduating, as my taste developed and my seven stone increased to eight, eight and a half and then nine stone, to the Tower, the Guinea, L'Étoile, Mr Chow's, the Rib Room and Gavroche. I would go for things with fancy sauces and com-plicated-sounding names, but Sidney ate very plainly – grilled fish or veal in butter. We also ate chopped liver and egg-and-onion at every nosh bar in London.

That was how it all began – full of the pain of Judy, and exploring London restaurants. And reading to each other. Talking about Johburg. Talking about our parents, our child-ren, our marriages, our families and our beliefs.

Sidney knew all about my world – he had known many

members of the Stiller family in Durban and the Cranko family in Johannesburg. He knew the London lefties of his generation, and in his schooldays he had been a close friend of Jack Tarshish, who was in jail with David. Sidney had fought the fascists on the Johannesburg City Hall steps and knew a great deal about the liberation struggle. We had the same terms of reference and we felt comfortable with each other. For the first time in years I did not feel alone.

At this time I was working as a bookkeeper for Henri Henrion – a leading designer. It seemed he designed everything you noticed: the LEB and KLM logos, the British flag on the tails of planes, Volkswagen, Blue Circle Cement. I applied for the job because it carried a big salary and it meant I could work in one job instead of three. Lately I had been spending so much time with Sidney, I had given up my weekend cleaning job and was getting very broke. I had never done bookkeeping but I thought, if I get the job, I'll soon learn – after all, lots of people do bookkeeping! I got the job and spent hours after work with an accountant friend, who first wrote reports for me and balanced the books, then showed me how to make entries and taught me to do the wages. In this way I was seen to be a first-class financial brain and Henri was pleased and made me a director of his company, Studio H Ltd.

One day I arrived at work flustered and late for an important client meeting, having been up the previous night with Sidney, who had flu, and to finish typing a thesis for the Hampstead Secretarial Bureau.

Henri asked, 'Norma! What's wrong with you these days?'

'Oh, Henri,' I said. 'In the middle of David, I've gone and fallen in love with Sidney.'

'Come here,' Henri said. He put an arm around me. 'Don't be so hard on yourself,' he said.

'I'll have to go to South Africa and see David. I'm absolutely terrified, but I *want* to go back. After last time, I didn't think I'd ever be able to face going back again – I don't know if I can even now.'

Henri knew what had happened to me the last time I had been

in South Africa, and he knew how much I needed to go home. 'When you look at it,' he said, 'they were trying to frighten you. Your life probably wasn't in danger. With the publicity the press gives your visits they have to be a bit careful about what they do. You have to make a difficult choice. They may want to keep you away from David – whenever you go back there's a resurgence of campaigning for the political prisoners. Only you can decide whether it's worth it to go. They may frighten you again. Perhaps Sidney'll go with you? He'd be *some* protection, I suppose. Apply for a visa and see what happens.'

Not wanting to leave Henri in the lurch in case my visa was suddenly granted, but knowing it always took time, I gave Henri six months' notice. But by the time I left Studio H, still no visa had come through. I had heard nothing. I registered at a secretarial agency and was hired out to legal firms as a temporary shorthand typist.

I continued to spend as much time as I could with Sidney.

One night I arrived at his flat in Rosecroft Avenue to find him in tears.

'Whatever's the matter?' I asked him.

'Oh, it's useless. What about David? I feel depressed.'

'I love you, Sidney,' I said, 'and I love David.'

'Well, but can you love both of us?' Sidney asked.

'Yes, I do,' I said. 'But who will understand?'

'I understand,' said Sidney.

'I'm doing a show at the Grosvenor,' Sidney said one day. 'Come along and have a look.'

'I've got nothing like that to wear,' I said.

'Wear your jeans. I've spent my life with models in "numbers". I'm sick of the trappings. Wear anything – you'll look wonderful anyway.'

The show at the Grosvenor was splendid. Sidney was urbane and handsome, self-contained and secure. Watching him at work that day I felt a deep sense of pride and I fell in love with him all over again. His clients would have a chat and a coffee with him and then just ask him to write out an order – they trusted him so much that he did not have to 'sell' to them. He was such a superb salesman that customers from New York, Paris and Australia came up to his stand with warm greetings and invitations to dinner, to their homes and their luxurious holiday retreats. Sidney is one of the most popular people I have ever met.

Sidney had always been in the fashion trade. His mother had supported herself and Sidney as a dressmaker, after his parents divorced. He'd hardly known his father and had a romantic view of a debonair, charming womaniser, a fantastic salesman, a successful big-stakes gambler. But when Sidney came to London to search for the father he'd never known he found a big-time sharpie – a Flag-cigarettenik, a Waldorf-*zetser*. His father dealt in the black market during the war and did his business in hotel lounges.

Sidney was bitterly disappointed by his father. But with his own good looks, his charm and his amazing sales ability, he had become the man he had imagined his father to be. He'd landed a job with Mary Quant soon after his arrival in London. She was just making an impact at the time and as her sales director he'd helped to launch her worldwide. Now he was with an Oxford Street company, had a posh car and an enormous expense account.

The rag trade didn't seem to go with the intellectual side of Sidney. He was extremely well-read and took only a few minutes to complete the *Times* crossword every morning. He'd been a successful actor, but had wanted a steadier living.

Now that we knew Sidney, life changed for Steven, Amandla and me. He had a beautiful daughter, Terri, who lived with Stella. She adored her mother and was understandably resentful of me. I think she had hoped her parents would one day get together again. Her brother, Jeremy, was uncomplicated and loving and Steven and Amandla enjoyed having an older brother. Jeremy was studying at Cambridge and now Steven only came home for weekends from Haberdashers' in Elstree.

On Sundays we got together and Sidney would take us to a hotel carvery, where the boys competed to see who could go back the most times for refills of beef, lamb and pork, potatoes and peas. It was lovely to feel part of a family again, to be able to refer to someone about the children's problems, successes and hopes. The kids talked about O and A levels – they were always taking one exam or another. We were usually full of high spirits and jokes. For a treat, after lunch, Sidney sometimes took us in the Jag through a car wash. The kids would act younger than they were, making believe they were in a ghost train and squeal and squeak and frighten each other as the green chamois strips slapped the windows of the car. Once Steven opened the window and we all got wet. I don't think any of us were used to being so happy and we made the most of every little outing or event.

I met Stella and became very fond of her, but she and Sidney were not comfortable with each other, so I did not see much of her. We lunched and chatted occasionally – we had many friends in common in South Africa and we had both been close friends of Judy's.

I was temping for a company of lawyers in Holborn, arriving each morning to mounds of work, thumping it out on an ancient typewriter, sitting on a crooked old typing chair. There was no security and no holiday pay, and I decided to look for a permanent job.

I started scanning the papers and registering with agents and found to my horror that, because I was forty years old, the secretarial world had closed down on me. Job after job had a 35-year age limit. I didn't even get interviews. In desperation I took a job in a small typesetting company, working on commission only, and then found that the slightly profitable balance sheet I had been shown was a fraud. The business was a loss-maker. Unless I made the company over from scratch, I wasn't going to earn anything at all. I tried to build up new business, with little success. My boss lied about the machines we had, showed clients work done by other companies, trying to pass it off as ours. Staff were sacked at whim. When I called in the NGA to unionise the company, I got twenty-four hours' notice to quit. But I had learned that with the same keyboard skill, a typist could become a typesetter and earn considerably more money.

Sidney and I discussed getting married. We did not want to hurt David. Happily, Joan visited England at this time. She became very fond of Sidney, and I had the opportunity to have long discussions with her.

'What do the kids think?' she asked.

'Well, it's difficult for them, you know. I think they'd want me to wait for David, but they like Sidney and life is exciting with him around. Steven says he thinks it would make me happy but he is cagey when I ask what about *him*, what does he think for himself. He says things like "Well, I like him very much but I don't want any father except Dad." Amandla isn't sure. She changes her mind about it every few days. I think she wants everything – David and Sidney *and* Jeremy and Terry.'

'Well,' said Joan, 'it's all very difficult. I think you should live with Sidney. I think you should *marry* Sidney. You need security – you've always felt insecure and we were brought up as the sort of women who have to be married. We can't just deny that – it's there. All our ghastly family's values are there no matter how we try to alter or grow. People like us can't really be liberated.

'You've been without David for six years. You've done well, let's face it. But you've been terribly lonely. We all worry about you dreadfully. What's the answer? You can't have no relationships, or just casual relationships – they're the least satisfactory. It's very difficult for you, I know. Because if you do decide to marry Sidney, people are going to be awful about it. They'll never stop bitching, judging you – because David is in jail.'

'I know all about that already,' I said. 'It's a funny thing. People who are sleeping all over the place, divorcing, separating, sorting out their own lives, get puritanical with me because David is in jail. They expect prisoners' wives to be virginal. I get frowns from some people when I eat out with a man. And I've heard all sorts of ugly gossip about the other wives. We have to try to live normal lives – whatever that means. It's the people outside – the people who didn't go to jail – who have so much to say, who make things difficult. I don't want to let David down – neither does Sidney. And I love David, you know. But I love Sidney too and I do want to live with him – marry him.'

'Well, then. Why don't you?' said Joan. 'I've spoken to David about it when I visited him in the last few months. He thinks it's a good idea. He's relieved that you have found someone as nice as Sidney. Imagine what it's like for him in there knowing what a battle you're having, picturing you lonely in London.'

'Does David think that?' I asked. 'I believe he imagines the chevra are friendly and supportive.'

'The *who*?'

'The chevra. That's what Sidney calls those members of the South African Communist Party in London. "Chevra" is short for Chevra Kadisha – you know, the Jewish Burial Society. Chevra is yiddish for "comrades". If anyone starts any activity that is not under their control, they "bury" them – immobilise them, or manoeuvre them out of the solidarity movement.'

Joan laughed. 'I thought you were a communist?'

'I am,' I said. 'There are many of us who don't recognise the chevra as communists although that's what they call them-selves. The chevra hold sway over the London ANC, and have influence in the Anti-Apartheid Movement and David's trade union, TASS. They're a very small, powerful group over here – mainly middle-class whites who left South Africa before the going really got tough.'

'That's terrible! How can you people be fighting among yourselves? Who are these people?'

'In the name of security, their activities and memberships and identities are kept secret. A guy called Brian Bunting inherited the South African Communist Party from his father. Brian's wife, Sonia, is a big mouthpiece in London – on many committees. The chevra have tremendous influence over the lives of all of us in exile.'

'How?' Joan asked.

'They have contact with the countries that help the South African struggle. They and their clique have the say in London about who does what – who types, who works in the office, who stands on committees, who gets into the Communist Party and who gets thrown out. I often wonder what the people fighting in South Africa think of all this. We know they call all this infighting the "London Problem".'

'But if they're no good, why do people listen to them?'

'Because the chevra speak in the name of the ANC over here. People of good will in this country who want to support the ANC wouldn't dream of challenging them.'

'What does David think about all this?' Joan asked.

'Oh, he's always known about it. In the sixties there were two lines of thinking: one was that South Africa suffered from a special type of colonialism, the other that South Africa was the victim of imperialism. David was an anti-imperialist. When the Party was formulating its programme, David was a regional representative to the conference and his members had voted for an anti-imperialist programme. The link man who was meant to tell David the date and venue of the meeting to decide the final programme said he had not done so because he was frightened David would be exposed to an informer. The meeting went ahead and the programme was adopted based on "a special type of colonialism". I wonder how many other delegates were similarly "protected". It may seem an abstract thing for people to get steamed up about but it has far-reaching effects for the liberation struggle. The whole political character of the coming South African revolution was at stake. The programme determined which class could emerge to lead the South African people, and how the struggle would be fought.'

'But David should have made it public – if he thought he was wrongly excluded,' Joan said.

'We believed that disagreements should be dealt with inside the Party. They shouldn't be the subject of public splits and attacks. This suited the chevra. With honest communists, not prepared to expose this sort of thing, they were quite safe to continue. Those who criticise the chevra are called "Trotskyist" or "ultra-left" – words used as insults which have no relation to their real meanings. Those who wish to expose them are in danger of being accused of siding with the South African

215

regime, of being called anti-communist or enemies of the movement. So most keep quiet.'

'It all sounds very dangerous,' Joan said. 'If David and you knew what they were doing, why did you get mixed up with them?'

'We felt we had to fight within the South African Communist Party for correct socialist policies. David had worked with these people and fought with integrity for years, and once he was in jail he believed that any differences would be forgotten. After all, the Party leadership in South Africa had appointed him the Communist Party representative to the four-man High Command of Umkhonto we Sizwe. He took that to mean they had confidence in him.

'David thinks the chevra are looking after the kids – after me. But they never did. I always thought that once you are in the movement, especially if your husband's in jail, your kids are my kids, my house is your house. We are one big family who care for each other. But that wasn't the way it was for me. All I got was criticism. I said to Sonia Bunting once, when I heard she'd been complaining and gossiping about Amandla being undisciplined, "Look, why don't you talk to Mandla? Why don't you tell her, "I don't think you should do this and that – your father wouldn't like it" instead of gossiping with the others and undermining my kids. Your own kids have a lot of advantages: a rich home, your inherited money, a good education, the best of everything. David is your comrade! I'm your comrade! My children are supposed to be your children!" She looked at me as if I were mad! What had she to do with my kids? She was the head of the London ANC political prisoners' committee. All that influence! And all they can do is criticise.'

'But the blokes in jail think we're all cared for – just one big happy family. It would break David's heart if he knew. But perhaps he does know. In his last letter to me he says he thinks Sidney and I should marry. He said he doesn't want me facing problems on my own.'

'Oh, I think David knows what a battle it is,' Joan said. 'You must do what you think is right. That is the only way to look at it. I don't understand about the people in London. It sounds dreadful.'

Before Sidney and I got married, we took our children to Yugoslavia for our honeymoon. On 23 August 1973, we were married. Our sons were witnesses and our daughters and a few friends came to the registry office. That evening friends gave us a big wedding party with champagne and a cake from Fortnum and Mason.

My mother flew over to visit and we moved into the Barbican. Our flat was beautiful but I hated it. Every time I entered the building, with its clanging metal doors and concrete walls, I thought of David in jail.

Hunting for a job proved fruitless and in November 1973 I opened a typesetting company, Red Lion Setters. No matter how much Sidney earned, he was a big spender and always broke. A friend of his lent me £2000 to buy an IBM composer. Henri designed my stationery. Sidney said, 'You're a Red, a Leo, and now you're a typesetter. So why not call it Red Lion Setters?'

The depression was biting and there was a power strike, which meant we had electricity for only three days a week. But I went ahead and rented a tiny room in Lambs Conduit Passage in Holborn.

Since my arrival in England in 1966 I had not officially joined the ANC in London because whenever I could, I went to South Africa to see David, and I didn't want to have any sensitive information in case I was interrogated. What little work I did for the movement was outside the London structures.

But as soon as I opened the doors of Red Lion Setters, I went to see the chief representative of the ANC in London, M.P. Naicker. In South Africa he had been a trade unionist and leader of the Indian Congress. I suggested that I could perform a useful technical function. As I only needed to earn a salary for myself, I could run the company as a free typesetting unit for the ANC in London. The clients I obtained would pay my salary. M.P. said he would raise it on the necessary committees and come back to me soon.

Sidney was against this. 'What for?' he asked. 'The chevra have broken your heart for years. Look in their publications. Where is David mentioned? Where have you ever been recognised? Look how they treat Steven and Amandla. These people in London aren't the real thing. They're residents here – they look after themselves. What have they done since they've been in England for the struggle in South Africa? What have they done for people like you? But, more important, what have they ever done over here for Nelson and Winnie Mandela or Walter and Albertina Sisulu – for the leaders of the struggle? No one even knows their names. That can't be an accident, can it?'

I argued with Sidney. 'They don't have to give me or David or any individuals credit,' I said. 'We aren't in this for what we can get. In this struggle, you have to give your all. We have to have some way to support the liberation struggle at home and, whoever these people are, they control the official bodies. There must be lots of sincere people like me who just want to do their share. Those people will understand.'

'Most of those people are casualties of the chevra,' Sidney said. 'Look around you at them – at all the South Africans who have been disbarred, alienated, swept aside, so that the same people can run the same committees. They're people of all kinds – communists, liberals, non-affiliated like me. I think South Africa is in a dreadful situation with the chevra. But what can the people in Africa do?

'The chevra sit in their posh houses in London eating chocolates, deciding who goes to what international conference and who heads this or that committee – and it's always one of their own chevra. Outside of their own little émigré knot they make no sense. It's the fact they have such influence that is so puzzling.'

Sidney continued. 'Look at what happened when Peter Hain made preparations to launch the Stop the Seventy Tour. The Anti-Apartheid Movement tried to block its formation and told Peter it would split the movement. In reality the chevra wanted to block it because they did not control it. Thousands of people participated in that successful campaign and the AAM virtually

218

doubled its membership. But the enthusiasm of all these people was not utilised in any other major campaign, and of course they began to drift away from the AAM.

'And look at TASS, for example,' Sidney went on. 'David's union formed the TASS Kitson Committee when David went to jail. They did a very good job for years. What happened? The chevra couldn't take over a union organisation so they diverted some of its office bearers into a new organisation, SATIS, Southern Africa the Imprisoned Society, which they controlled. After that, no discussion was allowed at TASS annual meetings!

'You and David had lived in this country and he was quite well known as a trade unionist so you were in a position to raise the question of political prisoners from a personal point of view and make it live for British people. The chevra don't want this, so they ignore you, never ask you to speak on their platforms.'

'Oh, Sidney,' I said, 'I can't bother about all that. No one can suss this type of émigré infighting. Our job over here is to get British people to support the liberation struggle. We can't hold back because there's this problem with the chevra. And it's complicated by the fact that the South African regime has infiltrated all the solidarity movements here with spies. Every now and then there is an exposure and spies are found. So the chevra get away with their manoeuvres in the name of security. In Africa they say the London Problem must be sorted out in London.'

'Well,' said Sidney. 'If ever that is done – if ever the chevra are dislodged, a lot of South Africans who want to be in the ANC in London – people now sitting on the sidelines, waiting for the clean-up – will enter the struggle. Then a real solidarity movement can be built. I only hope it happens in my lifetime.

'I just don't want you putting in a lot of effort and finding out you're blocked and wasting your time.'

'Well,' I said, 'British people can never understand all this. And I don't know that they can deal with it in Africa either. But I do know that even ANC chief representatives and black stalwarts who come here from Africa have to toe the line – or they get no cooperation and little regard. Do you know that even

219

members who have been on the national executive committee of the African National Congress, and sons of famous black political prisoners, have been cast out or railroaded out of London? Young black people who come over here to study have to accept the chevra rulings, otherwise they won't get their grants or accommodation or any other benefits from the London movement.'

Although Sidney argued with me, he understood that I had to try to go on working for the struggle.

As expected, M. P. Naicker came back to me a few weeks later and with a sigh of regret said that no technical unit was to be set up in London. He did not understand why – there was a great deal of work to be done. The London Committee had turned it down. Shortly after this, M.P. died of a heart attack on a plane, delivering printing to East Germany.

Of course eventually a technical unit was set up, and I trained the person who ran it – it just didn't include me. I was given work to do, away from the eyes of the chevra, typing documents, briefs and even books for black leaders and students, who came to me direct. Red Lion Setters grew, and from then on I ran the company and worked in it as a typesetter.

I kept applying for visas to visit South Africa. I was terrified but resolved that I would go home and continue to see David. After my marriage to Sidney, I applied as Norma Cherfas. I did not think my changed status would dupe them, but they might believe that with my re-marriage I had relinquished David.

In 1975 I obtained a visa and Sidney and I went together. I left Steven and Amandla with friends. Amandla, convinced that she, too, would give her life for the struggle, wrote:

My Dad's in jail but I don't mind –
He's making the world better for all mankind

He'll only be out when I'm 21
It's bad for me but it's worse for my Mum.

What I wonder while I'm still free
Is who will suffer When it happens to me?

· *12* ·

The plane journey on this trip seemed to be the longest imaginable and at intervals I wished the plane would turn around and go back to Heathrow. I was scared. Joan had arranged for me to have four visits and Sidney drove me straight to the jail.

I got through the numerous clanking doors as the warder in charge unlocked them and waited nervously in the waiting room. Captain Schnepel, in charge of the prison, came in and told me that I could have only one half-hour visit to David. I could not believe it! At first I tried to reason with him that I was entitled to four visits, two for each month, because David had saved up his visits for me and I had come all the way from London. He was implacable. 'You just got one visit to Kitson, OK? Half a hour. That's it.'

'No,' I said. 'I've got four.'

'Don't argue with me, Mrs Kitson, OK? You got just the one visit and that's final. Kitson's had his allowance. He's had plenty visits.'

I started to argue and shout at him and he did what most men do when faced with a worked-up woman: he got calmer as I got more upset and cocked his head and lowered his eyelids at the two warders present to show them how unreasonable I was and how reasonable he was. I began to cry. I was furious with myself. I had long ago decided never to show them a single bit of emotion. Coldness worked better than anything. It got you respect. But if you showed them they had got through to you with their ridiculous rules and strutting self-importance, it made them puff up their chests and test their petty power. But I never was very good at keeping my cool.

With wet, red eyes I was shown into a tiny corridor where three cubicles were separated by panels of masonite – the visiting room. A high wooden counter ran the length of the corridor and glass panels separated the visitors' side of the corridor from the prisoners' side. There were three stools for the visitors but when I sat on one of them I was too low to see through the glass. David was shown in. We pressed against the glass in greeting and spoke at the side through a square piece of masonite with holes punched through it. Then we stood back to look at each other. David took a small bunch of squashed marigolds out of his pocket. 'I grew these for you in the prison garden,' he said. 'I'm not allowed to give them to you, so they're just for you to look at.'

'I'm only allowed this one visit,' I blurted, on the verge of another flood of tears. It is an unforgivable thing to cry during a jail visit. Prisoners expect you to bring them cheer and warmth. David spent a few minutes consoling me.

'It'll be all right. They must have made a mistake. I saved all my visits for you.'

After the visit I found out that Captain Schnepel had looked at someone else's visit record instead of David's. It had all been a mistake. I was to be allowed three more visits.

David wanted every bit of news about Sidney. How did the kids get on with him? What was he like? What did he look like? Quite a few of the guys in jail knew him and thought he was terrific. David was actually proud of Sidney! Micki, who had visited last, had said Sidney was a great bloke.

'Yes,' I said. 'He's terrific.'

'It sounds as if it is really good for the kids. He sounds like a nice chap. I'm glad for you. I'm going to be in here for ages still, and who knows what will happen?'

'Nothing's going to happen to you,' I said. But I was frightened when he said that. Our friend Bram Fischer, a lawyer and leading member of the South African Communist Party who had been in prison with David, had died there. David looked ill. He had been suffering from an allergy for a couple of years when he was in a wood workshop. There was no protection against the sawdust and nothing seemed to help him get well.

Outside the jail Sidney was waiting for me in the car. This first visit to David left me very upset. He had been cheerful enough and had done his best to put me at ease, but I had got off to a bad start with Schnepel and I was still shaking from the clanking doors and prison smell. Now I could cry without restraint and I did. I could not explain to myself, or to Sidney, why I was in such a state. We drove back to Johannesburg to my sister Joan.

I felt I was being closely watched. Every time I left my sister's house, I had the feeling I was being followed. Sidney would not let me out of his sight and this gave me a measure of protection.

People we had known in the sixties had got richer. The suburbs of Johannesburg glowed like jewels with massive red, blue and gold flowers in the beautifully tended gardens. The huge houses gleamed with white paint. Thick green leaves and luxuriantly coloured *begonia cherera* shaded stoeps polished to a gleaming red. Crystal aquamarine swimming pools glittered in the sunlight. Even the roadsides had flowerbeds and carefully cut grass shapes these days. The mine dumps gleamed and twinkled gold on the Johannesburg horizon. Egoli (City of Gold) – as black people called Johannesburg – had changed from an ugly city to a suburban paradise.

I had never been more terrified. I determined never to return. There was something about the gleaming beauty of everything that showed the enemy to be firmly entrenched. White South Africa was displaying its confidence, and everywhere I went arrogant signs of it shouted at me: new buildings, shopping centres, brand-new factories, huge new housing schemes.

Yet the people who lived there were frightened. I could feel it everywhere. Many of the women I met took sleeping pills, tranquillisers, headache pills and pills for their sore heads, backs, stomachs, knees and necks. Every bathroom cupboard that I peeped into in wonder held rows of pills – uppers, downers, painkillers and lots of bum pills. It seemed everyone in Johburg suffered from haemorrhoids. I didn't have the nerve to ask why.

Front doors had locks, mesh, chains, bolts, knockers and

bells. Windows were barred and crisscrossed with burglar proofing. The door leading from the kitchen to the rest of the house was also bolted and barred – locked against the servants of the household. There were enamel signs on the front walls of houses, giving the name of the security company who had installed the system in the house, to deter intruders. Burglar alarms would go off by mistake, and their ringing had become a common sound in Johburg suburbs.

Every house had a gun and some men carried them as naturally as one would carry a pen in a pocket. The women had either little gas canisters – like breath sprays – in their handbags or dainty guns. Many of the women now went to afternoon gun practice the way they used to go to cookery or art classes, and often talked about their sons who had been conscripted into the army. There was some talk of the advantage of the army 'making a man of' some young boy, but there was fear in parents' eyes and most of the families we saw either accepted conscription as an inevitable horror or else got their sons out of the country before the draft. Although South African propaganda shrieked that the army was fighting against the 'total communist onslaught', many parents knew that their sons weren't going to fight communists. They were being sent to the front-line states where the South Africans made constant military incursions against peaceful surrounding nations. Or, worse, they could be sent to areas of unrest inside South Africa, to shoot fellow South Africans in the townships and rural areas. A popular war-resistance movement had formed and helped to get many of the young men out of the country.

The Johburg jokes had changed. At nearly every house I was asked if I had heard the latest:

'This guy was at his golf club and he phoned home. Jim, the gardener, answered.

'"Where's the madam, Jim? Call the madam."

'"Master, the madam she's busy."

'"Never mind busy, you cheeky bugger. Just call her."

'"Please, master, the madam she's busy with another master in the bedroom."

224

' "Bloody hell! Now look here, Jim. You know my study?"

' "Yes, master."

' "You look in the top drawer, underneath the new shirts. You'll find my gun. You go into the bedroom and you shoot that master and then you shoot the madam. When you've done that, you throw the gun away in the garden. You go quick, quick. Then you come back to the phone. I'll be waiting for you. OK?"

' "Yes, master."

'The master waits, hears two shots, waits ages, and finally Jim returns.

' "Where the hell you been? Why you been such a long time?"

' "Please, master: I took the gun from the drawer in your study. I went to the bedroom. I shot the master and the madam. I took the gun to the garden. I threw it in the swimming pool . . ."

' "Swimming pool? What number *is* that?"

With two and a half million guns in white hands, there was a lot of shooting in Johannesburg. Often, during family rows, someone would take out a gun and shoot. The white civilian death toll mounted.

It was sometimes difficult to pick up friendships during these visits. Privileged South Africans made excuses for the way they lived and put up defensive barriers that made ordinary conversation impossible. Simple things I asked them appeared to be loaded. I'd say, 'How are you getting on?'

'OK. It must be terrible living in England with all those race riots. Notting Hill Gate, wasn't it? Dreadful! We heard that the blacks just ran loose against the whites. How many got killed? It sounds like you've got worse race problems in England than we have here.'

Or I'd ask, 'How are you doing?' and be met with long explanations, the purpose of which was usually to show that they did not operate the apartheid system themselves.

'You know, I pay my girl more than any other in this area. Honestly, she does next to nothing. Every five minutes she's off to the townships and I'm for ever signing her pass. All the girls in this street start work at 6 am, mine only starts at 8. And I let her bring her child here the other day. I could of got fined for it.'

It was the same with my little brother. Sidney and I went down to Durban overnight to see Mom. The family gave a dinner for us and welcomed Sidney. Mangelwurzel was there on holiday. We hadn't seen each other for years and had never got to know one another well. When he was seventeen he had married Pam, in Rhodesia, and they had three children. Mom wrote to me about Markie in her letters telling me how kind he was to her and how he was battling to earn enough to keep his family. I felt well disposed towards him.

He greeted me with a smile. 'Back from the land of the *rooineks* for a while, I see.' (The English are called rednecks by South Africans because the fair skin on their necks gets burned red from the sun before it tans.)

'Hello, Mangelwurzel.'

'How's England?'

'Fine – and you?'

'It looks to me as if you people in England sit around criticising South Africa most of the time.'

'Well, that's not true, but if it were, it wouldn't be such a bad thing, would it?'

'You don't have to be so superior.'

'I don't feel superior. What's the matter? What do you mean?'

'I know you've always looked down on me because I work in Uncle Mervyn's factory.'

'Now why would you think that? I've never looked down on a factory worker in my life.'

'Well, then because we manufacture uniforms for the Rhodesian army.'

'I don't understand why you're so defensive. I haven't seen you for years. I don't feel critical towards you at all. It's up to you what you do with your life. Like everybody else, you probably just do your best.'

'I suppose you're quite prepared to see this country run by ignorant blacks.'

'Why? Are you happy it's run by ignorant whites?'

226

'The whites have had *thousands* of years of civilisation, that's the difference.'

'You mean after a thousand years the best the whites here could do was develop *boeremusiek* [Afrikaans folk music]? Or did it take a thousand years to learn to cheat people out of their land? Or do you mean the thousand years to make teargas and bullets? Which civilisation are you referring to? Are *you* more competent to vote than Mom's cook?'

'Ag, man. Anyone can see you've been living in England. You speak a hang of a lot of bullshit.'

'What's bullshit?'

'You believe everyone's equal, don't you?'

'No, I don't. Anyway, you were talking about civilisation, not equality. How are the children?'

'Well, one thing's for sure. They not going to get mixed up in politics. Look where it got you.'

Mangelwurzel and I did not hit it off. He told me that someone had asked him, 'Would you feel upset if your sister married a kaffir?'

'Oh, yes,' I said wearily, 'that's an old one.'

But he continued. 'I said, "Only if I had the hell in for the kaffir."'

Having established his hostility to me, that was that.

This time when I visited Johannesburg, the black people walking the streets looked different. They didn't jump into the gutters to let you pass. They were prouder, they wore better clothes. The government allowed only those black people who worked in the city to live in it. They could hide millions of unemployed, sick, elderly and young black people – all those that white industry and white homes didn't need – in the bantustans, barren tracts of land, far from white eyes. But in the cities it looked as if black people were doing better.

It was strange to rise at six o'clock and go for a walk with Sidney. Only barking dogs and black workers were abroad at that hour: white South Africa slept. Walking down the street past the houses with their drawn upstairs curtains, black people called out greetings to each other. Some played guitars, sitting

227

relaxed on the kerb before the white world swung into its demanding morning. And some sang in the street. Front steps were being vigorously rubbed and polished, gardens were being dug and watered in the cool of the day, newspapermen were delivering, chauffeurs were shining big cars, milkmen swung their crates down and went round the back of houses to offload cartons of milk, cream and orange juice, and to pass words with the maids at the back of kitchens. It was a black world. Soon the madams would be heard calling 'Annieeee! Sarah! Betteee! Where the hell *are* you?' and the black people would disappear, leaving the streets to the white men on their way to work and the white kids with satchels on their backs and hair slicked down on their way to school. But now they greeted us as we passed, an unfamiliar sight to them – white people, at six o'clock in the morning!

Before returning to London, I visited Pumi. She was working for a posh madam in Saxonwold, a rich suburb of Johannesburg. She bought me green cream soda and I sat with her in her tiny corrugated tin room, with its iron bed built up tall on bricks. All servants prop up their beds like that to stop the creepy-crawlies getting on their beds and to be able to store things underneath them. Pumi wanted every fine detail about Amandla and Steven and to know how David was managing in jail. When I told her how the children had grown, and what subjects they were learning at school, she nodded proudly. When I said that David looked funny in khaki with short hair, but that he was cheerful, she wept a little and put her arms around me.

'It's a sin that someone like David should be in jail,' she said. 'David has always been a happy person. He will keep happy, even in jail. Have you noticed that when people are fighting for a common cause, they are also fighting for their personal happiness? That is something that is not affected by walls and bars. But he must miss you and the children.'

Pumi promised to continue writing to us. We had kept up a correspondence over the years and she always signed her letters 'I remain, here, Pumi Ndlovo'. I was homesick even before I left to return to London.

Going to the jail from rich, beautifully decorated Johburg homes was a contrast I could not get used to. One minute I was looking at elegant tables laid with an array of shiny cutlery and four kinds of glasses, or sitting beside gleaming swimming pools being served trays of cakes and sandwiches, and the next it was time to visit David in Pretoria. Someone would lend Sidney his huge American car and we would speed to steamy hot Pretoria, arriving outside the forbidding brick walls. I stood in the heat, waiting to be let in, and was led to the waiting room through clanking doors, past black prisoners endlessly polishing the floors. Then into the cubicle-like room. A few minutes' wait and David, in baggy clothes, would appear behind the thick glass with a wide smile of welcome. I'd glance at my watch to be sure I wasn't going to be cheated of any of my thirty minutes and the prepared words would fly out of my head while I stood looking at him.

But David was used to this sudden paralysis in his visitors and was practised in relaxing them. I can't remember what we spoke about – the words were nothing. I just watched as he looked at me, blew his nose on a big red jail handkerchief, or fingered the base of the glass between us, wishing I could touch him.

The last day of our stay came. I was to have the final really long phone call to Mom in Durban, have my last swim, say goodbye, for ever, to David's mother, who was ill, and his father. It was my last chance to talk to Joan face to face. I was to pay my final visit to David until his release. I was determined never to return to South Africa until liberation.

Over the years there had been many farewells, but now there was a finality that bit deep. I went through the day blindly, feeling such a sense of loss and devastation that I can barely remember the events. But I do remember a tear sliding down the cheek of my mother-in-law, Chris, as she cuddled me goodbye. Joan cried at the airport.

I did not recover from my feeling of paralysis after the last visit to David until I was on the plane. When I had gone to the jail on that last occasion, I made notes of the bits of news I'd forgotten to tell David. On the final visit before every one of my returns to London, I let him know the most important piece of South African news. The prisoners were allowed no news broadcasts or newspapers at that time and there was nothing the boers could do if I quickly slipped in an item at the end of the visits. This time the visit was terminated before I had a chance to mention that Chief Buthelezi, the puppet leader of KwaZulu Bantustan in Natal, had revived *Inkatha*, the Zulu nationalist movement.

On the plane I recalled, with regret, all the things I hadn't said and would not be able to write in our heavily censored letters. Sidney was understanding. We chatted and played Scrabble and 'I'm not Nebuchadnezzar, nor am I...' When I cried, he comforted me.

'Well, at least now that I'm not going back again,' I said, 'I can work properly in the ANC in London.'

'I was waiting for you to say that,' Sidney said.

'Well, why don't you join too?'

'No,' said Sidney. 'I know it would be a waste of my time. I know too many people who have been bruised trying to get things done. I don't fancy banging my head against a brick wall.'

'Well,' I said confidently, 'I'm just going to do whatever I'm asked. Johburg made me feel positively sick. South Africa is heavy with decadence. It's become tangible. Even though you know everyone is scared and carrying guns and all that, they're so strong and so arrogant.'

In 1976 I applied for readmission to the ANC in London and was assigned to a unit.

Soweto was the lull before the storm. In 1976, the youth of South Africa rose up. On 16 June, the black youth peacefully demonstrated against the injustices of their lives. The world was shaken by the indiscriminate slaughter of hundreds of young school students in Soweto. Two days later Alexandra Township rose and then the University of Zululand, Tokose, Natalspruit and Kathelehong, Vosloorus, Tembisa, Kagiso and the University of the North. On 20 June the young people of Seshego rose and the day after in Duduza and in the townships

230

surrounding Pretoria: Mamelodi, Mabopane, Atteridgeville and Hammanskraal. The following day they rose in Lekozi, and at GaRankuwa in Bophuthatswana. On 23 June they rose in Jouberton and on 18 July at the University of Fort Hare. Witbank, Middelburg, Carleton, Biopatong and the Zulu Training School in Vryheid, and Ndwedwe followed.

Listening to the reports of our people engaged in those life-and-death battles, we were shocked to hear that they were meeting bullets and teargas with stones, using dustbin lids as shields.

In August the uprisings continued at New Brighton, Montshiwa, Mdantsane, Langa, Nyanga and Guguletu.

In 1976, after the Soweto uprising, when thousands of black school children demonstrated against their oppression and protested at their inferior education, taught in Afrikaans – the language of their oppressors – Nomzamo Mandela had been accused of fomenting the trouble. She said:

'I was there among them, I saw what happened. The children picked up stones, they used dustbin lids as shields and marched towards machine guns. It's not that they don't know that the white man is heavily armed; they marched against heavy machine-gun fire. You could smell gunfire everywhere. Children were dying in the street, and as they were dying, the others marched forward facing guns. No one has ever underestimated the power of the enemy. We know that he is armed to the teeth. But the determination, the thirst for freedom in children's hearts, was such that they were prepared to face those machine guns with stones. That is what happens when you hunger for freedom, when you want to break those chains of oppression.'

South Africa was never to be the same again. A new generation had arrived. The police shot indiscriminately at babies playing, at children on their way to school. Mass funerals took place. Fifteen-year-olds were sent to prison on Robben Island, parents could not find their children and scoured hospitals and morgues. Many fled the country and many went into military training at ANC camps. Younger children were sent to the new ANC school on land given by the Tanzanian government – the Solomon Mahlangu Freedom School.

Our ANC unit agreed that we should collect direct material aid outside the Brixton Tesco. As only a few unit members could make it, and there was no active anti-apartheid group in South London, the people from my office came to help. We stood outside the supermarket with baskets and placards explaining that the goods were for the camps, crèche and school in Africa. At first the regular stallholders in the street were suspicious of us, but when they found that we were there every week they began to support us because we were collecting for Africa. Local women brought us their jumble, people offered help for the struggle in South Africa and asked where they could go to learn and give help and we encouraged them to join the Anti-Apartheid Movement. Shoppers gave generously and we had to arrange transport to take all the goods to the office each week.

After about six weeks the collections were called off. The reason given was that people in Brixton were poor. By collecting for Africa, we were depriving Brixton. Some of us were upset about this. I felt the friends we were making in Brixton would soon have become a core of solidarity in London.

Sidney shook his head at these developments and said sadly, 'I told you so.' We had a deep understanding and love for each other which we were never to lose. Sidney and I were friends at the deepest level and I could talk to him about most things, though I was never his intellectual equal. There was a world of knowledge that he possessed and constantly added to – I never found out how. He remembered everything he read and every actor in every film or play he ever saw. He knew the news from every country and was equally up-to-date in City gossip and the literary world. He was educated and cultured and, beside him, I felt I was just a crude South African.

The day after Sidney and I had got married, we had had the first of several arguments about, of all things, my name. This subject surfaced from time to time and became more and more hurtful for him. I had not realised that I would now be called 'Mrs Cherfas'. It had been bad enough, when I married David,

232

that I had become Mrs Kitson. I lost touch with many friends of my child- and girlhood who knew me as Norma Cranko. Now I wanted to go on being called Norma Kitson. This hurt Sidney very deeply and was always a contentious issue between us. Of course it hid much deeper feelings in both of us about David. For a while I became Kitson-Cherfas but I couldn't sign or call myself a double-barrelled name – it just wasn't me, it made me want to laugh.

'But you're my *wife*,' Sidney said.

'I remember,' I said, 'when my mother married Oscar and called herself Goldberg. It was terrible for us children to have a different name from our mother.'

'Why?'

'It made me feel like an orphan. And I don't want Steven and Amandla to feel like orphans.'

'Well, they won't. Anyway, there's nothing wrong with a double-barrel name. Or you could just call yourself Cherfas.'

I felt appalled. 'It doesn't sound like me. It sounds pretentious – like someone else. I wouldn't mind Street-Porter or Dustbin-Lid – I can relate to that, but Kitson-Cherfas! Do you know I once went to school with a girl called Rosemary Faith Llewellyn Davies Webb? She tried to stow away on the *Vanguard*, which was the ship Princess Elizabeth and the Duke of Edinburgh were on during their visit to South Africa. She fell in love with a sailor. She had lots of taffeta dresses and a pair of shoes with high heels.'

'What's that got to do with it?' Sidney asked. 'I don't know what's with you. What's in a name?'

I would not give way. I was in my forties and I did not want to change my name. Sidney felt I was holding on to David, putting him between us.

I didn't have an answer. What Sidney felt was the truth.

I received a letter from David each month, the regulation 500 words. At first I shared them with Sidney and we'd have warm chats about my feelings and how David must be feeling. But after a few months I would take David's letters out of the letter box before Sidney could see and keep them to myself. Sidney must have realised what I was doing, because he knew David would not stop writing, and I think he was deeply hurt.

David's sentence was due to end on 18 December 1984, and on New Year's Eve when the year changed to 1980, I began to think about David coming out. I had been married to Sidney for seven happy years, but for the next eighteen months I lived in a subliminal panic. I didn't know what was wrong with me and I went to the doctor. I began sleeping badly and Sidney often had to move to the spare room to get a night's sleep. I felt I shouldn't go away on holidays. I didn't want to speak to anyone and I shut people up. I closed down communication with Sidney and I stopped wanting to go out to films, friends or restaurants. The doctor said I was overworking. I was. I spent hours longer than necessary at the office, but I was working erratically and became snappy with clients and with the members of Red Lion Setters.

In July 1981, not fully aware of what I was about, I packed a bag and moved in with an ANC woman friend in Hampstead. Sidney visited me, asking me to return. I said I couldn't. He understood much better than I did what was happening. I denied that it had anything to do with David, but he knew and I knew that I was preparing myself, preparing the way for David's return.

In 1980, I had been elected to the ANC women's committee and became a member of its propaganda subcommittee. Here my typesetting skills were put to use producing leaflets, cards and documents. But the women's committee could barely function. Communication with the chevra who ran the organisation at the office was so difficult that the permission we needed to produce leaflets, cards, T-shirts and other material was seldom forthcoming. Our logistics committee, intended to raise material aid for the struggle, barely existed. Our youth group, set up for the children of ANC members, virtually went out of existence for lack of support. Our fraternal committee, set up to make links with women's organisations throughout Britain, faltered. No one was allowed to address public meetings unless vetted by the chevra. Thinking that we should improve our

234

public speaking, we ran workshops – but the chevra kept a tight rein on who could appear in public on behalf of the ANC in London.

My close friend at this time was Carol Brickley. She had come to work at Red Lion Setters in 1976 as an artworker and, soon after, became a director of the company. Carol was a communist and her group produced a monthly newspaper, *Fight Racism! Fight Imperialism!*

We planned to take our annual leave together in 1981 and visit Zimbabwe which, the previous year, had become independent. Carol made appointments in Harare to see members of the Zimbabwe government to get interviews for her newspaper. She took me along with her. We visited Chitingweza camp where the Zanu and Zapu soldiers were joining together, and beer halls where we met the local people.

We made our way to Kariba where I was to cross from Zimbabwe to Zambia to visit the ANC head office in Lusaka. Red Lion Setters had sent down an IBM composer and items for their use and I collected two suitcases of the things our comrades were asking for – tape recorders, calculators, Letraset, coffee, em rules, nonreproducing pencils and the like.

In Zimbabwe the ANC chief representative, Joe Gqabi, whom I had first met in the fifties in South Africa, came to see us and I spent some time every day with him. He had been imprisoned on Robben Island until 1975. I did not discuss our London problems with Joe – he needed clerical and other assistance, which I gave him – but he must have heard rumours that were circulating from London. Before I left for Zambia, he held my arms and said, 'Just carry on, Comrade Norma. Whatever they say, we know you're doing a fine job for the struggle.'

A few months later, Joe Gqabi was killed in Harare – a bomb was planted in his car.

Leaving Carol at Lake Kariba, I made friends with a border guard and got a lift to Lusaka. The British engineer who drove the car made regular weekly sorties into Zimbabwe for stores. He complained bitterly about living in Zambia – it was so awful and there were shortages of everything. I couldn't understand why he worked there if conditions were so bad. 'I earn £35,000 and get a free trip home once a year,' he said. 'So it must be worth it.'

Poor Africa, I thought.

Driving to Lusaka was a frightening experience. The South Africans had bombed the road for miles and driving was difficult. There were huge holes and boulders in our path and sometimes we had to track right around a stretch of road and meet it some distance ahead. The land was laid waste and children lined the road offering bits of amethyst in exchange for a drink. At one point the engineer stopped his car and opened the boot, extracting from crates of beer one single bottle, which he gave to a group of children. They handed him a fist-size rock of amethyst and fell on the beer, taking a quick gulp and then passing it, one to the other. They were dying of thirst.

In Lusaka, I was taken to a safe house where a number of ANC people were living. Conditions there were difficult. The South Africans were always on the look-out for ANC houses. A number of bomb attacks and raids had taken place in the front-line states, and our people had been killed. This meant that our comrades had to move often, and strict security had to be observed.

The house I was taken to was bare but spotless. No one complained about the spartan conditions. We sat on the floor, chatting. For the first time I was listening to accounts by young people who had been students in Soweto during the 1976 uprising. Some had walked hundreds of miles to escape the police brutality. Most had relatives who had been killed by the boers. Some had lost sisters or brothers in the uprising and searched in vain for them in hospitals, jails and morgues. Many of their young friends had been maimed by police bullets.

Some of these youngsters were hoping to join MK and others were being sent abroad to study and were waiting for their places in colleges and universities.

After some hours spent chatting and walking around the newly planted garden, my stomach began to rumble and I said, 'I'm hungry.'

'Are you *hungry*?' a young freedom fighter asked with concern. Some time later I noticed his absence and was told he had gone to look for something for me to eat. Much later, in the pitch-dark, he came back with an orange. I shared it out – a *skyfie* (segment) each – but everyone tried to get me to have theirs because *I* was hungry. The food for meals, which was probably delivered by comrades from some central depot, had not arrived at the house and no one had eaten for two days. When food did come, it was beans and offal. These warm, friendly people, whose lives were full of hardship, offered me their pillows and shared their bedclothes in an attempt to make me comfortable. When I objected, one young woman said, 'We're used to living like this – you aren't. Don't feel bad about it. We want you to enjoy being with us.'

Here in Lusaka people asked interestedly for news of David. We had political discussions and exchanged ideas. This was uplifting, it had never happened in London.

I was taken to the women's house. A meal had been prepared and women gathered to chat and welcome me. I was presented with an ANC dress – made out of yellow material with *Amandla!* imprinted on it. I was delighted to find such a refuge for women. They had made a base for themselves, with curtains and furniture, so that, even though they might live in a safe house some way away, they could come to this base and be together.

They mentioned the London Problem and were off-hand about it. 'There's always been trouble in London,' one of them said.

'I feel that work is always being held back there,' I replied. 'That's very worrying. I can't understand it.'

'We know about the delays, the quibbles and quarrels. We see the women's committee minutes. But we can read between the lines. You're someone who proposes and then does a lot of the work. We appreciate that. Don't worry about the problems.'

'It's easy to dismiss like that,' I said. 'But important things get shelved or held up. Can't you people here do anything about it?'

She looked down. 'The problem is, we just have to wait for a lot of that generation to die. Many of them did good work when they were young, in South Africa. Much effort has been spent trying to sort out London – too much. What matters is what happens inside South Africa. We have to sort that out.'

'But London is important,' I said. 'If we can get real solidarity there – a lot of people involved – in the heart of the imperialist world, then it will assist the struggle at home. For instance, there's never been a proper campaign there for Nelson Mandela or the political prisoners. I think there is support in England – it just never gets tapped.'

'That's why we love you,' another woman said. 'We know that whatever the problems, your work continues. And if there's support, you and people like you will tap it. We rely on that. We have to.'

There has always been a special quality, a warmth and political intensity among South African women. Back in London, where I met with coldness and hostility and the intricate bureaucracy created by the chevra in the London ANC, I would often think of the simple statements made by those women, and of the warmth of my reception in Lusaka.

I met the head of the ANC Department of Information and Publicity, Sigashe Sizakele. He wanted to launch a training project in Lusaka for office workers for the ANC, and he took me to a technical base to see the printing and other machinery that was available. He was setting up the project and would call on me soon to spend six weeks at the base to train typists and typesetters. When I returned to London, I must arrange to free myself from Red Lion Setters to be able to do this work.

I wanted to do this task. From time to time I had taught typing for the movement, and the thought of working in Africa, under this eminent, warm man, was exciting.

Back in London Carol agreed to run Red Lion Setters during my absence. She was always willing to do anything for the liberation struggle in South Africa and she helped me prepare suitable teaching manuals and collect the things I would need for the training – rubbers, carbon paper, stencils, Tipp-Ex.

The months passed as I waited to be called. Everyone at Red

Lion was collecting materials for the course I was to give. I heard nothing. I should have known that it was not to be.

In 1983, at the funeral of Dr Yusuf Dadoo, chair of the South African Communist Party, I met Comrade Sizakele. He greeted me coolly. 'You did not respond when I called to you, Comrade Norma. You were to be involved in Operation Blue Eye.'

I explained to Comrade Sizakele that I had made preparations to go to Lusaka and had written to him but had heard nothing further. I had enquired at the London office, and they said they knew nothing of the matter. He looked at me unbelievingly.

Life for our people in exile in Africa is hard and very dangerous. Back in the life of luxury we led in London, I thought of them constantly, those people in exile in Africa – from our beloved president Oliver Tambo to the youngest freedom fighter – who live seven days a week in the struggle, deprived of their families and of every single comfort.

· *13* ·

Joan Amelia Cranko – Joan A. Sachs – Joan A. Weinberg – Alison Weinberg – Alison Berg – Joan Alison Weinberg. A portrayal of my big sister's life and her changing image. It never changed really. She was always searching, when it seemed to me she had found: always felt inadequate, and who, I ask myself, could ever have been more adequate than she? Always slimming, her figure was trim; always reading self-improving books, and what could a Dale Carnegie teach her? She meditated, did yoga and read Chinese and Indian philosophers. To me she was wise, sympathetic and loving.

She viewed the world as a perfect, magical place, and thought the imperfect thing was herself. She tried all her life to change herself. She never knew how nice and how beautiful she was. And perhaps because of her – because as a child she had encouraged me to love myself – I was her opposite. I thought I was OK and that the world was wrong. I wanted to change it.

I took her name changes in my stride up to the Alison. After all, the others were the devastating identity drops that all women went through on marriage. It was when she called herself Alison that I balked, and I could not, at first, remember not to say 'Joan'. She bore it with patience but one day said earnestly:

'Can't you *help* me?'

'With what? I can't take it seriously – you changing your name. What's Alison mean?'

'Look, Norm. It's serious. I know people joke about it. I don't want to be a Joan. I want to be an Alison.'

I could never get over it. I have always thought it much better to be a Joan than an Alison. But I realised then how serious and important it was to her and I never forgot to call her Alison (or Ali Pushka) after that – until she died. Then I thought of her as Joan.

Joan Amelia Cranko was the plump blonde baby with electric blue eyes and frizzy hair, and also the fat ungainly teenager, sometimes red-eyed, sunk in unhappiness, addicted to peppermint crisps, but more often bright and outgoing, with lots of boyfriends who bought her silver flapjacks – as powder compacts were called. She wrote hilarious stories, listened to 78s of the Ink Spots and Harry James and played boogie on Dad's Bechstein.

Joan A. Sachs was the young bride who left Durban with her piano-playing German dentist husband, Rolf, singing German songs in their Vauxhall car, to make a new life in a new town – Odendaalsrus. I sensed trouble early because he pulled the teeth she thought should be filled. But she was loyal to him – except that she advised me to go to another dentist. She wore a white uniform with a wide belt around her slimmed-down waist, peroxided her hair to a more dazzling blonde, and made friends with all the young couples. She joined the dramatic society, played bridge, gave birth to Robbie. She wouldn't let our mother touch him because she felt so bitter about her own babyhood.

I don't know how the Sachs marriage ended. I told Joan all my secrets – every tiny thing. But she was the big sister and she kept her unhappinesses to herself in case she should discomfort me.

When she married Norman it was a different ball game. He was in another class. He was big and warm and lovely. She loved him so much she gave up smoking – just like that!

'*How*?' I asked her wonderingly.

'He said we could get married on condition I stopped,' she said.

'Oh, hell, how could you let yourself be blackmailed like that?'

'I really love him, Norm.'

She believed in true love all her life – the Hollywood kind – but the men in her life disappointed her, although to me

241

they looked and behaved like film stars.

She bought lots of sheath dresses and black stockings and high-heeled shoes, put away the white cotton nighties – even though they were thin and had lace – and became svelte. I don't know what happened to the tiny diamond Rolf Sachs gave her as an engagement present – I think women used to have to return them when their marriages ended. Now she had a great big diamond, and new friends. A different class of bridge altogether – straight Acol.

They built a house with a swimming pool in a new suburb of Johannesburg. Norman put every conceivable gadget into the house. It was fully robotised before electronics. You could hear the baby cry through a plastic box, if you were sunning yourself at the pool, the phone rang everywhere, and Norman had a special machine under his pillow so that he could listen to music all night without disturbing Joan. They bought the latest fashion furniture – light sapele mahogany, with dramatic black and white curtains, and a six foot six bed. Joan was no more than five foot but Norman was over six foot tall. When Joan was pregnant with Tessa she lovingly crocheted hundreds of little squares with a bright blue border, sewed them all together and made a huge bedspread to fit the bed. Tessa was such a beautiful baby that my throat caught every time I looked at her. By then Joan had relented towards my mother for having all of us raised by cruel Nurse McGrath, and allowed her to cuddle Tessa. But after the birth Joan went into a deep depression, and it lasted for a couple of years.

As soon as she got over these troubles, she became pregnant again, and after Lindy was born she fell into an even greater depression. This lasted for about five years and Joan's marriage to Norman started to fall apart. Norman tried to patch it up and she stuck it out for many years because she didn't want her three children to have the chaos that we had had when our parents divorced.

When she got well, she wanted to be independent of Norman. Being a dental receptionist was all she was qualified for. Now she cast around for a way to earn her living. There was a dog

242

parlour for sale in a local suburb and she became enthusiastic about it.

'Dogs!' I said aghast. 'How can you spend your life with dogs?'

'Oh, Norm!' she said. 'It's a lovely little place in a new shopping centre. And I'll have my own life.'

'Why don't you read Marx?'

She laughed as if it were a joke. 'That's communism,' she said. 'Everybody doing the same thing. I couldn't bear that.' She had the warped South African view of Marxism and was frightened of the very thought.

'But I am a communist,' I said.

'Oh, well, but you're just growing up,' she said, as if it was a disease I'd grow out of.

It rested there. We never reconciled our views of the world. We accepted that we differed and never argued. I went on urging her to read Marx and she would send me her latest philosophical discovery, usually concerning how to change oneself from within.

Norman bought her a station wagon with cages in the back. He did the books and she became a society dog-parlour owner with a very nice line in rhinestone collars. Ladies brought their poodles for different styles of haircut and for rinses in shades of pink and blue. Sometimes she got the cuts mixed up and did Mrs Cohen's dog pink with shaved legs and Mrs Grant's blue with puffed out ankles, and then she got into trouble with the clients and became quite upset. She shampooed Rhodesian ridgebacks, Alsatians and other big fierce dogs, of whom she was rather frightened. She worked very hard, expanded the business and sold rabbits and goldfish. She changed her name to Alison when she fell in love with Howard – a six-foot shiny blonde WASP.

She didn't think much about it when she left Norman. She just upped and went. Howard worked for a big American company, he was rich and she didn't have to bother about the practical side of life. She met him and his wife Marge playing bridge. Norman and Marge were rather upset and I thought it

243

would have been very neat if they both got together as well. But they didn't.

American companies don't like their executives getting divorced. Howard was sent to their London office. Joan said he was being promoted; I suspected he was being punished. Joan was to follow, and then they would be married.

Steven and Amandla, still at school, and I were living in Hurstwood Court in Temple Fortune, north London, then and we were excited at the prospect of Joan/Alison coming to live in London. When Howard arrived in England, he came to see us and I was quite taken aback. He was *so* American! Over dinner with the kids he spoke to us about golf – golf was his passion. I couldn't believe it. But he also told us all how much he 'lurved' Alison and how hard it was on Marge. He painted a picture of the deserted Marge as if she'd been his mother. She had baked lots of apple pies, partnered him at bridge and acted as his caddie at golf, and generally seemed to have been a sort of adjunct to his passions. I started to get nervous for Joan/Alison. Before she arrived, he took me to see the St John's Wood flat he had rented. It had a sunken bed with sunken lights and a sunken bath in a sunken bathroom. Black and white. Underfloor c/h. Gold taps. I thought: Wonderful! But is it a place for living in? Alison was wildly delighted and showed it to me all over again, even the closet shelves that had smelly paper – a fruit smell that was supposed to keep clothes fresh. And she showed me the special sachets that came from America to keep your broeks smelling of oranges.

Alison was full of plans. There was talk of Howard being transferred to Tokyo – the American company apparently couldn't send him far enough, and it wasn't certain how long their London sojourn would last. She was dying to see London – all the places she'd read of and I'd written about. She wanted to shop at Harrods. Howard would have none of it. He wanted her at home in the flat. She phoned me one morning early:

'Norm, I can't stand it.'

'What?'

244

'He says he wants *different* kinds of canapés in the evening with his drinks. Marge always used to make *five* different kinds.'

'What's a canapé?'

'Oh, well, we call them snacks.'

'Tell him to *gey kush*. Tell him to go get stuffed with his snacks together,' I advised her.

'Oh, Norm! Be serious. I mean it. He wants me at home all day. He says he'll take me shopping on Saturdays. He won't buy me a car. I've got nothing to do. He suggested I knit him a jersey! He's made arrangements for bridge three nights every week with the most *dreadful* people. He only mixes with the Americans who work in his company! They're so *boring*. Last night I had to cook a meal before we played and it was a failure. I thought I'd try a new recipe. He got terribly *angry*! I felt awful. Norman used to say to people "Help yourself to one of our failures" and defend me but Howard started asking the couple to excuse *him*. Oh, God, what shall I do?'

'Come and see me. I won't go to work today. Come over and talk about it.'

'I can't. What if he phones?'

'It sounds as if you're more frightened of him than in love with him.'

'Don't be ridiculous.'

'Come over then.'

'OK, I'm coming. How do I get there?'

She came with her suitcase and she never went back. In a matter of weeks, Howard married his young blonde secretary and I heard they went off to Egypt where his American company sent him. Alison and I had an exciting holiday in London – I slung in my job to be with her and when we were both flat broke she returned to Johannesburg. Before she left she'd airily told Norman she wouldn't be needing anything so he could keep all the furniture. The kids, including Robbie, who was Rolf's son, stayed with Norman as well.

She returned to South Africa broke, to build a new life. Dad helped her buy a partnership in a marriage bureau in the middle of town. Eventually it became her own. She rented a tiny one-bedroom flat in central Johannesburg, became Alison Berg, elegant and businesslike, and practised Canadian Air Force exercises. She got so wrapped up in bringing lonely people together – especially old ones – that she never made much money at it. She arranged for all her lonely hearts to meet and have Christmases together and she started a granny-sitting service for old lonely women. When she ran out of sitters, she went and sat with them herself. The *Rand Daily Mail* published an article praising her social work. There was always a lonely person in her office. She offered them sandwiches and Postum and was so friendly and encouraging that her clients would walk out into the world with confidence.

Something is dripping on the bathroom floor. I try to focus. Wobbling, I pull the towel from the rail and hug it to me. Then I remember that a long time ago I was going to wipe the blood with it. It is coming from me. I came into the bathroom because I must have some water. I kneel over the bath, hang my head under the tap. Switch on the tap. The water flows over my head. There is a searing pain in my jaw and my left leg is stiffening. I am looking into the bath water, pinking with my blood. My throat is dry and I cannot seem to swallow. There is a warm place under my head but my body is cold, very cold. A door slams shut. The cold is reaching up into the place in my head. The towel falls into the bath. I cannot close my mouth properly – nothing meets.

The doorbell rings. Damn! I am just getting ready to go out – I have an appointment with the dentist. I hop to the door, putting on my other shoe as I reach it, and open the peephole. Oh, hell! What do *they* want now? Steven is in solitary – no, he is on the plane now. Close the peephole and unbolt the locks on the door.

They come in shouting at me. I run backwards in terror, into the bedroom. They come after me, hitting out. I feel a terrible blow on my head . . . Something drips on the bathroom floor. I try to focus. Wobbling I pull the towel from the rail and hug it to me. Then I remember a long time ago . . . The doorbell rings . . .

Steven is in solitary. No, he's on the plane . . . I run backwards in terror, into the bedroom . . . The doorbell rings . . .

I sit up. All is quiet. I am in London, in Highbury, in my familiar bedroom. All is comfortable. I switch on the bedside light. I am still frightened. Not all the barbiturates, Mogadons or tremazepams prevent this recurring nightmare. Is it a nightmare or is it what really happened to my sister Joan/Alison, being replayed through my brain somehow? The doctor said time would deal with my shock at Joan's murder. And time *has* helped. Sometimes I go for several hours without thinking about her. Now my jaw doesn't go into muscular spasm, useless, as her broken jaw must have been. Now I do not feel a choking sensation and sometimes when the doorbell rings I do not spin into panic. Sometimes I can even talk about her – not often. When I do, I feel very brave and then I usually slip away somewhere to calm myself. Occasionally, now, I do not get a feeling of terror when I reach for my towel in the bathroom. I am ashamed of my 'nightmare' and ashamed of not taking mourning in my stride. Psychiatrists, I am sure, have a name for it.

She phoned me from Johannesburg on 6 January 1982.

'Oh, Norm! You have to be very brave. I've got some awful news for you. Steven has been detained.'

I felt my scalp tighten and I must have shown signs of distress because Carol, who was working next to me, jumped towards me. But to myself I sounded calm, quite businesslike. 'What happened?'

'It was after a visit to David this morning. He was waiting to be let into the jail and he had his notebook and pen, as usual, to note anything David wanted. He went in and after the visit he went back to Robbie and Ruth's flat. They came and arrested him this afternoon – they said he'd been drawing pictures of the jail.'

'What do you mean?'

'Hello! Norm! Are you all right?' The line started to go fuzzy. Carol took the phone and I heard her speaking to my sister for a long time.

'What do you want to do?' Carol asked me when she put the phone down.

'Get Amandla!' I began to cry.

I waited, paralysed, until Amandla would arrive from college.

Each December since he was sixteen, Steven had spent his holiday in South Africa in order to visit David. I had had to fight down what I thought were irrational fears for Steven. I felt I was being neurotic when, year after year, I telephoned the British Foreign Office and arranged with them to have his plane met and to keep tabs on him. Now, for the first time in nine years, I had not done so. Steven, politically aware, had never been politically active. As a boy of thirteen he had wanted to join the Anti-Apartheid Movement and our ANC comrades had advised him against it. 'Your mother and Amandla are both involved,' they'd said. 'Your duty is to be free to visit your dad. That's your political task.' And so he'd stayed out of everything. TASS, David's union in England, had formed the TASS Kitson Committee when David went to jail, and they undertook to pay Steven's fares to see David.

I could not bear the thought that those bastards had got Steven. Perhaps they had arrested him to get at David. Recently our letters had either not reached him or had been terribly delayed. They were trying to break David. There were hundreds of detentions at that time and Neil Aggett, a doctor and trade unionist, was killed in detention within days of Steven's incarceration. The South African authorities were making the ridiculous allegation that Steven was attempting to arrange a breakout of the political prisoners. I felt icy with fear.

Amandla came in and put her arms around me.

'We've got to get him out,' I said, crying into her shoulder. 'We've got to do something to get him out quickly!'

'We will, Mom,' she said. 'Don't you worry, we will.' She was angry and her anger gave me a boost. She brushed tears from her face and we sat looking at each other, drawing strength, as we always did, from each other. Once she'd arrived things started moving. She and Carol were a formidable team, and they started directing operations. I telephoned the London ANC office to

248

give them the news and ask what we should do, but there was no one in authority there who could tell me. They said someone would phone me back – but no one did. Amandla telephoned Mike Terry, the executive secretary of the Anti-Apartheid Movement. He said that the movement was not geared to 'this sort of thing over an individual'. She telephoned Ken Gill of TASS, who said that they were a trade union, unable to respond instantly to a campaign of this type, but would participate in whatever we decided to do.

We felt the only hope for both Steven and David was to create an uproar of protest in England that would embarrass the South African authorities enough to force them to release Steven. The South African regime was extremely sensitive to pressure from Britain. They spent millions of rands duping British people about the conditions in South Africa. Only recently every MP in Britain had received a glossy book, depicting the virtues of the bantustan Venda. The production costs of this book were more than the total gross national product of Venda – where children died of starvation and the people were in dire need.

We sat around at my office thinking what to do. There were nine people on the staff at Red Lion Setters and we decided to form the Free Steven Kitson Campaign. From then on everyone at Red Lion Setters threw themselves into work to secure Steven's release.

'I'll phone Auntie Al back and get more information. Carol, if you and Gail could phone the press, Lizzie and Derek can phone trade unions and organisations. Kim can phone the Foreign Office. No, Mom, you just sit where you are for a while. There'll be plenty for you to do later . . . '

We made lists of everyone we could think of to draw into the campaign. Amandla called people to an emergency meeting and picket outside the South African embassy to protest against Steven's detention.

At this time I made a friend who was to stand by me with a loyalty that, in times of weakness, gave me the strength to carry on. Many left-wing groups came to us for their typesetting and that way I had met David Reed in the early seventies. His group, the Revolutionary Communist Group, believed that only if Ireland and South Africa were liberated could a socialist Britain be possible. They therefore supported the South African liberation struggle. David had a very clear political head and a magnetic quality of leadership. In a country like Britain, where competition to be *the* Marxist group has caused so many splits and factions, he drew a lot of fire from the left. But he was a brilliant Marxist-Leninist, and he proved a good friend.

The moment he heard of Steven's arrest, David came to the office to help and he, his wife Anne and their daughters, Susan and Helen, were to help our family from then on.

Amandla and I did not sleep for days. I remained suspended, in a deep state of shock, and all I could think was 'Get him out . . . get him out'. Those words kept drumming through my head. Amandla lived up to her name. She held me together, saw that I ate, sat with me in the bath, dealt with the phone calls, directed operations.

We held pickets outside South Africa House, got questions raised in the House of Commons and saw that articles and reports appeared in the newspapers. We appeared on television and on radio programmes. At this time Mark Thatcher went missing and there were letters in the *Guardian* comparing the fuss made over him and Steven.

We bombarded the Foreign Office in London to such an extent that they got their consul, Mr Miller, to telephone me from Johannesburg to tell me he had been to Pretoria, not to worry, Steven was fine. He would give me no details but confirmed that Steven was in solitary confinement.

'What do you mean, he's fine?' I asked. 'Don't you know solitary confinement is torture?'

'Mrs Kitson, I've seen Steven myself,' he said. 'I won't say he's altogether well. He's a bit pale, but you'd expect that, wouldn't you?'

'No,' I said. 'I don't expect my son to be pale. You should be creating merry hell,' I said. 'Steven is a British subject and he's being held for absolutely no reason.'

'We're negotiating on the matter at the moment, Mrs Kitson.

As soon as they've finished interrogating him, they'll let him go.'

'What do you mean "finished interrogating him"?' I asked. 'About what? You should be pressing them to bring him to court if he's done anything wrong, not condoning detention.'

I tried the man's patience. God save me from British diplomats for the rest of my life!

I knew very well what solitary confinement meant and I knew my son was being tortured. I said so when I was interviewed on BBC television news. They changed the BBC rules on interviewing after that because they said there was no proof that he was being tortured. However, I don't think anyone has emerged from detention in South Africa untortured.

I feared for my son. I knew that Steven was strong and, as he had not been involved in politics, had no information that would be useful to them. But he was ill-equipped to deal with the South African security police in detention, with the physical ill-treatment that detainees routinely undergo. He had grown up with the stories of David's and my detention and the horrors it gave us, and he had his own frightening experiences as a child in South Africa in the 1960s.

As it happens, his interrogation was worse than even I imagined. A friend in London had asked him to obtain some music cassettes by a South African group called Juluka. Seeing this word in his diary, his interrogators took it to be the name of a contact he was going to make. They wouldn't leave him alone about it. They punched him in his stomach and knocked his head against the wall. His nose bled profusely. They made him stand for hours, throwing buckets of cold water over him and, when he sagged, threatened to throw boiling water over him. They assured him he would serve a sentence longer than David's.

Before Steven was sent to the interrogation cells, he was taken to a clinic for a medical examination. This terrified him. He knew full well that his interrogators were not interested in his wellbeing. The doctors at the clinic in Pretoria did not even ask why they had to examine Steven. Theirs was a routine job for

251

the security police – they wanted to gauge how much physical maltreatment his body could withstand. The evil role played by these apartheid doctors was exposed by Bronwen Murison in *World Medicine* (23 January 1982).

One of Steven's worst experiences was listening to the agonised screams of other prisoners being beaten up, and he witnessed one of these beatings on a black boy who could not have been older than fifteen. This sound was to torment him in the years ahead.

They tried to implicate Steven as one of five people who had planned the escape of three white political prisoners in 1979. He had never even met the other accused, three of whom were later to be imprisoned, charged with this offence.

My sister Joan went to visit the jail in Pretoria every day. She spoke to Colonel Malan, in charge of the case, insisting that they bring Steven to trial if they had anything on him, or release him. She took Steven clothes, toothbrush, books, food – none of which he was allowed to have – and every time she went to pester the military in control of Steven, she insisted on seeing higher and higher authorities. When she came back to Johannesburg she phoned me through the meagre news of whom she had seen and what they had said. She started making complaints that she was not allowed to see Steven. She employed a lawyer to make representations. She also realised the effect it would have on David and she visited him and comforted him as much as she could.

My mother was distraught at Steven's arrest. She was ill and could not travel to Johannesburg – and Joan did not think the family would have permitted her to do so. Joan tried to comfort our mother, chatting to her on the telephone and trying to relieve her anxiety.

But Joan herself was anxious. She telephoned me twice or three times a day from Johannesburg and now and then her voice became unsteady with emotion. She had taken Steven on his visits to David in her car, and she knew better than anyone that he had done nothing.

Ever since I left South Africa in 1966, Joan had been David's main visitor, his sole, steady contact with the outside world. At a time when everyone was frightened and stayed away, when to show friendship and support to a banned, imprisoned or marked person was to endanger yourself, she befriended David. When the family, friends and even servants of the suspected were also detained, my sister Joan wrote letters complaining of prison conditions and lobbied for us. She did it first out of love for me and her deep sense of duty, and later I believe she did it for love of David. As the political prisoners were slowly upgraded over the years, the number of visits and letters they were allowed increased, from one every six months to one every three. Then one a month. When they were upgraded to A, the prisoners were allowed two half-hour visits and three 500-hundred word letters a month.

For fifteen years Joan regularly travelled from Johannesburg to Pretoria for a thirty-minute visit to David, at first taking with her his elderly mother and father and then, after Chris Kitson died in 1978, just Fred. She badgered our friends to take the other visits when David was allowed more than one a month, kept a roster, if necessary drove them all the way up to Pretoria. Then she telephoned us in London to let us know how David was. She saw to it that he was never without a visit. When the prisoners were allowed to see films, she sewed a curtain-screen for them.

From the earliest days in 1964 she had helped us. She was one of the women who each day shopped, cooked and delivered meals to the hundreds of detainees. When John Matthews was detained – he was number four accused in David's trial – she delivered meat to his house every week. She looked after David's father, having him over to her office for chats and to lunch or dinner at weekends. Fred loved her.

Six days after Steven's arrest, on 12 January, Joan phoned to say that he had been released and had been escorted to Jan Smuts airport where he'd got on a plane to London. Steven had been popped like a pip from an orange because of the demonstrations and representations of British people. He would be arriving the following morning.

I could not believe it was my son who emerged from the plane at Heathrow. As I took him in my arms, he sagged and wept on my shoulder. He was pale, thin and looked tormented, with red-rimmed eyes.

The press had been asking us for news, and immediately they heard of his release, members of the Free Steven Kitson Campaign arranged a press conference at the offices of Red Lion Setters. David Reed took us to a hotel to have breakfast and to give Steven a chance to wash before meeting the press. I had ten minutes alone with Steven.

'They wanted to know who was in the ANC in London, Mom. I'm sorry. I'm so sorry, I cracked.'

'What did you tell them?'

'I didn't know exactly who any ANC members were. But I knew that Shireen was. That's what I told them. And I said you were.'

We were staying at Shireen's house in Hampstead. 'That information is not secret,' I said. 'You did nothing wrong.'

But, like most detainees who have been undermined by constant questioning and belittling, Steven felt guilty. At his press conference that morning when questioned why he had drawn and photographed the prison, he replied that he had done it so that his grandchildren would see where his father had been held.

'What grandchildren?' I asked him afterwards. 'What were you talking about?'

'They didn't believe me, Mom. I just had my usual notebook in case I had to remember any messages from Dad. They kept saying I'd drawn and photographed the jail. They didn't believe me. I had to admit it. And then they asked me *why* I had done it. When I couldn't answer they punched me. I couldn't think of what to say – and I knew I had to say something quick. So I said that – about grandchildren.'

'But you're out now,' I said. 'You didn't have to say that this morning. These were British media people, not interrogators.'

Frowning, Steven looked at me. Then he suddenly smiled. 'Oh, yes! But they sounded just like interrogators asking me all those questions, didn't they? Part of me doesn't know I'm out of that cell. All the way in the plane I was scared to fall asleep. I was frightened if I did, I'd wake up and find myself back in the cell.'

'You'll be OK, Stevie,' I said. 'You need some rest and some food.'

It was to be many months before my son was his normal self.

The day after Steven's release, on 13 January 1982, my sister Joan was found battered to death, her jaw broken, her head over a bath full of blood, clutching a towel. Blood all over the flat. No sexual attack. No forced entry. She had a dentist's appointment that afternoon. They said it was suicide, until I made it known that I had taped our conversation a few hours before her death. Then they said it might be murder but that they didn't know she had anything to do with David Kitson.

The case has never been solved. The police put forward a variety of theories and said an arrest was imminent. They contradicted their own statements to the press. They tried to smear her. They said they had seized 'documents' from her flat, implying that she had been politically active. We never found the autobiography that she had been writing, or her history of the Cranko family and their black forebears that she had been working on. Just one poem.

> Barren of events –
> rich in pretensions
> —my earthly life.
>
> Obscurity – my real name.
> Wholly unto myself
> I exist.
> I wrap no soul
> in my embrace.
> No mentor worthy
> of my calibre have I.
>
> I am all alone
> between failure
> and frustration.
> I am the red thread
> between nothingness and eternity.

The inquest was delayed. We were told the coroner had a cold. When seven months later it was held, the Johannesburg *Star* reported, 'An unknown person was responsible for the death of Mrs Joan Alison Weinberg, the sister-in-law of political prisoner David Kitson. Mr C.J. Botha found the cause of death was "multiple injuries and haemorrhage: asphyxia due to pressure on the neck". No arrests had been made and no murder weapon found.'

· 14 ·

For two years Amandla, Steven and I had been increasingly worried about David, who had been transferred, with the other political prisoners, to death row in the Pretoria prison.

Three political prisoners had escaped from the maximum-security section of Pretoria Local prison in 1979. In revenge, the authorities transferred the other white political prisoners, including David, to the maximum-security jail – we were told, to the section for the criminally insane. It turned out that the jail they were now being held in was for prisoners condemned to death. An average of two people a week were hanged a few yards away from their cells. The South Africans were efficient about their hangings – there was room for six people to hang at any one time. This prison was built into the side of a hill, freezing cold, and had no heating. The cells were tiny. The jail had no facilities for long-term prisoners. The South African attitude is that the lives of those who are awaiting death are going to be short, so they may as well be brutish.

In all his years in jail, David had never complained, but in January 1981 we got a hint of how bad things were. He wrote:

The current cold seems to have contracted the operative parts of the bird of happiness into immobility, but it will warm up soon, I keep telling myself.

And in July 1981:

I have given up running for the nonce. It's just too cold for me out there in the morning. Mind you, it's not much warmer in here.

In October 1981, he wrote:

We have been having a dreadful time, weather straight from Antarctica, seemingly never-ending...

257

As soon as she heard of the transfer to death row, my sister Joan had begun to agitate for David's removal. And I started putting pressure on the Foreign Office in London to get them moved.

The first phone calls were encouraging.

'There's really nothing to worry about, Mrs Kitson,' one gentleman in the Foreign Office told me. 'They're being moved within three months. They're just fixing up the jail where the prisoners escaped – making it safer, you know – and then David and the others will be moved back to Local where there are proper facilities.'

'Three months from when?'

'Well, they haven't given a date, Mrs Kitson. They don't respond well to pressure, you know. But they have said definitely three months. I think we can take their word for it. We don't want to upset them.'

'Why? They've upset me a lot.'

Polite diplomatic laugh. 'Yes, well, I understand how you must feel. But I assure you . . . I think a *little* patience. We've been assured that Mr Kitson is in excellent health.'

'What state of health is Mr Mandela in?'

Another laugh. 'Mr Mandela is not a British subject, Mrs Kitson.'

'He's a citizen of the world, you know. He will no doubt be the next South African prime minister – then you'll look a bit sick never having stood up for him, won't you? And anyway, is David British? Do you recognise David as British? Why haven't you given him a British passport? Why don't you claim him as British? You people go on about people like Sakharov and Walesa, because it suits your rotten political purpose. But what about *British* David Kitson? None of you make statements or TV documentaries about him. Why?'

'I'll pass on what you have said, Mrs Kitson.'

I had to be content with that. After four months had passed, I phoned the Foreign Office again.

'We've been in touch with them *today*, Mrs Kitson. And we've been assured that the prisoners will be moved within three months.'

'But I was told that a few months ago.'

'Ah, yes. Well, they had a few problems with the rebuilding, we understand. But things are going smoothly now and it is with some confidence that we tell you that we anticipate the move soon.'

This had gone on every three or four months through 1980, 1981 and the beginning of 1982.

There were various changes in staff throughout this period, but no change in the placatory, smug sounds which emanated from the Foreign Office. There was a period of about six months when I did not telephone them. I felt so impotent whenever I had one of these mindless conversations. So they phoned me.

'I thought I would telephone you, Mrs Kitson, to let you know we have been making progress in the matter of Mr Kitson's removal from Pretoria Central.'

'You mean from the prison for the condemned – why can't you people call a spade a spade?'

'Yes, well, if you will just give me a chance . . . '

'Just get to the point, will you. What's the progress?'

'We anticipate with a fair amount of assurance that Mr Kitson is going to be moved within three months.'

'Is only he being moved? What of the others?'

'We are not at liberty to discuss the other prisoners.'

'I see. And what makes you confident that this promise will be met?'

'Oh, we have been assured! We have been in close touch with the authorities there.'

'Yes? Well, let me know when the move takes place. I'm not happy to have my hopes raised only to be dashed every time I speak to you people.'

'A little patience, I think, Mrs Kitson. Of course we know it's hard for you. But a little patience . . . '

'It's not hard for me. It's hard for David and the others with him. I think you people are utterly heartless phoning me like this.'

In May, feeling more wretched than ever, and overworked at Red Lion Setters, I decided to get out of London for the

259

Whitsun weekend. Steven was working at Rolls-Royce in Bristol and he invited me to go up and visit him there.

On Whit Sunday the telephone rang in the house and Steven's flatmate called, 'It's for *you*, Norma!'

'Me?' I said, mystified. No one knew where I was. I picked up the receiver.

'Ah, Mrs Kitson,' said the familiar drippy voice of British officialdom from the Foreign Office, 'I thought it would be worth getting hold of you because I have some rather good news about Mr Kitson.'

'He's been moved?' I asked excitedly.

'Well, no. Not yet. But I've been assured that the move will take place within three months.'

'How dare you telephone me here – how did you get this number? How dare you persecute me with your rubbish?' I shouted.

'Ah, Mrs Kitson, your anxiety is understandable. But I thought it was only right to let you hear the good news.'

'You look here,' I said. 'I've stood nearly three years of torment from you people. If he's *not* moved within three months this time, I'm going to mount a nonstop picket outside South Africa House until he and all the others *are* moved. I don't know what you get out of this sort of behaviour, but this time I'm going to call your bluff and show the world the type of complicity that you people are engaging in.'

Our experience over the years had shown that when there were campaigns for the prisoners, there were direct positive results. When activity died down, conditions for them worsened. Within three weeks of the 1969 Whitsun march from Oxford to London organised by the Ruskin Kitson Committee, which had formed at Ruskin College in 1964 to campaign about David's imprisonment, the prisoners had been upgraded to A, which meant three letters and two visits a month.

In response to the prisoners' campaigns inside the jails for study facilities, better conditions and upgrading, we had rallied people, held demonstrations, spoken at meetings, constantly putting on pressure to help the prisoners' demands. When

Steven's arrival after detention, 1982.

ANC President Oliver Tambo and Steven.

Nomzamo (Winnie) Mandela and Amandla in Brandfort, 1983.

Carol Brickley and freedom fighters in Zimbabwe, 1981.

Nelson Mandela went to jail in 1962, black prisoners were not permitted to wear shoes, and they had to campaign for basic essentials. Political prisoners had so few rights in jail that they had to campaign to see the jail regulations under which they were being held, to have books, to have visits and letters, to get magazines and newspapers, news broadcasts, music – and remission. Whenever we managed to join or mount a campaign, there was some result, sometimes tiny and seemingly insignificant, but always a result. The South African regime was forced to make little adjustments in the face of Western criticism.

These small gains – better food, a film once a week, better clothing – seemed paltry to many hard-pressed campaigners in Britain, who could not gauge whether their efforts were any use, but they made a difference to the lives of our prisoners. When the prisoners were upgraded, it meant a remarkable improvement in the quality of their lives. Just as importantly, these campaigns made more British people aware of what was going on in South Africa and brought them into activity against apartheid.

Some people believed that it might be dangerous to take up the question of political prisoners – the authorities might retaliate and prisoners would suffer for it. Yet time and again we heard both from released prisoners and from jail visitors that the prisoners wanted those on the outside to do everything in their power to agitate for better conditions, remission and release.

In January 1982, the Free Steven Kitson Campaign had brought hundreds of people into anti-apartheid activity. SATIS, with the support of TASS, the Anti-Apartheid Movement and the ANC, had been urging us to wind up the campaign – we had won massive support in the country but it was outside their control. Now they wanted us inside the Anti-Apartheid Movement. TASS offered to pay the expenses of the campaign. Steven was free and Red Lion Setters had suffered a financial setback because so many of us had been concentrating on the campaign to the detriment of our clients' work. I was eager to get the business going properly again. But we did not want to lose the support of the campaign's members. Many of them were already in the Anti-Apartheid Movement but had never been assigned to a group. Many were disillusioned about the efficacy of the AAM local groups yet wanted to give solidarity to the South African struggle.

Before the closure meeting, Des Starrs of TASS and also the SATIS chair, exacted a promise from us that, if we wound up the campaign, members who wanted to work for political prisoners would be able to help in the TASS Kitson Committee. But after we wound up, Des explained TASS was only open to its union members and that SATIS did not accept individual members. Only national organisations could affiliate – if invited to do so. We faced the departure of many activists.

With assistance from the AAM, the members of the Free Steven Kitson Campaign formed the City of London Anti-Apartheid Group in January 1982. Members of the staff of Red Lion Setters formed most of the committee and our office became the Group's headquarters.

The Anti-Apartheid Movement had been set up at the request of Chief Albert Lutuli, then president of the ANC, to campaign in Britain on South Africa, but even after more than twenty years of existence, its membership was small, it had almost no influence or active support from any group of British people, and there was virtually no regular activity they could take part in. The Anti-Apartheid Movement was controlled by the chevra.

Under the auspices of SATIS, whose office was that of the Anti Apartheid Movement, the chevra held infrequent pickets outside the South African embassy. These were usually silent vigils – during which people stood around chatting socially. Singing and chanting by the demonstrators was discouraged. They failed to recognise that Britain in the eighties was not the same as Britain in the sixties or even the seventies. They looked upon the British police as their friends – with whom they, as middle-class whites, could always negotiate. As long as they stood there for an hour chatting, the South African embassy officials made little complaint. When young black youths began to join their pickets and were harassed or arrested by the police,

262

the chevra accused the youths of confrontationism, and refused to help defend them. When it looked as if a large number of black and white youths wanted to demonstrate against apartheid South Africa, they tried to drive them away from the pickets, sending their bully-boys to insult them, telling some British black youths that they were not really black because they were not from Africa, or that they were not allowed to sing 'our' liberation songs. Or, as they told a British black youth leader, 'We don't want you here.'

I had tried, without success, to get a hearing on the ANC political prisoners committee since 1979 to see what could be done about campaigning to move the prisoners from death row. In May 1982, after my letter to the Foreign Office threatening a nonstop picket outside South Africa House, I telephoned Ruth Mompati, ANC chief representative in London, to ask her permission to take the plan forward to City Group. She said it was an excellent idea and that she did not understand why there were not more frequent pickets of the embassy. She asked what I would do about the running of Red Lion Setters and how City Group could involve the numbers of people required. I said I would tell the staff at Red Lion Setters that I wanted extended leave, and to raise with City Group plans for mobilising the picket. Ruth was encouraging and said I should go ahead.

On her arrival in London at the beginning of 1982, Ruth Mompati had called an ANC general members' meeting and informed us she had been sent by ANC head office 'to solve the London Problem'. At first she created problems for the chevra. She felt none of their constraints. She sanctioned solidarity meetings, logistics collections, had no objection to any ANC member speaking in public, pushed aside bureaucratic objections in unit meetings, and generally operated in a way guaranteed to encourage anti-apartheid activity. After a couple of years, she was recalled to Lusaka.

Steven and Amandla were enthusiastic at the idea of a nonstop picket.

Steven said, 'I'm sure City Group will agree. People want to show in a direct way their detestation of apartheid. If we had a

263

day-and-night demonstration, it would be a focal point to express this feeling. We could get the trade unions involved, political parties, MPs. We could have the black, green and gold liberation colours flying outside the embassy. It would be great.'

'It would,' Amandla said. 'We could spend the months before starting the picket going to colleges and schools, mobilising, explaining through Dad's case the position of Nelson Mandela and all the others. If we went and told them about Dad, it would bring it home to people.'

'I think a good date to choose would be David's sixty-third birthday,' I said. 'That's when the Foreign Office say Dad will be moved. If he isn't, we'll be prepared to go ahead then. It gives us three months to organise. We'll have to do so much! It's terrifying. I don't know how I'll be able to last day and night.'

'We'll have to organise our times,' Steven said. 'Mom, you'll have to be there during working hours and go home every night for a good sleep. I'll have to go on working, and I'll be there overnight.'

'I'll have to give up my typing course,' Amandla said. 'I'll be free to be there most of the time.'

'It sounds terrifying,' I said. 'Let's see what the members feel.'

Red Lion Setters agreed that I could have extended leave. City Group was enthusiastic and people started thinking how to reorganise their lives to be on the picket. Planning and mobilising began.

A couple of months after Joan's death, her son Robbie visited David. My nephew phoned me anxiously.

'I thought I'd phone you, Auntie Norm. I don't want to worry you, but I went to see Uncle David and he can hardly talk. He's very sick and he's got a cough. It sounds like bronchitis. I asked them to let him see a doctor and they said they would, but I thought I'd phone you anyway in case there is anything you can do.'

There was nothing I could do.

'I *must* go and see him,' Amandla said. 'I don't see that we have a choice. We can't just leave Dad. No one in South Africa

264

has given us any news of him for months now. He can't say much in his censored letters and now Robbie has confirmed that Dad is ill. Auntie Joan isn't there to see to things. One of us *has* to go.'

Steven agreed. He had, since childhood, attended campaigns for the release of his father, but he had not joined the Anti-Apartheid Movement or any political organisation because he felt if he did he might not get a visa to South Africa. Now, after his detention, he was keen to take part in anti-apartheid activities. He was himself prepared to face further harassment and return to South Africa to visit David, but his visa application was refused. We were fearful and uncertain about Amandla's proposed visit. To date, she was the only one of our family who had not wound up in jail.

After much heart-searching, it was decided that Amandla would visit South Africa in March 1982, with Stanley Clinton Davis, Labour Party shadow spokesman on foreign affairs, and Hazel Selbourne, a friend from our earliest days in England.

Stanley Clinton Davis went with a double brief – to protect Amandla, and as our family lawyer. He tried to see David, with no success. He attempted to see ministers and to raise the question of remission. He was treated rudely by the regime's representatives and he complained vociferously about them. He managed to get the authorities to agree to let David have a British passport.

The visit was frightening for Amandla. She expected arrest and detention and we were relying on the outcry about Steven's frame-up earlier in the year to protect her. She found David's health poor and when she telephoned us in London, although she tried to allay our fears, we knew that she was upset and fearful.

The press had published her photograph and news of her visit and she was widely recognised. She received courtesies and surreptitious salutes from black people wherever she went. She visited Dr Nthato Motlana, veteran community leader and head of the Committee of Ten in Soweto, but did not attempt to seek out any political friends because she did not want to draw attention to anyone.

At a press conference on their return to London, Stanley Clinton Davis gave his vivid impressions of the horror that South Africa was. He roundly condemned the apartheid regime and went on to address many meetings in Britain to express his repugnance at the system in South Africa. When he was appointed European commissioner, Stanley never let the apartheid issue go. Had the Anti-Apartheid Movement had a person of this calibre on their team, its ranks would rapidly have swelled.

A CBS *Sixty Minutes* television team had been trying to make a documentary on Winnie Mandela. The South African authorities would not permit them entry to interview her, so they approached the London ANC office for material. None was forthcoming. As our family had been in the news – with Steven's arrest and Joan's murder – CBS asked me if they could film a documentary on me. ANC members are not permitted to have media coverage, write articles, speak at meetings or perform any public function without permission so I referred them to the London ANC office. In any event, it was up to the ANC to say which of our members should be documented. There were outstanding women in London at that time. Adelaide Tambo, the wife of our president, was here. So was Bongi Dhlomo whose husband had been on Robben Island and Esme Goldberg, whose husband was serving life, sentenced in the Rivonia trial with Nelson Mandela; Eleanor Khanyile, whose husband William had been murdered in a raid on an ANC home in Matola. There were also young freedom fighters and students who had left after the Soweto uprising.

CBS's attempts to meet anyone from the London ANC proved fruitless and they returned to me saying that unless they could start filming immediately – delays in trying to get permission had used up most of their scheduled time – no programme on South Africa would be made at all.

I telephoned the ANC chief representative, Ruth Mompati, and she told me to go ahead.

On Easter Sunday the CBS seventeen-minute television film was shown in the United States to an audience of 60 million. As

266

a result, I was asked by the All People's Congress and Workers' World, two American organisations, to visit the United States to address meetings.

At the London ANC office, Ruth Mompati gave me a letter of introduction to the chief representative in the United States. Ruth arranged for Hilary Rabkin of the ANC political prisoners committee to supply me with badges, leaflets and speaker's notes to get support for the picket in the US.

The tour went well. The meetings I spoke at were packed. I saw little of America. I was flown from one city to the next and driven from meetings to television studios and radio stations. Sidney, Pauline and her husband Terry accompanied me.

I met only two kinds of American people. One lot was Cheryl-and-Hank. The Cheryls were model-thin, suntanned, usually blonde, over five-foot-six-inch women, who wore lots of thin gold chains around their necks and wrists. The Hanks, also suntanned, were over six foot four with big shoulders and each wore one gold ring. This group drove long, shiny tin cars very fast and spoke incessantly about the American depression which, they said, was caused by the Japanese. They felt President Reagan had given the American people back their fighting spirit which, they said, had been lost after Vietnam. It seemed to me that none of the Cheryl-and-Hanks recognised any other part of the world but the United States. At home they had freezers and electronic gadgets to open their garages and air-conditioning that suddenly blew at one without warning. Radios switched on automatically and their houses contained no books. Electronically primed garden sprinklers started squirting plants at dawn and dusk. They had bars where highballs, Cokes and every spirit was served. On top of the bar counters, computers perched, coughing out rolls of paper.

The other group of Americans I met were mostly Black, Puerto Ricans, Mexicans or American Indians. They were worried about whether their homes would be 'gentrified'. I thought this preoccupation odd – I'd love to have someone come in while I'm out and improve the interior of my home and gentrify it. But after a while I understood that 'gentrification'

267

meant that property developers, who have an eye on a street of dwellings as an investment, regularly cause fires to rows of rent-controlled houses. That gets rid of the tenants and then the developers build expensive condominiums on the burnt-out sites. The ex-tenants cannot, of course, afford to live in this new housing. In South Africa they do similar things, but with bulldozers. And they get similar results: a lot of people with nowhere to live. The parks in New York are full of people sleeping rough.

This second group came in all sizes, shapes and colours and were warm and hospitable. They shared takeaway meals on the run, offered me books, records and anything I admired. They wanted to 'roll back Reaganism' – they didn't think America needed a fighting spirit, not if it meant fighting everything progressive. They thought of Reagan as a cowboy film actor strayed into politics. They spoke about world recession, lived mainly in communities in poor housing and were discriminated against by white America.

At one meeting I addressed I met Dennis Banks, leader of the American Indian Movement. At his office in a private house the following day, we did a filmed interview together. People were crowding around to see and speak with him. He was so knowledgeable, kindly and magnetic that I thought of him as the Nelson Mandela of the United States. Dennis Banks was constantly harassed by the American authorities, and shortly after I left to return to England I heard that he was jailed.

In New York, the day before my return, I telephoned Amandla and Steven. Amandla was upset.

'Mom, I think there's trouble. I think the chevra are going to put the mockers on the picket.'

'Why?'

'There's a message for you to phone Ruth as soon as you get back. City Group has sent out the leaflets and invitations announcing the start of the picket to all the organisations, trade unions, MPs – everyone – and we've had some enthusiastic replies. I told Ruth that but she just said not to send anything else out until she's had a chance to speak to you.'

As soon as I arrived in London I phoned Ruth, to learn from

On the picket line: Vanessa Redgrave, Steven, me, Ian Mikardo, Amandla.

The picket line.

UB40 on the picket.

Sidney on the picket.

Joe and picketer.

the ANC office that she would be out of London until 'the end of August'. No one else was available or knew what she wanted me for. In desperation I arranged to see Sonia Bunting, head of the ANC political prisoners committee. She said we could go ahead with a family campaign for David, but not mention the other prisoners – that was the work of her committee. I said I could not separate David from the movement to which he was giving his life. Sonia arranged a meeting with Mike Terry of the Anti-Apartheid Movement. He said if I was campaigning only for David, the AAM could not participate in the picket. The AAM was set up for *all* political prisoners. It was catch-22.

Des Starrs of SATIS and TASS said he would never set foot on the picket and he never did.

The big four – ANC, AAM, SATIS and TASS – in synchrony, inexplicably pulled back at the last moment.

We went ahead. The nonstop picket started at one o'clock on 25 August 1982. City Group members lined up with newly painted placards, leaflets, petition forms and song sheets. Trade unionists came with their banners; MPs and party leaders addressed the demonstrators. There was singing and chanting. All the left groups came down, selling their newspapers, taking photographs, making speeches. UB40 and other pop groups played on the street. Poets and mime artists performed. Someone brought three chairs and Lord Gifford arranged with the police that we could have them there permanently for the elderly, sick, disabled or pregnant demonstrators.

When Ruth returned at the end of August she denied having given permission for the picket. 'Where are the minutes of the meeting you say took place, Comrade Norma?'

'I spoke to you on the phone first, Ruth, so there were no minutes. Then I met you in your office before I went to the States and we discussed all the plans for the picket. You gave me letters – everything I needed. There was a march and a demonstration in the United States on 25 August in solidarity with the picket. You must remember.'

'The office committee has no knowledge of this. You went ahead and planned it on your own.'

'No, I came to you for permission. And you gave it.'

'I'm only an individual.'

'No, you're the chief representative of the ANC in London. I did not approach individuals.'

'Well, what's the trouble, anyway? You're on the picket.'

'The trouble is that people in prominent positions are being telephoned and told that the ANC does not support the picket and they shouldn't go to it.'

'I know nothing about that. I'll investigate it.'

Back on the picket, MPs, councillors and trade unionists came to tell me about calls they had had from members of the ANC telling them not to attend. Panicked, I tried to get a hearing on the ANC political committee. Instead they wrote me a short letter saying they did not like the wording on some of the leaflets.

I wrote back, 'Which wording? Please give me guidance. Please, can I have a meeting to discuss all this?' But there was no reply.

When Joe fell in love with Renata on the picket, I shed a few tears. Joe had given up his TGWU (Transport and General Workers Union) job to run the picket. He said to me when he came down to Trafalgar Square on the fifth day:

''Kin hell, you Kitsons are living on this 'kin pavement day and night. You'll all be 'kin dead in another week. I'm here to relieve you. From now on, I'll be here day and night.'

A mate of his, Phil, who had been in the British Army and wore fatigues to the picket, joined, and the two of them ran a tight ship.

At first we were a thin line of City Group members and friends of our family, but soon people passing by, students from colleges, schools and dole queues joined us, and stayed. Many came as shy individuals, knowing little about South Africa. Amandla's powerful voice rang out, chanting slogans and calling on people to sign the petition. Steven and I taught liberation songs, and soon we became a family.

Ruby fell in love with Chris, our City of London Anti-

Apartheid Group secretary, and then with Dale. Everyone fell for Colette because she was so caring. Richard fell for John in the SWP from the Central Poly and then for Mark, a punk. Yvonne, only fifteen years old, from a care home, and Maddie, a white Rasta woman, fell for Steve. I fell for Eddie, a member of the Revolutionary Communist Group, and Mary, from the British CP, did too. Sam and Simon from a North London college fell for Amandla and we all fell for the Greenham women. I think there was a point where life was so hard on that pavement outside South Africa House that we all fell for each other. We were keeping each other going, feeding each other, protecting each other from the police and the weather, welcoming guests who came to picket for an hour or two, fighting for our viewpoint, so, although there were so many of us, we were a real family. If, for any reason, Billie Wells, Nick, Mandy, Sharon or Diane didn't come to the picket, we'd get worried and ask each other if we thought they were OK. Like any family, we cared and we had a common cause – to demonstrate against apartheid South Africa and to move the political prisoners from death row to conditions where they could survive.

When Carol came down to the picket from Red Lion Setters, which she was running in my absence, she brought us leaflets and placards. She was well loved and had been elected convener of City Group. Everyone would stop to chant, 'Viva Carol, our convener. No one tougher, no one meaner. Have you ever been to see her? Viva! Viva! Carol.' Everyone went to Carol for help. She was our rock.

At first I was scared by many of the young people, with their spiky hair and studded belts and shaved heads. I had never mixed with groups of young people and I was even more frightened by those who wore fashionable clothes and make-up. But as we got to know each other – the animal liberationists, CNDers, young liberals, ecologists, graduates, punks and working people in their jeans and jackets, the fears that many of us felt for each other went, and in that process we drew together. For the first time I realised how important it was to get to know people of different generations. The Pickies in their sixties and

271

seventies petitioned and sang with everyone else and a respect grew among us. Relationships formed across the age barriers. At first, most youngsters called me Mrs Kitson. After a while, many called me Mum, and then some began to call me Comrade Norma. The word 'comrade' came with difficulty. For many of them it was a new, alien word, considered very un-English, with no place in their everyday relationships. As the days passed, we were on first-name terms.

There were passionate arguments on the picket. The police were harassing the demonstration, arresting us haphazardly, and the Pickies voted in a set of rules. These were always hotly debated and were re-voted each evening. Armed struggle or passive resistance was the big question for a number of the Pickies. Many demonstrators became vegetarians. I was educated by the students, animal liberationists, ecologists and the conservationists. I had never met so many unemployed, unhoused people of all ages and I learned social manners from them.

There were times when I felt people came to picket just to get a meal or shelter under our umbrellas, but this did not worry the youngsters. They gave food and comfort to anyone who wanted it. They welcomed everyone, whether they stayed five minutes or hours. My unconscious, which I discovered had accumulated a series of scales of means-testing and grading of people by their clothes, manners, age, education and demeanour, was challenged. At the beginning of the picket I had automatically chosen older people or those with political experience to steward and keep the discipline. But young people soon claimed responsibility and became the mainstay of the demonstration.

But at first the main organising was done by me and Joe. I didn't think he was the type to fall in love – not when I met him. 'Bloody bourgeois 'kin concept in'it?' he'd said. 'All these kids dying of love and romance. Saving their sandwiches for some green Pickie who's only been here a few hours. 'Kin stupid. 'Kin middle-class.'

'Oh, be kind to them, Joe,' I said. 'They don't *have* to come and stand out here in the rain getting harassed by the cops.

272

They're good kids.'

But no one was kinder than Joe, with his tough exterior and brusque manner. He was strict with everyone except me and the old campaigners. He was respectful to our regular over-sixties Pickies – Rene Waller, Joe Marcus, Vera, Daphne and, of course, our oldest City Group member, Frank Sully, who was eighty-three and who came down to hold the banner for hours.

No matter how tired the youngsters were, when the police came around at 6 am and started kicking their heads – sticking out of the sleeping bags – Joe would jump out of his, stand up, shake his hair out of his face, and shout, 'Wakey, wakey, you lot. 'Kin get up, *now*!' If anyone didn't respond instantly, he and Phil would go and pull them, eyes blinking, to a standing position, before the police had a chance to make any arrests. Then he'd stand them in a line and give the day's orders. 'Right, you 'kin lot. We want four volunteers to go to Harry's for teas. You, Kim, there. You look in the bucket and see if there's enough money for sandwiches. Then you lot can have early 'kin breakfast.' (Late breakfast arrived with the bakers' union delivery at about seven o'clock: sixteen loaves of brown and sixteen loaves of raisin bread.) When the volunteers had put their hands up, he'd send them off and continue. 'Right! Keep that line *straight* now. I want four volunteers off to the launderette to wash all the sleeping bags. What's the matter with you 'kin people? Get your ruddy hands *up*! Right, then, off with you lot. Phil, you sort out four of them to get going with the broom and dustpan and get this bloody place cleaned up.' And Phil's team would sweep the blue tarpaulin which marked our territory.

Joe organised four people to get signatures from the public on our petition, two to hand out leaflets and someone to take round the Picket Book. Everyone who came onto the picket signed in every day. When he had given his morning orders, he'd sit on one of the three chairs in our 'lounge'. Steven, Richard, Billie or Charine would start the morning singing with 'Mandela Says Fight For Freedom'.

Coming up from the Charing Cross underground at eight

o'clock every morning, I could hear the singing, and above it Joe's voice: 'How many 'kin times do I have to tell you? When the thermos flasks and food get dropped in, put them in the kitchen area. Wait for Comrade Norma before we break for second breakfast. Right? We're a 'kin *group*, not a lousy load of rotten individuals. Right?' As soon as the Pickies caught sight of me they'd get the line to start a liberation song, and as I approached one of them shouted, 'Viva Norma Kitson!' and they responded, 'Viva! Viva!' Then I'd sit next to Joe and he would hand me a plastic cup of coffee and give me the night report.

'After you left at midnight, Maddie had a go at night security. She wanted to go off for a pee and said she didn't want no men accompanying her. A lot of the women don't like the rules. And they say the men are 'kin sexist. I've explained a hundred times to them what democracy means – that the rules are voted in by the majority and the rest just have to obey them or get out. I reminded her Frances got attacked by fascists when she went for a pee on her own. You can talk till you're blue in the face. We got a bunch of 'kin anarchists here, I can tell you.

'We had twenty-six sleeping over last night. Two sleeping bags short, so Phil and I sat up with security. We'll either have to send people away or get more sleeping bags. I'll leave you to do something about that. Security got the whole lot up singing when a bunch of fascists gathered near St Martin's at about three o'clock. There are full notes of police activity in the Picket Book – and Paul took a lot of photos when they started threatening to arrest us. Andy and Gordon were on the banner most of the night, relieved by Ivan and that young war resister, what's-'is-name, Alasdair. We got some visitors at 'kin two o'clock. A jazz band came over to play for us after they'd finished their gig. We all enjoyed it – and then a discussion got going about violence. There were some Young Communist Leaguers here and some Workers Revolutionary Party kids, not to mention a women's libber, those two Catholic girls and of course our regular lot. I think young Matt clinched it all when he told everyone about the bantustans. These kids are really

274

getting on top of things. The visitors ate the leftovers from the meal Cranks delivered. So the food's all gone. I'm going to have a wash, OK? You all right?' Joe wore the chief steward's red armband like a decoration, and he handed it to me.

Soon all the regular Pickies were organising, and we had fifteen-year-olds chief-stewarding. Feeling the need to give more tangible support, the youngsters held a social at the Adelaide Centre and raised £200 for the ANC youth section.

They became knowledgeable about the South African struggle and its leaders, gave speeches through a megaphone to the public passing by, organised street meetings, sent delegations to the Labour Party and trade union conferences, and every day sent people off the picket to address meetings or give out leaflets in schools and colleges.

Joe looked worried one morning when I arrived. 'Some white bloke saying he was from the ANC came down late last night and told the kids not to sing ANC songs,' he said. 'Quite hostile, he was. Don't understand it. Must be a boer. But I thought we'd better wait for you before doing anything, so Amandla and the other bleeders made up their own songs. Here they are.' He passed me a sheet of paper.

I'll give you One O
The people's Freedom Charter – O
What is your One O
One is worker's unity, and ever more shall be so.

Two, two the shield and spear
Freedom in South Africa.

Three, three the Black, Green and Gold
Four for the years of the Treason Trial
Five for the arms of Congress
Six for the letters of AFRIKA!
Seven days a week in struggle.
Eight – the Rivonia heroes
Nine for the women in August.
Ten for the points of the Charter

275

It's been a hard day's night
And I've been shouting like a frog
It's been a hard day's night
I should be sleeping like a log
But when I look up at you [the South African embassy]
And see the things that you do
I know I'm doing what's right.
When you're gone, everything's going to be right.
Till you're gone, we will just stand here and fight – fight!

Way down south – in Africa
I mean south – South Africa
The system there is apartheid
Based on a racist state
With apartheid – you have racist laws
With apartheid – you have fascist wars
So come on people – let's unite!
This is one struggle – one fight!

'They're good,' I said.

'So what are we going to do about the freedom songs then?'
Joe asked.

'There's no ban on songs. Let them sing whatever they like,' I
said. Joe looked worried. We had been asked not to wear ANC
colours, not to mention Nelson Mandela. Young men who had
escaped conscription in the South African army and formed a
war resisters' group in England had become a strong force on
the picket. After a few weeks they came to tell me that they had
been threatened if they went on coming to the picket their
papers to remain in England would not be granted. I could
never work out the connection – which, one after another, they
repeated to me with such regret. Most of them left, one or two
stayed.

While the chevra in London did everything they could to
switch off support for the picket, messages acclaiming our
demonstration came from Africa and from South Africa.

The picket peaked every day from five o'clock as people
joined us after work and passers-by were petitioned and
leafleted and addressed. By seven o'clock we were weary and sat

down on the pavement. A discussion would take place with everyone crowding round. From this grew the Pavement University. The Pickies voted in Nelson Mandela as chancellor, and chose freedom fighters in South Africa as their board of governors in absentia. Rules were adopted: anyone could put their name and subject forward, lectures would be voted in by a show of hands, each person present having one vote. Every 'lecturer' would receive a degree in pavement philosophy. A chair was elected each evening. Speeches should be not more than ten minutes so that two or three lectures could take place every evening and discussions held. People rushed to put their names down to speak at the Pavement University. ANC leaders came to address the university. Lawyers, MPs and councillors put their names down. Most of the Pickies wanted to speak. When Tony Benn MP addressed the picket, the audience was so large we had to move into Trafalgar Square.

Four weeks into the picket, it was decided to hold a rally at Conway Hall. Not knowing what support we would get, the Pickies, liaising with Carol and the City Group committee, invited speakers from nearly every political party and group. Our platform spanned from the right of the Labour Party to the left of the Left. The main speakers were young Pickies who had never addressed the public before.

The picket grew. One hundred and ninety-six MPs had signed an Early Day Motion before the start of the picket. The motion read:

This House calls on the Government of South Africa to provide immediate remission of sentence to Nelson Mandela, Walter Sisulu, Ahmed Kathrada, David Kitson and other political prisoners who, in most instances, have been imprisoned for many years.

Stanley Clinton Davis, Michael Foot, Roy Hattersley, Denis Healey, Tony Benn – Labour MPs came every day. The Pickies tried to ensure that an MP or VIP would be on the picket because this often stopped the police harassment.

Lawyers offered to help with the defence of those arrested. A doctor volunteered his services. Kevin, an accountant, became our treasurer and Richard was elected our cultural attaché and everyone submitted their stories and poems to him and groups performed sketches and plays on the picket.

Colleges and unions pledged to attend every week. The Fire Brigades' Union made a line in front of picketers being threatened with arrest. 'They'll have to take us first,' said a fireman. The Electricians' Union offered to provide us with underpavement central heating.

'How will we pay for it?' Kim asked naively.

'Don't you worry your head about that,' the electrician said. 'We'll go in nifty and wire you up to South Africa House. Then they'll pay for it.'

The staff at Caseys, the local hamburger joint, gave us free hamburgers. The staff at Dixons gave us free rolls of film. Harry's tearoom gave us early morning teas. Cranks gave us a feast of health food each evening. The people who worked and lived around Trafalgar Square became our life-support system. They passed each day to and from work, dropping in food, thermos flasks of coffee, sleeping bags, umbrellas, clothes and books. Newspapers were delivered each morning. The Post Office Union delivered our mail addressed to 'The Picket Outside South Africa House'. Florists delivered bouquets and pot plants from well-wishers. Busloads of picketers from all over Britain came to spend their weekends on the picket. Visitors came from Italy, Sweden, Switzerland and the United States to spend the summer on the picket. Representatives from all over Africa came to join us.

In October there were only four days when it did not rain. That's when Renata joined us. She was a tall, stately German nursing sister. Joe succumbed to her charms. He stopped swearing. He got his hair cut. He went with Billie Wells to buy new clothes and then Joe bought Renata a bunch of flowers.

Amandla teased Joe. 'I thought love was a bourgeois concept. Who's fallen for Renata, then?'

'I thought you were meant to be giving out song sheets instead of standing around here gossiping. I thought you were writing your speech on the Freedom Charter for tonight's Pavement

University? Mind you, some chance *you* have to get picked if all you're interested in is me buying Renata a bunch of flowers.'

'I've got a good chance to get on tonight,' Amandla said. 'Look at the back of the Picket Book. There's only sixteen names down for tonight's university and one of them's Phil. He's put down to speak on antique clocks. No one's going to want that. I thought you said it was bourgeois to fall in love.'

Joe blushed deeply and ran his fingers through his unfamiliar short hair. He spoke so gently to Renata that Phil told me Joe had gone soft and that's when I shed some tears. We had all gone soft. We were all offering everything to each other. We took anyone who had no home into our homes. The Pickies pored over newspapers to find jobs for those who wanted them. When two drug addicts joined us one night, Chris took them to hospital and five weeks later they came back and said they were cured.

Sidney, a founder member of City Group, came to the picket often after work. 'It's magnificent what's going on here,' he said. 'This is what the Anti-Apartheid Movement has needed for a long time.' When he heard of the daily troubles from the chevra he shook his head. 'They'll never forgive you for having a successful campaign – never.'

'Don't be silly,' I said, still naive. 'Whatever problems and infighting there are, they *are* against apartheid. And this picket is demonstrating what support there is in this country if it is tapped.'

Sidney put his arm around me. 'The continual optimist, that's what you are,' he said. 'Come and have a bite to eat. You look tired.'

I shrugged his arm off. 'I'm not a bloody optimist,' I said. 'I'm just a realist.' Sidney laughed.

When Liz, a nurse, was pregnant, she decided to have a sponsored labour. Matthew, our youngest City Group member, earned over £300 for City Group by delaying getting born. Gerald, Matthew's dad, was one of the mainstays of the picket.

The Pickies wrote comments, stories and poems at the back of the Picket Book:

The amount of good will here is amazing. The other day I got a free taxi ride at 2 am when the driver heard I was coming to sit outside South Africa House – and he got a free lecture on apartheid all the way!

I joined the Picket on 25th August. I stayed until 8pm and returned the next day at 8.30 am only intending to stay an hour or so and have ended up staying day and night to see it through. It is interesting to watch each police shift and see their reactions which seem childish and provocative.

After banging my head against the brick wall of apathy in Epsom for 15 months, and Godalming for a year; after trying to mobilise, without success, interest in the heroic struggles in South Africa, Namibia, Lebanon, Ireland; after efforts to set up a Direct Action group with no response at all; imagine my feelings when I came to Trafalgar Square for the picket on Thursday last and found people prepared to continue this into an all-out continual demonstration of solidarity! There is life after Epsom!! I am a believer again. My efforts have not been in vain. May the Picket flourish and *succeed*, Victory is Certain!

I had just arrived in London as a tourist from Switzerland and was walking around. From Trafalgar Square I saw people standing on the pavement with banners. I came to see what it was. I signed the petition and stayed for a while – I guess maybe because Amandla, in her singing and fighting has got the power to retain people's attention. I don't know how it happened but I joined. Now I guess I will stay as long as I can. I feel personally involved in this struggle because this action is not abstract – it is something direct to be able to do.

I came to this Picket because I oppose racism in England – and because I hate my foreman, love my Mum, am bored with my trade union branch and I want to overthrow the system of privilege which pervades this country. It's good to stand alongside the youth, because they speak the truth.

This is one of the few things I have no doubts about. People walk around with the idea that their personal lives and problems are separate to those of other individuals and nations. Nobody can be under any of those illusions when it comes to David Kitson's case – which is the whole case against apartheid. The Kitsons have given me and others an opportunity to do something positive about it. Thanks. I've learnt more in the last few days about myself, my ideas and what we're up against in this country than all my years at College.

280

MANDELA

Rain, rain, rain, listen to the rain drum
On the plains of Africa
Hear the rain drum
On the tin shack roofs of Soweto
Hear the rain drum
On our heads on the picket
Mandela, Mandela, Mandela, Mandela, Mandela, Mandela,

Businessmen pull down your shutters
The rain will drum on your window pane
Mandela, Mandela, Mandela, Mandela, Mandela, Mandela,

Deep in the forest
Hear the parakeet screech the name Biko, Biko, Biko – Steeeve!!

In London town
Two white cockroaches
Stroll down the aisle
Of St Paul's Cathedral
Never thinking of Mandela.

In Africa the storm gathers
The hooves of the herds as they wheel on the plain
Are thundering the name
Mandela, Mandela, Mandela, Mandela, Mandela, Mandela,

For the roar of a lion
Brings skyscrapers down
Raises up the shanty town
We will release that lion – his name?
MANDELA

ANOTHER STEP ON THE ROAD

This is a saga of apartheid
White man in prison for black man's fate
One of many fighters – David Kitson
Mandela-man – to a person we're with him.

Outside the embassy on the picket
Only by fighting will we lick it.
Outside in weather – rain and cold
We'll never give up. We'll never fold.

They claim power with guns and might
But victory's ours 'cause we know we're right
We know that one day we shall win
And good will triumph over sin.

In this land of trouble and strife
I now claim 'The struggle's *my* life'
So then the question's one of time
This here picket is a bold front line.

The International Monetary Fund
Provides the weapons so more get gunned.
But watch your pockets, watch your money
When South Africa's free
They won't give *you* their honey.

To the people goes the power
Smashing down apartheid's tower
All who'd stop us are the same,
Police, spies, *and* he who hides under *the* name.

Here we're just a British few
Standing firmly, standing true
Standing for David and those like you
Mandela-man – we follow too.

On 1 November I left the picket to attend my ANC unit meeting. I ran into a barrage of hostility. The picket had been discussed at the previous month's meeting, which I had not attended, and the minutes were read out to me. They ended, 'Norma Kitson was instructed to close the picket.' I had never had this instruction at all. No one had even spoken to me. Those present at the November meeting said it was not their recollection that that was the outcome of the previous month's discussion. But the set of minutes could 'prove' I was undisciplined and disobedient. It was on record.

There was jubilation on the picket when on 8 November the prisoners were moved from death row into a prison with long-term facilities. There was a mass victory picket. We had achieved the first demand of the picket. With the eyes of the world on his health, David had been sent to a clinic. The Red

Picketer addressing rally at Conway
Hall, 4 October 1982.

Frank Sully, 85, and
'Rolihlahla' Hamilton.

The Pickies.

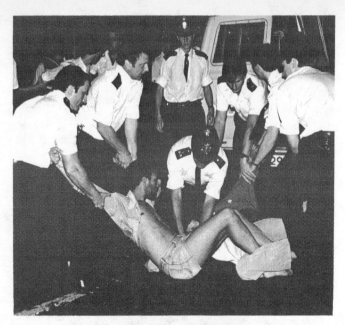

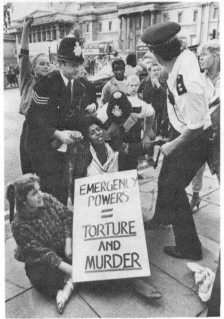

Arrests of Pickies.

Cross had visited the jails. Doctors had been to see the prisoners on Robben Island and in Pretoria.

I discussed our position with Carol. In the face of strong opposition from the London ANC, the movement to which I had belonged for thirty-one years, how could we continue the picket?

At the Pavement University I got voted in to speak on the future of the picket. With mixed feelings, I put forward the reasons why the picket should end: picketing was only one aspect of anti-apartheid work. We must leave the pavement to do all the other things the Anti-Apartheid Movement does. In the discussion one of the youngsters asked, 'Like what, for instance?' I fumbled. While on the picket we had had street meetings, material aid collections outside supermarkets, had formed the City Group Singers who sang at benefits, had sent public speakers to the Labour Party and TUC conferences and to colleges and schools, had demonstrated outside Barclays Bank, South African Airways and Rio Tinto Zinc, had collected 25,000 signatures on the Free Nelson Mandela petition and had participated in the big event of the year organised by the Anti-Apartheid Movement – a cycle ride for Nelson Mandela.

Mr Sully, eighty-four, said, 'I want to participate in a campaign for Mr Mandela, but I don't have a cycle.'

'Hands up everybody with bicycles,' Andy said. Four people raised their hands. 'Well, there you are, then,' he said. 'There are over a hundred of us on the picket at the moment. If you want to organise a small meaningless campaign – go for 4 per cent of activists.'

That night after the Pavement University I felt I had left the Pickies confused and angry. One after another had knocked down my arguments for going off the picket. We decided to have a full meeting of the members of City Group and supporters, to vote whether to continue or to leave the pavement and put our energies into other anti-apartheid work. I would need to canvass for support and bring new arguments for the big meeting.

I was in a state of conflict when I addressed the meeting at Friends' House. Inside I knew that, with the enormous support we had, the picket should continue until liberation, building up on that pavement. The South Africans had complained to the British Foreign Office – we were an increasing embarrassment to them. They had had to close the front doors and the staff went through the side entrance. Visitors to their weekly embassy dinners were put out when they saw us and tried to hide from our photographers.

On the other hand, it would be a good thing if the young people were encouraged to become more organised. We had been living on the pavement for seventy-six days. Amandla had given up her typing course and was sleeping on the picket. Steven had managed to keep his job, but he was exhausted. He was living on the picket and going to work each morning. Red Lion Setters was suffering from my three-month absence and the hostility from the chevra was mounting.

We were to spend eighty-six days and nights on that picket before we won our demand to have the prisoners moved. We saved David's life. And when the picket ended, there could not have been many people in London who did not know about Nelson Mandela, Walter Sisulu and the liberation struggle in South Africa.

Most of us on the picket wanted to continue until Nelson Mandela's release, but the chevra's work was beginning to tell. Rumour and gossip was rife. It was becoming public knowledge in England that the ANC was against the picket.

On 18 November, by a small majority, City Group voted to end the picket. Many of our members were disgusted.

City Group continued to picket the South African embassy every Friday evening.

After we stopped the picket, the Anti-Apartheid Movement told us we had to stick to the square mile of the City of London and all our members had to live or work in the City. The City of London is full of banks and building societies. Ordinary people do not live in it. The name of our group was chosen with Chris Childs, a member of the national committee of the Anti-

Apartheid Movement, but we had always been active in Holborn and Westminster as well. We applied formally to work the area of Holborn, Westminster and the City. The AAM did not reply to our letter and told their supporters that we were intransigent and had refused to obey them.

By 1985 City Group had 450 members and were one of the largest anti-apartheid groups in Britain. In February of that year we were expelled from the Anti-Apartheid Movement on the grounds that we did not confine our activities to the City of London.

In 1983 Amandla visited David again. This time Richard Balfe, Member of the European Parliament, accompanied her. The *Rand Daily Mail* printed a large full-colour photograph of Amandla and this time she received a warm welcome from progressive people who saw her.

There was a new feeling abroad in South Africa. The struggle was gaining momentum. Walking down a Johburg street, in the centre of the city, Amandla saw a van stop and a heap of newspapers thrown into the middle of the road. Black people flew out to grab copies. The paper announced the formation of the United Democratic Front – a mass overground resistance organisation had formed in South Africa. Amandla was given one of these precious papers to take back to London. South Africa was in ferment.

Amandla made two visits to David. To her relief, she found his health improved.

'He's so strong, Mom, and cheerful and relaxed. You'd never think he was in jail. He's full of news about his studies and he wanted to know all about Steven and you and about the new flat. And he's pleased Sidney and us are still good friends. He says Sidney is one of the family.'

The highlight of the 1983 visit was when Amandla met Nomzamo (Winnie) Mandela in Brandfort. Richard Balfe arranged with the British consul to take Winnie a heater and supplies of paraffin as a gift from the British Cooperative Wholesale Society. Nomzamo had been without heating. She gave Amandla an ecstatic welcome and later described to me on the telephone how much this visit had meant to her.

In 1977 Nomzamo's home in Orlando had been raided and she was banished to Brandfort, a small town in the Orange Free State, where she was confined to a tiny wood and breeze-block house, under constant surveillance by the police. Nomzamo said, 'When they send me into exile, it's not me as an individual they are sending. They think that with me they can also ban the political ideas . . . I couldn't think of a greater honour.'

The apartheid regime had tried to isolate Nomzamo. Instead she drew the local people of Brandfort to her side. She opened a youth centre and a crèche and defied the signs that said WHITES ONLY.

Nomzamo was delighted to see Amandla. They spoke about the South African struggle and Amandla told her about the activities of City Group and the 86-Day-and-Night Picket. Nomzamo encouraged Amandla to continue the struggle. For the first time in her life, Amandla was getting wholehearted support where it counted. Nomzamo inscribed a book, honouring the political work we had been doing. Amandla met Zinzi Mandela, and was treated lovingly in Brandfort.

It was a far cry from the public meeting in London that Amandla had attended when she gave out leaflets for the release of Nelson Mandela. Solly Smith, then the ANC chief representative in London, had shouted at her, 'You – you Kitson girl! Go away! You're insane. If you give those out here, I'll have you chucked out of this place.' When she had gone to help in the ANC office with the preparation of the ANC *News Briefing*, a weekly publication of news from the South African press, Gill Marcus had thrown her out because, she said, Amandla was a member of the Revolutionary Communist Group.

'I'm not,' Amandla had said.

'Yes, you are. You're a *secret* member of it. You can't come in this office any more. ANC policy is, no one can work here who belongs to a British organisation.'

'But I don't belong to any British organisation except the

Anti-Apartheid Movement.'

'You're not allowed to help us here any more.' And Amandla had had to leave.

Similar treatment had been meted out to Steven. He had tried to join the ANC choir and was accepted but not told of their practice sessions or performances. Young black ANC members came to the house to teach him the songs. But when he joined the choir singing in public he was told, 'You're not wanted here.'

Steven was asked by the ANC women's committee to help run a batik workshop to produce goods for their annual bazaar. He was praised for his work by the ANC president, Oliver Tambo, but never invited by the London ANC to continue the workshop.

Both Steven and Amandla were snubbed by the chevra.

In Johannesburg Amandla talked with members of the United Democratic Front, trade unions and the community. She met Cyril Ramaphosa, head of the South African National Union of Mineworkers, and Helen Joseph, the first person house-arrested in South Africa and an intrepid fighter. She discussed the class struggle with Father Mkatshwa, church leader Beyers Naude, Raymond Suttner and Guy Berger, who had been in jail with David. She was due to meet with Albertina Sisulu but on the day of their appointment, Mrs Sisulu was arrested. Zwelake Sisulu went to Jan Smuts airport to see Amandla and published her news about the picket on the front page of *The Sowetan* newspaper.

She returned to London brimming with confidence. David was well and cheerful. Now that we had the blessing of so many fighters we must step up our activities, she said.

Events were sharpening in South Africa – and they wre sharpening in Britain. At a time when people in Britain needed to draw together in solidarity against apartheid, every left group was riven with splits and conflicts. These hostilities in the solidarity movements were shaping into a confrontation just as David was due to be released from jail.

287

On 10 December 1983, the telephone rang in my Islington flat. I scrambled over Steven's rucksack, hockey stick, suitcase, files containing his computer and maths doodles, and all the other paraphernalia my son had brought into my life. He had left his job at Rolls-Royce in Bristol to be settled in London by the time David was released. He was home- and job-hunting.

It was Lynne, Stanley Goldstein's ex-wife, in Johannesburg. 'Norm! Fantastic news! David is going to be released on the 19th!'

I was stunned. There had been so many false hopes and broken promises over the years. 'Nineteenth of what?'

'This month! *Norm!* He's getting exactly one year's remission. Isn't it *wonderful*?'

'How d'you know?' I asked warily.

'It's not official,' Lynne said. 'But Stanley went to see him today.' Stanley was Lynne's ex-husband and the ex-husband also of my friend Micki. 'Stan says he has it on good authority – from one of the top jail boers. Anyway, David's been separated from the other prisoners. He's being held in a different section.'

I began to feel wobbly. 'Oh, really?' was all I could manage. If David had been moved, it was a sure sign. Prisoners were always separated before they were released, so that they could not carry messages out.

Lynne went on, 'Stan says David wants to spend a couple of weeks with his father after his release. He's always been fond of his dad. You know David, with him there's only one party to hostilities – he just doesn't recognise that sort of thing. And poor old Fred isn't well now – well, he's ninety! Stan's house is a bit crowded at the moment, so we've arranged for David to stay at my house. I'll look after him – don't you worry.'

'But it's so *dangerous*', I said. 'I won't be happy till he's on a plane to London.'

'Well, we all think that. But David told Stan he's adamant. He's got things to do here before he leaves for London. Isn't it *lekker* [wonderful]?'

'Yes. Yes,' I said. 'It's dead *lekker*! Thanks. Thanks so much, Lynne.' I held the receiver away from my ear, looked at it and then put it down. I sat on the couch, moving Steven's books, coats and cushions to make room for myself. I felt weak. Such excitement was welling up in me that I suddenly leaped up. I stood a moment, then ran down the narrow passage to the bedroom where Steven was watching the telly.

'That was Lynne on the phone. Dad's coming out on the 19th! Stanley confirmed it with the boers.' Steven looked at me, excitement and doubt twisting his face. 'I think this could really be it, Steve!'

We telephoned Amandla, who shared a flat with Richard and Charine from City Group in Camden Town. 'What makes you think it's for real?' she asked.

'Lynne was quite sure.'

'Well, wait for me. I'm coming straight over.'

Steven whooped. 'I'm going to Chapel Street market right now to buy a Christmas tree. *This* year we're really going to celebrate Christmas.'

I sat and waited. Perhaps this was it. Lynne had been so sure! Perhaps David was really going to be released. Everything came into my head at once. The feel of David. His funny smile. Food! Sweets! We'd have to get lots of food in. We must get new sheets. I'll ask David Reed or Pauline to drive us to the airport. David coming home! I'll buy a new pillow. I sat on the couch in a tangle of thoughts. We'd have to move. Knowing that David's sentence was up on 18 December 1984, for the first time I had applied to the International Defence and Aid for help – the fund set up during the Treason Trial in 1956 to pay legal costs and to help the families of political prisoners. We would need to buy a place big enough for the whole family. They had agreed to give us £10,000 towards the purchase of a house. Friends! I'll phone *everyone*, write down everything I have to do. But first I must let the ANC know. Solly Smith, the chief representative, did not sound enthusiastic.

'I've got *such* good news,' I said. 'We've just heard from a Johburg friend that David is being released on the 19th of this month.'

He was distant and made a harrumphing noise.

'He's coming *out*!' I said as if I hadn't been understood.

'That's nice.'

'On the 19th!'

'Oh yes?'

'Of *this* month. He's being released a year early – almost exactly a year.'

Silence.

'Hello! Are you still there? I thought I'd phone you before telling anyone else because you probably want to, I don't know – whatever! Arrange a press conference, or for him to be met, or a party, or *something*!'

'Well, thanks for phoning.'

'Shall I phone you when I get any more news?'

But he had put the phone down.

Amandla and Steven arrived together. We opened a bottle of Perrier and a carton of tropical fruit juice and sat looking at each other while I tried to remember every word of Lynne's phone call. Amandla said, 'I'm going to phone Lynne back. I want to get the news first-hand. We've waited a long time to hear this, and I don't believe it. Why are they doing it? They never give something for nothing.'

Amandla and Lynne had a long chat. Lynne confirmed the arrangements. David would stay with her and her friend Malcolm at their house for a few weeks and then he intended to come to London.

Steven went out to get a Chinese takeaway and I went to have a bath. Lying there in the warm water, I remembered the tear-streaked face of the little boy of seven on the evening of David's arrest in June 1964. The plainclothes security police had left. The cars had driven away and the house was silent. Amandla was asleep in her cot and Steven, and I were standing near the bookshelves from which the police had randomly taken some of our books.

'Will they bring Dad back soon?' Steven asked.

'I don't know.'

'We were in the middle.'

Silence from me.

'Mom, I'm talking to you. We're right in the middle.'

'We're all in the middle of David,' I had said to him.

'We are in the middle of *The Incredible Journey*. Will he come back and read it to me?'

'Yes, one day.' And now, twenty years later, the 'one day' was perhaps ten days – or a few weeks – away.

I got out of the bath and took down the file of David's letters, leafing through them. He had been skilful keeping in real touch.

To Steven aged 16 (1972):

When Alison visited me recently she told me that you had shown her how to enamel copper and now she is teaching Lindy and Tessa. She said that Mummy had got a new stove. I am often curious about the flat and its contents. Would you please tell me about it, stove, fridge, television, record-player, favourite records, car, bike, the lot, and how they are arranged.

To Steven aged 17 after an operation on his foot injured in a rugby accident. David had been sent to work in the jail garden because he developed an allergy to dust in the jail woodwork shop. (1973):

That was a most entertaining and charming letter you wrote me. I only hope that when you answer this early in December (please) one will not have to break your footbones to inspire a similar articulacy.

Once over the immediate effects of their cuts or fractures the inmates of a surgical ward are full of beans. When I had an appendectomy in Highgate Hospital in 1955 they had me up the next day. I had to walk a million miles from my bed to a chair by the wall. Ten days later I went off in my pyjamas with Mummy in a taxi.

If you consider it, a square with a perimeter of 10 is completely definable. Using the calculus of variations to find its side length and area is like using a steam hammer to crack a nut. It's alright as an exercise I suppose. I'm glad you like the subject, because it's going to loom large in your life quite soon, being used more and more in problems of optimum control and efficient rocket trajectories etc. In fact one of the problems dealt with is that of a 'bang-bang' control, so it would have been more appropriate to have ended your problem with a bang-bang instead of a boom-boom. In my Applied Maths III exam,

291

just written, I had to start with the motion of a particle described by classical mechanics (Hamilton's formulation of Newton's laws), and by means of transformations involving the calculus of variations end up with Schrödinger's equation, representing a wave motion.

It being that time of the year, Ma lizard has delivered so that there are several tiny lizards scuttling around the yard. When a lizard is attacked, it drops a bit of its tail off which then wriggles like mad, attracting all the attention while the lizard makes its escape. Then it grows a new tail. It seems that the birds like lizards' tails, because some of the babies have no tails at all now. I suppose you could call them manx lizards. I caught one and let it run about my hand, but it kept on taking off.

To me (1976):

Dear Norma, What do you mean, my Muswell Hill room was bare? I distinctly remember that it was furnished with a shilling gasmeter, to say nothing of two beds, the little one without sheets because I had hidden them. Then there was a bookshelf, a utility sideboard, a couple of wardrobes, a row of pewter and hardly enough room to swing a cat. However due to my flair for arrangement it looked uncluttered. One need not mention the kitchen, complete to the last detail, even a half-eaten pilchard casserole, ag! I mean steak and mushroom.

To Amandla aged 13 who wanted to be an actress (1975):

When I was a young student I got involved in a production of 'You Never Can Tell'. As I arrived late for the audition the only role left was that of the second waiter. So I also took on the job of stage manager and subsequently spent some years stage managing plays and shows in Durban. Once I played the whole Greek army in a production of The Trojan Women. First I dragged Cassandra off, then I tore Andromache's child from his mother and finally I set the whole of Troy on fire. I had a suit of Greek armour made from Coca-Cola bottle tops and had to wiggle from one side of the stage to the other behind the scenery, without rattling, in order to work the curtain. The whole Greek chorus used to watch my progress while Hecate was making her final speech to see if I would get there in time. As a matter of fact I always did.

Later that evening, surrounded by the empty foil dishes, Amandla said, 'I don't think we should say anything – to anyone – except really close friends. It's not official yet. We don't know what's going to happen. Today's the 10th. Let's wait till the 14th – that's Friday. By then we should have heard more. We'll still have nearly a week to let everyone know before he's released.'

I wanted to broadcast the news, but Steven agreed with Amandla. 'Let's just keep it to ourselves till we hear more.'

Amandla had to go to college, but Steven and I roved the estate agents and streets, looking for a house. We felt we should stay in Islington. David's father, Grandpa Fred, had been born there and that is how I had got my British citizenship – as a patrial. David's family links were there. Islington proper was much too expensive but Highbury or Stoke Newington would do fine. Even if we couldn't move quickly enough to be in the house when David came, it was as well to buy something as soon as possible.

We heard no more news from Johannesburg. Monday 19 December came and went. The Christmas tree dropped pine needles over everything and we threw it away. I despaired of ever seeing David alive again.

On Saturday 21 January 1984, Lynne Goldstein was found murdered in her home in Craighall Park.

In March we moved into a house in Highbury. We did not now expect David out before the end of his sentence in December. In the evenings, when we weren't at City Group meetings or at the weekly Friday evening picket of South Africa House which we had continued since the ending of the 86-Day-and Night Picket, Steven made bookshelves for David's room. I sewed a patchwork quilt for him and, with Amandla, made patchwork curtains as well. The members of City Group helped us prepare the house for David's return. They cleaned, decorated and moved furniture, gave us gifts and drawings. I cooked and stocked up the freezer to bursting point. People had heard about David's sweet tooth, and boxes of chocolates and sweets starting arriving for him from the day we moved in.

City Group continued to flourish. The GLC subsidised a

small office for City Group where we held regular meetings and, with the steady increase in our membership, our work was stepped up. Our major campaigns now were for the release of Nelson Mandela and all Southern African political prisoners and to close down the South African embassy in London. Recently the South African embassy in New Zealand had been closed down by the direct action of the New Zealand people. We had no hopes of a quick success – Britain's more extensive involvement in apartheid would make our task a lengthy one – but we were sure we would eventually succeed if we got support.

I attended unit meetings of the London ANC most months, and with each meeting, in the year preceding David's release, the atmosphere towards me got progressively more hostile. I had thought that closing the 86-Day-and-Night Picket would have mollified our antagonists. Rumours had been spread that undesirables ran the picket, that the youngsters behaved badly, that the picket was racist because it was an action for one white prisoner. None of these things had been true but a different spate of rumours was issued each month and this left many ordinary members of the London ANC suspicious.

What perplexed me was why the London ANC or the Anti-Apartheid Movement had not stepped in to take over the running of the picket. I was a member of an extremely disciplined organisation and the ANC could have directed me, told me to leave, instructed me to close it down, or put in other ANC members to lead it. City Group members would have been delighted to have acted in accordance with ANC wishes.

The ANC said they had no right to interfere with the Anti-Apartheid Movement. This did not answer the point why I, an ANC member, had received no instructions. In any event, a high proportion of the membership of the AAM national committee were ANC members, and they had never had any hesitation in influencing the AAM.

Instead, the London ANC had stayed away, given us no guidance and left me to stick out like a sore thumb – the only active ANC member in City Group. The chevra now accused me of self-promotion – and worse.

They said City Group was run by Trotskyists; that it was run by the Revolutionary Communist Group; that it consisted of unemployed, badly dressed, confrontationist youth. In vain did I explain that City Group was run on democratic lines, with participation by a broad section of British people. I took documents, leaflets, news cuttings and albums of photographs to show unit members. They refused space on their agendas to discuss the picket or its aftermath. I could not understand why they wanted us to turn away hundreds of anti-apartheid supporters. All these people, so far as I was concerned, were welcome. We represented many trends and we didn't ask people to account for their political affiliations. Among City Group members were a clergyman, two Islington councillors, a Westminster Labour councillor and some MPs. The only requirement for joining City Group or participating in its activities was that one had to be opposed to apartheid in South Africa and racism in Britain.

The attacks against me and City Group increased. In the face of the successes of City Group, people were being told our politics were 'unsound'. But I was the one who, in 1983, had recorded Sonia Bunting's radio broadcast which told British people that Nelson Mandela should be released from prison 'because he has paid his debt to society'!

'What debt?' I asked her in terrible anger.

Sonia maintained that she had not been very well and more-over she had made a 'genuine mistake'. Her supporters stood by her. But so great was the rage of some of our black comrades at this 'genuine mistake' that one went so far as to threaten her with physical violence. All who spoke out against her for this 'genuine mistake' were hauled off speakers' lists and out of committees.

Although in South Africa I had been a Communist Party member in good standing, had been a member of Congress, had carried out actions for Umkhonto we Sizwe and had been part of the underground technical committee, I was never admitted, in London, to the South African Communist Party in exile.

Sonia and Brian Bunting had left South Africa several years

previously, and now that David's release was imminent they were getting anxious that he should follow the line of the chevra. Nothing was more guaranteed to bring shivers of insecurity to the chevra in 1984 than the criticism of them implied in David's statement from the dock in 1964: 'I could run or stand. So I stood.'

IAN DAVID KITSON
Extract of statement delivered from the dock in the Johannesburg Supreme Court on 18 December 1964

I am a white South African who was born in this country. I went to school with South Africans, to University with South Africans and fought in the war with South Africans. I feel an affinity with white South Africans.

As I grew up, however, and came to think for myself, it became difficult for me to reconcile the oppression of the black people here with the philosophical outlook of the Western civilisation we whites purport to defend. Clearly the situation was contrary to the Christian tradition in which I had been reared.

The only organisation I could find which stood for equality of opportunity, regardless of race, was the Communist Party. Later, I came to accept the Marxist standpoint that mankind can only achieve its complete liberation with the achievement of communism. Today communism is a swearword which is directed against a multitude of sins. Different people understand different things by 'communism'. For my part, I saw communism as a movement against racial discrimination and oppression.

I found that when I got married, domesticity made bigger demands than devotion to ideals. I also found that I was still a South African at heart and wanted my children to be South Africans, so I came back to the land of my birth. I came back from England, where I had gone to further my career, with the clear intention of not taking part in any kind of political activity at all but of devoting myself to my family. This attitude was buttressed by the fact that the Authorities knew about my past, for my passport was confiscated on my return. I lived this way for about a year.

Then, Sharpeville took place. The Active Citizen Force was mobilised. In the Emergency, hundreds of innocuous people were arbitrarily detained. In view of my past, I could easily have been one of them. The

Government, supported by the majority of the whites, had turned a granite face to the Africans and their fellow-sufferers and had flouted the mainstream of development along which the world is going. This is still the case.

I could run, or stand. So I stood. It was natural, in view of my past, to find a home in the South African Communist Party. At least my participation would show that I stood alongside the Africans and their fellows. It showed the world that another white had chosen the side of humanity. In view of the Nationalist opposition to Communism, nothing could underline my detestation of apartheid more than being a Communist.

I joined Umkhonto we Sizwe for the same reasons that have been set forth at length by Nelson Mandela in another Court, namely that there were no lawful methods of effective opposition which remained open.

I do not see how I could have done otherwise.

· *15* ·

'They never close doors.'

'Why?'

'Well, they haven't closed a door for years, have they? So they're just not aware of it. It's terrible, especially in winter.'

'You must be careful what you give him to eat. Just think of all the things he hasn't eaten for twenty years – curry, cakes, anchovies.'

'I don't think I've eaten anchovies in twenty years,' I said.

'And alcohol. You can't let him have any alcohol – it'll probably kill him after being on the wagon for all that time.'

'We don't drink,' I said.

'Of course he'll be an incredible male chauvinist pig. I mean, twenty years! He'll want his grub on the table, his women a certain shape, and you'll have to learn to obey him – you know what men were like.'

'David was never like that.'

'He'll probably want to go to bed at nine o'clock every night – they're used to a very strict routine. He'll need a doctor – a socialist one, of course. You'll have to get on to the Socialist Medical Association. Ask for Audrey Thomas, she'll help you. He'll need a proper check-up after all that chest trouble.'

'Have you thought of sex?'

'Yes.'

'I mean, after twenty years! There was a code among the politicals – they never practised homosexuality. A lot of them have got prostate trouble. You can't expect him to be able to perform. And anyway, he hasn't had the company of women for all that time.'

'Don't let a dog near him. They've had killer dogs guarding them. He'll be terrified of animals.'

'He made friends with chameleons, a lizard and birds in jail,' I said.

'They get very tired – they're not used to all the stimulation.'

'You'll have to get a psychiatrist for him. It's been proved they all have nervous breakdowns after a couple of months. It's the strain of decision-making and all the different choices and things they have to do.'

'Remember, he went in just as the Beatles were becoming known. He missed the miniskirt era and women's lib. The world was in black and white – there wasn't even colour television.'

'There was no television at all in South Africa then.'

'He won't get on with the kids, so don't expect it. Don't forget he hasn't even *seen* children for years. Most of the kids leave home – with aggro – the minute their father comes out.'

'They haven't been caressed or cuddled for ages. A lot of them don't like it – they've got used to not being touched. He'll probably be withdrawn and even cold.'

I tried to shrug off the advice so many people gave me. To them David was a 'they' – a well-known, documented phenomenon. But at night I found myself lying awake with doubts. Had it been right to buy the house? Could we ever have a full relationship again? Many marriages had broken up when the man came home. If I couldn't expect to get back the David I had known, whom was I planning to welcome? A complete alien.

I decided to play safe. David would come and live in the Highbury house if he wished. I would assume nothing. We had been good friends for nearly thirty years – nothing could change that. Given time, a closer relationship might develop. I had changed too. I could hardly remember what I'd been like twenty years ago. Perhaps people would warn him about me. Now I was used to my independence, used to living alone. I played Bach and Prokofiev, he liked Beethoven and Mozart, but we'd weathered the difference in taste before. I tossed and turned, worried. I had been longing for David's return since the day of his arrest in 1964. But would it be *David* who returned? Perhaps, as everyone seemed to think, we were embarking on the impossible.

When I tried to express my fears to Amandla, she was sympathetic but dismissive. 'Oh, Mom. Stop worrying! It's not as if we haven't been in touch with Dad all the time. So you'll have a few problems – *nu!* Show me what relationship doesn't.'

Steven was more philosophical. 'Look, if it doesn't work, it doesn't. We'd all be silly not to anticipate a lot of problems. But we won't know what they are till he's here. At the moment we have to worry about whether they'll ever let him out.'

'But Steven, Susan told me they all go to bits after a couple of months – it's documented.'

'So he'll go to bits and then we'll deal with it. At the moment *you're* going to bits. What do you think is the worst that can happen?'

'He won't like me.'

'He loves you – he always has.'

'I've changed.'

'Of course. And so has he. You'll both explore the changes.'

'Well, maybe he won't like you and Amandla?'

'He loves us all, and if he doesn't, he will, because we'll all be so nice to him. You know, he's very proud of us. The prisoners who have been released and visited us have all gone on about how he boasts of our achievements, however trivial. He's followed all our doings throughout the years. He's pleased as punch with us – always has been. Read his letters again.'

He rushed upstairs to get a file of David's letters and read me excerpts from them and I felt reassured.

To Norma

You shouldn't worry so much. You know what happens to worriers according to the ancient Simian proverb. Joan, who visited me early this month, said that she had a long letter from you. I love to hear about the doings of you, Sidney and the children. Lots of people have told me about him. So I have a mental picture of him. Now he's one of the family, I look forward to hearing everything.

I am most interested in the affairs of Red Lion Setters. Tell me all about it.

To Amandla

What you should realise when you write to me, is that I want to see everything through your eyes. No matter how trivial or mundane you may think your daily activities, they are of interest to me. So tell me about the Welsh Harp, the cows up the road, the statue in the road, the little shop in Shaftesbury Avenue that sells French drinking chocolate, your shopping in Temple Fortune or Golders Green, the boys and girls you play with, your school, its teachers, Victoria's kittens, the Harwich train, the new aluminium tube trains, the rain in Kensington ... whatever you think of.

To Norma

I certainly approve of all your doings. However sometimes I get nervous that you might bite off more than you can chew. But keep fighting!

But I was wary. I set aside the biggest bedroom in the house for David. I put a television in it so that it wouldn't be confused with a cell – so that David could live his private, sexless, nervous, tired, animal-hating life in comfort. My small bedroom was next door. Steven built bookshelves and we put his books from twenty years ago in them. For years I had been buying him clothes, tracksuits, pyjamas, shirts and socks, and Amandla took them out of their boxes and put them tidily into the drawers we had bought.

When I went to buy a bed for him, even Mr Litvinoff in the pine shop had advice.

'Mrs Kitson,' he said. 'Be careful. If you get a bed that's too soft, he won't be able to sleep. Prisoners' beds are hard. Get him a hard bed, otherwise you'll break his back.'

I bought a hard bed. After he had survived the brutality of the apartheid regime, I did not want to be responsible for breaking

301

his back.

Sidney promised to take Poopy to live in the Barbican if David was frightened of dogs. I had bought a dog in July 1984 after my Islington flat had been raided and my papers rifled. Poopy was my guard-dog. I invited the kids from City Group to eat all the frozen curries I had prepared and filled the freezer with stews and steak-and-kidney.

I rearranged the furniture, fussing over David's room. I was getting tense, waiting for David. As February slid into March I started ticking off the time. Ten more months to wait.

Despite the distance between us – and we had not seen each other for nine years – I had grown closer to my mother. We spoke to each other every week. One afternoon at work, I received a telephone call from her.

'Hello, darling. Can you hear me?'

'Mom, why are you whispering? I can't hear you properly. Speak up.'

'Listen carefully,' she said, 'I've got news for you.'

I shivered and strained to hear her. 'OK, Mom, go on then.'

'I've formed an organisation for blacks.'

'You've *whaat*?'

'I've formed a lift-scheme organisation for blacks – to take the nurses home.'

'Mom,' I said. 'It's no good whispering on an international telephone line. It's tapped. Whispering doesn't help. Don't say anything that will get you into trouble. I'll find a way to get someone to pick up a message from you if it's important. The security police just play back the tapes and they can hear everything.'

'Oh,' she said. 'I don't pay any attention to *them*. Auntie Bea is in the other room. The family would kill me if they knew.'

I had to laugh. Even now she was more frightened of what the family might say than of the apartheid regime.

In Durban there were scores of black nurses who attended sick whites in their homes. They went off duty at odd hours of the night and risked mugging and attacks on the streets. Driving in her car one night, my mother had been flagged down by a frightened black nurse and had given her a lift home. Then Mom started organising the people in Durban to give lifts to get the nurses to their homes safely. 'What if that girl had been my daughter?' she said. I thought of Phineas, Sixpence and the others she had so uncaringly discarded years ago. My mother had changed a great deal.

Her action in setting up the lift scheme was so unusual that the press became interested and the *Natal Daily News* published a story about it. That blew my mother's cover with the family.

For ten years or more my mother had suffered a bad back. In the past year she had had an operation in Johannesburg. Now she was recovered, she wanted to pay us a visit. Clarice, Ricky and their three kids had settled in Australia, as had Robbie, Joan's son, with his wife Ruth and their baby. Mom planned a round trip in 1984 – London, Australia, London, South Africa. Later she planned to visit Tessa and Lindy, Joan's daughters, living in Israel. Mangelwurzel was now living in Durban, having divorced Pam. He was a great comfort to Mom, visiting her often.

We suggested she should come over in the English spring, well before David's release. I did not think I could cope with a convalescent mother, Red Lion Setters – which was having increasing financial problems – and David just out of jail.

Sidney drove me to the airport to fetch Mom, now seventy-nine. She emerged through customs in a wheelchair, giving me a terrible fright. She could barely walk. She was still glamorous, with beautiful hands and feet. Ronnie used to say, 'You could eat off Mom's feet, they've never been used.'

I took a week's holiday and went with her to a health farm, to try and get her mobile. When she had returned to Durban after her operation, her sisters had been concerned, fussing around her, treating her like an invalid, and she had become virtually bedridden.

We swam every day, limbered up in our leotards, took spa baths, exercised to music, chatted in the Jacuzzi, and by the time the week was up, Mom could not only walk, but run. She had made friends with all the women and two men had fallen in love with her and invited her out.

Sidney fetched us from Tring and came to our Highbury house in the evenings to play rummy with Mom when she wasn't going out. I discovered that Mom had many friends in England – she had invitations most nights to theatres and dinners and to spend weekends out of town. While I was at work at Red Lion Setters during the days, Mom shopped, cooked, moved the furniture, bought pot plants for all the rooms, filled vases with flowers, and continued the preparation of David's room, buying a bedside light, a clock – 'Little things that men like,' as she put it.

Now, at the age of fifty, I rediscovered my mother. Although she still missed and mourned Oscar, whom she had loved since she was eighteen years old, she had come into her own in the years since his death. Living by herself was very hard for her, but she had so many friends and new interests that her life was full and satisfying. She had begun to take painting lessons. She had discarded many prejudices about whom she could befriend, and had ceased being competitive with women. She still played poker – but not bridge. 'They don't play Culbertson – he's out of fashion,' she said. 'It's all science now. They've reduced everything in this world to science. Everything's by rote. People go around calling themselves good card players who've got no proper card sense at all.'

'Do you remember,' Mom said to me when we were sitting in the lounge after dinner one evening, 'how I used to go on about Grannie being friends with Greeks? Well, lately I've made friends with the most loving Greek family. I see them every week. I don't tell the family, of course. But I really look forward to it. I don't think I ever understood my mother. I was always frightened she was going to make some dreadful social gaffe and disgrace us all. But looking back now, I see her differently. She was a brave, self-contained woman, wasn't she? Isn't it sad – for me to discover it now? She was younger than me when she died.

Do you know what else I found out?'

'What, Mom?'

'Arabs are Semites. I always thought they were anti-Semitic, but they're not. And not only that: they're very much like us. They don't eat garlic or onions on Friday nights – we don't because we go to shul; they go to the mosque. And they all play *klaberjas*, though they call it something else. And backgammon – they call it shesh-pesh. They're really just like Jews. Anyway, we're more like them than English. I don't know what all the enmity's about. Don't ever tell the family I said that.'

One evening I walked into Mom's bedroom to find her sitting at the dressing table in tears.

'Whatever's the matter, Mom?' I asked. 'Are you unhappy here?'

'It's nothing, darling. Of course I'm not unhappy. It's wonderful being with you.'

'It's Joan, isn't it?'

From the moment of her arrival at the airport, it was as if Joan was there between us but neither of us could mention her. I felt I might burst into tears and reopen wounds for my mother. After Joan's murder, she had taken to her bed for months, unable to face the world.

'Sometimes,' my mother said, 'I can feel her hand in mine and see her blue eyes looking at me, like she used to when she was a little girl, and I hear her saying, "Don't worry, Mommie. I'm fine now, really." I try to hang on to her hand but she just melts away. Who would do such terrible things to my Joanie? She didn't have an enemy in the world. Everybody loved her.' My mother started to cry again.

I put my arms around her. I could not talk about it. I was holding Joan too close to share with anyone.

After that I knocked when I went into her room and I noticed that her eyes were often red. Alone, my mother gave way to her pain and tried to find a private comfort.

After three weeks, Mom left to see Clarice in Australia.

My mother had run up and down the stairs, chatted on the phone, bought occasional tables and a whatnot, made Steven and Amandla their favourite dishes, taught me how to make apple crumble, and filled our lives with movement and light. Her absence left the house silent and lonely. Steven, Amandla and our friends drew closer. Red Lion Setters was slipping into bankruptcy. One of my close friends from my London ANC women's committee days, who had staunchly supported City Group and had defended the attacks against my family, suddenly became hostile and joined forces with the chevra.

On 11 May Steven, Amandla and I called a meeting of friends to discuss the possibility of a final campaign to get David released. He had been separated from the other prisoners for months and we feared he was being held in solitary confinement. We gathered at the house, sitting around the circular table Mr Humphreys had bought us so many years ago.

Just as everyone was seated and I had made a pot of tea, the telephone rang. It was the Foreign Office to say David had been released and was at Stanley Goldstein's house.

We phoned Stanley. He knew nothing of David's release and thought someone was playing a cruel joke. We phoned the Foreign Office and they said they would get back to the authorities for confirmation. I sat trying to hold myself together, between expectation and terrible anger. David had disappeared. I had visions of him being assassinated, of a car accident – or was this another false alarm?

At about five o'clock Steven rang Stanley's house again. There was a long wait and then he passed me the phone.

'David!'

'Oh, you! Norma? Am I talking to you?'

'Where have you been?'

'The boers lost their way in the car. They told me at lunchtime today I was being released. They aren't used to Johannesburg. We had to stop at a stop and buy a map. Then I navigated them to Stanley's house.'

'Oh, *David*. Hello! How are you?'

'Feeling bloody silly at the moment.'

'What's the matter?'

'As we arrived in the car, Stanley rushed out to say Steven was

Mary Barnett, David and me on a Friday-night City Group picket.

David's arrival at Heathrow, June 1984.

David and Matthew (the youngest member of City Group).

on the phone. Well, cars have changed since I was in one. Instead of a handle, there's a sort of lever. I just grabbed what I thought was the doorhandle and pulled off the ashtray. I've messed up the boers' car.'

'Oh, David! You're the same you!'

'I'm just the same all right, how are the kids?'

I passed the phone to Steven and then Amandla and then we passed it around to each other again. A few minutes after we had put the phone down, David rang back and spoke with the three of us again.

Our friends went to telephone the news, leaving Mary Barnett, Carol and Adelaide Tambo with us. Soon people began to arrive, bringing food, champagne and gifts. Flowers and telegrams arrived.

Three weeks after David's release, Fred Kitson died. It was as if he had waited all those years to greet his son out of prison. David spent two weeks with his father and then had to wait for his exit permit to leave South Africa.

In London we were on tenterhooks waiting for David. The phone bill mounted and so did my excitement. There was talk of my meeting David in Africa. A newspaper offered me a large sum if I'd go to Nairobi and give them an exclusive story.

In Johannesburg, David was lionised by the young political activists who saw him as a father of Umkhonto we Sizwe and a hero of the struggle.

On 20 June 1984, Steven, Amandla and I sat twitching in a private cubicle at Heathrow airport waiting for David to arrive. I did not, for quite some time, recognise him as he walked towards us. No one had told me that his brown hair had turned grey. He took me in his arms and then reached out and encompassed Steven and Amandla in the embrace and the four of us stood there with our arms around each other.

Then we went to meet the crowds. It was an ecstatic time, the most colourful welcome there had ever been at Heathrow – so the television reports said. Everyone was shouting and singing, waving, calling and rushing towards him. Members of his trade union, TASS, touched him as he walked by, and some wept.

307

They had campaigned for him for twenty years. In 1969 they had offered him a fellowship at Ruskin College for life. Scores of City Groupies sang freedom songs and shouted slogans. Ruskin College sent a delegation with their banner. And of course friends came – lots of friends. There were bright trade-union banners, placards, ribbons, singing, cheering and weeping. The police tried to rush us through the crowds but David stopped every now and then to greet someone.

The ANC chief representative, Solly Smith, supervised the garlanding of David and hailed him as an ANC leader. The television reporters were hungry for interviews and mobbed David, shouting questions at him as we walked to the car.

At home David examined the house from top to bottom, fiddling with the gas jets of the cooker, opening the freezer and the fridge, looking in cupboards. With pride we showed him his bedroom and he nodded with approval and touched everything. But when I showed him my bedroom he said, 'Nonsense, we haven't waited all this time to sleep in separate rooms.'

'We have to get to know each other again,' I said.

'Well, how do you do then,' and he put out his hand to shake mine, and then took me in his arms. He examined Steven and Amandla minutely, touching their ears, fingering the backs of their necks, pulling up sleeves and running his hands down their arms and backs. Then he made them take off their shoes and looked at their feet.

'What are you doing, Dad?' They giggled.

'I missed all of your growing up. Now I want to see what I've got.' Then he looked in our mouths at our teeth.

When I made steaks for dinner, he picked his up and looked underneath it.

'What you looking for?' Amandla asked.

David chuckled. 'Nice and thick, isn't it?' And he ate it so quickly that we all looked at him.

'No point waiting around, is there? Why are you three so slow?'

He cuddled me and the children constantly, touching us and running his fingers through our hair.

308

Poopy took an instant liking to David, who asked when he'd last been for a walk. So we all went to Clissold Park while David threw sticks and Poopy brought them back to him. Steven, Amandla, David and I kicked a ball to each other. I was jealous. From then on Poopy was David's dog and slept at his feet. Then David wanted to go to a shop.

'What sort of shop?'

'Let's walk up to the local shops.' In the Blackstock Road David bought a bag of Mars bars and ate four of them on the way home. He looked through all the newspapers at the newsagent's and examined a freezer of ice creams, discussing the merits of each before buying two for each of us. We passed a chemist's shop called Motala and he went in. He had known a Mr Motala, a merchant, in Durban in the forties. This turned out to be his son. They had a chat about Durban and how the Indian market had burned down and about the Motala family.

At home, David made bacon and eggs for dinner, while Steven, Amandla and I lay around exhausted.

That night, when the children had gone to bed, David came and stood at the door of my bedroom.

'I don't want to sleep in that big room alone,' he said.

'Well, I will. You can sleep in here.'

'I want to sleep with you. Move over.'

'Don't you think we should wait a while – see how things turn out?'

'No. We know how things are going to turn out. Anyway, that bed's too hard.'

I moved over and opened my arms to him. From then on we were to sleep tightly cuddled up every night. After a week I got so used to it that I couldn't fall asleep on my own when he had to be away.

The next day David moved all the things out of his cupboard and brought them into my room, hanging them up among my dresses. We were inextricably together again.

David had kept himself very fit in jail. Now he ran around Clissold Park with Steven and Poopy every morning and also did exercises. Neither imprisonment nor age had impaired him and he did not suffer prostate trouble. But he had a cough and developed colds easily.

David's press conference took place at the Africa Centre the morning after his arrival. He had kept abreast of South African affairs, gave an analysis of the current situation and reaffirmed his total dedication to the liberation struggle in South Africa. He pledged to carry out whatever he was called upon to do by the African National Congress.

We arranged a welcome-home party on the first Saturday after his arrival. David rose early and and I heard peculiar sounds coming from the front of the house. He was washing the windows. Then he mowed the lawn and swept the garden and stashed the debris into bins. Steven, Amandla and I, having made our beds and cleaned our rooms, were lolling in David's room, where we were accumulating the news reports of his release, piles of correspondence and a growing list of telephone calls for him.

David called us. He had made breakfast – bacon, eggs, mushrooms, tomatoes and toast.

Amandla yawned and I flopped into the chair.

'What's the matter with my family?' David asked. 'None of you has any energy.' Amandla and I groaned. Steven, competitive, danced like a boxer and he and David threw a few friendly punches.

David had emerged fresh, energetic and ready to play an active role in everything.

Over four hundred people came to our house. Andimba Toivo ja Toivo, leader of SWAPO of Namibia, recently released from Robben Island, sang and danced with us and paid tribute to David and to the people who had campaigned for David's and his own release. Leaders of the GLC, MPs, councillors and ANC comrades mixed with college students and unemployed youths. City Group Singers sang under the leadership of Adelaide Tambo – a good friend and mother to all South Africans in London – and James Phillips, a famous South African singer with a voice like Paul Robeson. Everyone brought a feast of food and drink. Former political prisoners posed for photographs outside the house.

Steven, Amandla and I were relieved that the chevra had not so far shown hostility to David. In fact they had welcomed him as an ANC leader. David himself was slightly puzzled at this. He had never been an ANC member. No whites were allowed to be ANC members inside South Africa until recently. He had been a member of the Communist Party since 1940. In the 1960s the South African Communist Party had delegated him to act on the four-man national high command of Umkhonto we Sizwe. But we explained that now no public distinction was made between ANC and MK members, and that whites could be enrolled as members of the ANC. The Communist Party operated, in London in any event, secretly inside the ANC – so everyone in the movement was called an ANC member.

Our relief was shortlived. Although he had been acknowledged in public, the chevra never in fact admitted David into the ANC, MK or into the South African Communist Party. He was never assigned to any unit or branch. Having acclaimed him, they kept him out in the cold. He tried to go to Lusaka to get instructions from the ANC head office, but was blocked from doing this.

Shortly after David's arrival he was summoned to the ANC office in London. He thought he was going for a briefing session so that he could represent in his talks and at his meetings the main themes the ANC wanted raised, or to be told current ANC policy in relation to meetings. He was not briefed at all. Only one topic was discussed – their distaste for City Group.

David was appalled and explained to Solly Smith, the chief representative, and to the office members present, that incarceration in death row was the worst time he and his colleagues had spent in jail. The head of the prison had told him, when they were moved, that the picket outside South Africa House had caused the move from death row to take place six months earlier than it had been planned. These six months had been vital to his health. How could he speak out against the group? What problem had it caused the ANC?

When David suggested that the ANC use its influence to get

the AAM national leadership to meet with City Group to resolve their differences, Solly Smith said that the ANC could not interfere with the activities of a British organisation. He told David he was not to join City Group. David agreed not to do so.

David left the ANC office distressed and bewildered. In South Africa people had lauded the efforts of City Group and of his family. He went through the City Group tapes, videos and leaflets, looking for a clue to the hostility. He found none.

A few months later David was summoned to a meeting with two leading members of the South African Communist Party. They were also members of the London ANC and of the National Committee of the Anti-Apartheid Movement. They wanted him to speak out publicly against City Group at the annual general meeting of the AAM in November 1984. David's refusal to do this was the source of his later problems with the London ANC.

'I can't speak against City Group,' David had said. 'I have met a few hundred of these people and I find them laudable. I think the stand they make is noble. I have been to a Friday-night picket outside the South African embassy, and I think they're necessary and that they're in line with Anti-Apartheid Movement policy. My family are members of City Group. I have encouraged them in all my years in jail to follow this path.'

The South African Communist Party made no further contact with him.

David offered to withdraw his nomination for the national committee of the AAM. He offered not to attend its annual general meeting, but they did not want that.

At a meeting with Brian Bunting, David asked why, during his absence in jail, I had never been admitted to the South African Communist Party in exile in London. Brian said I had not submitted a curriculum vitae. David looked at him in amazement.

'Do you mean you want her record *in writing*?' he asked. 'Copies of it would arrive on a desk in Pretoria if Party members did things like that. It's a dreadful security risk! Norma worked with some of the leading members in the underground and some

312

of those people are here in London. She can be personally vouched for. I will not permit her to write out her actions, which were mainly in the underground, and submit them to anybody. Some of those activists are still in South Africa.'

Brian repeated that I would have to submit a CV.

David had run into a barrage of hostility at a time when he needed support from his friends. It was difficult for him to adjust to being out of jail. At first David was lost in our big house. He forgot where he put things and complained bitterly. 'I used to have one shelf and I knew where everything was. There's too many things in this house.' He mislaid his glasses, pens, letters and notebooks.

For weeks our telephone never stopped ringing. Friends wanted to see David, organisations wanted him to speak at meetings, newspaper reporters wanted to interview him and he appeared on television chat shows.

Television centres are big, bustling, unnerving places and I was wondering how he would cope. He was greeted by the interviewer as if he was suffering.

'David, (pause) how *are* you?'

'I'm coping,' he said.

'Just coping?' she asked with great sympathy.

'Well,' he said, looking at her with a twinkle in his eye, 'I'm even prepared to live it up!'

Everybody expected David to be an invalid, but he was right on the ball.

A reporter asked him, 'What did you miss most in jail?' He thought for a few seconds how to respond to this difficult question and then said, 'Bacon and eggs.' We were awakened in the small hours of the morning by people offering to make him bacon and eggs. When the next reporter asked the same question, David said:

'When I was last asked that question, I said 'bacon and eggs' and our sleep was disturbed for weeks, so now I'm going to say what I missed most was cuddles.'

On the third occasion he said, 'First I was woken at all hours of the day and night for bacon and eggs. Then I was bruised and

313

battered every time I went into the streets with people clutching me. So I think what I missed most in jail were the collected works of Karl Marx.'

Sidney was a regular visitor at the house. He and David became firm friends and David considered Sidney a member of the family. They chatted while they cooked lunches and dinners together.

My mother returned from visiting Clarice in Australia. I was desperately trying to sort out Red Lion Setters, which had now sunk dangerously into debt, so David drove my mother around London for the two weeks of her stay, shopping and sightseeing. When she left for South Africa I realised that, since her return from Australia, we had hardly had time for a proper chat.

David was speaking at meetings nearly every night. Steven, Amandla or I would accompany him. We were getting weary but David never flagged, never complained.

'I have to do it,' he said when I asked him to take it easy. 'I'm a Mandela-man. I was a casualty of the struggle and now I've just got to get on with it.'

'You'll burn yourself out,' I said. 'You're entitled to a bit of a rest.' But he was adamant. If anyone wanted him to speak at a meeting, he consented, whether it was in London or in Scotland.

We attended a reception at the Soviet embassy in London and were invited to visit the Soviet Union. Neither of us had ever been there before and we looked forward with great excitement to the trip.

We were due to leave London on 10 August. The night before, a large meeting had been planned at Hackney Town Hall to celebrate South African Women's Day. David had eaten no supper and was hungry. Before the meeting began, he went off to look for something to eat. He came back with a kebab. That night he complained of a sore stomach.

We were guests of the Central Committee of the Communist Party of the Soviet Union and were taken to a magnificent hotel in Moscow.

On our first morning we were taken to a polyclinic for a

314

thorough medical examination. Everywhere David went, people wanted lengthy chats with him. They wanted to know what it had been like in jail and how he was coping now. In the Soviet Union people were delighted to discover that David could speak Russian. He had studied it at Ruskin College in the fifties and again in jail, but after a year the authorities forbade him to continue his Russian studies. After a friendly talk, the doctor asked:

'How are you?'

'Fine,' said David. 'I ate a kebab last night. I don't think it agreed with me. I've got a bit of a sore stomach and a bit of diarrhoea.'

Panic ensued. The clinic swung into action. Nurses rushed out, doors opened and closed. Here was someone recently from Africa with a stomach complaint. A string of dangerous diseases and infections had to be ruled out. David was rushed to an isolation hospital. Our hotel room and all our possessions were fumigated and I was moved to another room.

Of course his stomach cleared up after a couple of days but they wanted to keep David in, waiting for test results and for observation. I was worried. David was in isolation again. I was not able to visit him. Imagining he must feel imprisoned again, I started making urgent efforts to get him out. Most people think the Soviet Union is run by the Communist Party. I began to think that it was controlled by the medical profession. The Party officials were fully supportive. They agreed with me that it was dreadful for David to be held in isolation. They made strong representations to the doctors, who argued the medical grounds. It took a directive from a member of the Central Committee to clear the matter up. In fact, David was having a ball. The hospital was in the country a few miles outside Moscow, in beautiful surroundings. Here David had made many friends. He was perfecting his Russian and spent his time chatting with patients in the hospital. In one of the wings he found some ANC comrades who had been sent to the Soviet Union for medical treatment. Nurses and doctors were giving David loving attention.

When he was passed as fit, we went to Sochi, a health resort on the Black Sea.

During these two weeks, among kindly people, in luxurious accommodation, I got to know this wonderful Martian-man who had emerged from jail after nineteen years and seven months. We had so much to tell each other, so much to catch up on, that we talked late into the nights, sleeping in the afternoons and dozing on the beach.

The guests at the resort arranged a meeting and David spoke about South Africa. I taught everyone the song 'Mandela Says Fight For Freedom'. Our birthdays are a week apart and our official interpreter passed the word around. On the 18th and then on 25 August the management and guests celebrated with us and we were showered with gifts.

I had got my David back – the same David: loving, political, concerned. He had missed sweets in jail and ate them throughout the day and night – in the morning I would find a pile of toffee papers next to his side of the bed. He was so loving that, even reading, he would reach out for my hand. He wanted me close to him always – and I wanted to be near him. Sometimes at night I would awaken and touch him with my finger to make sure I was not dreaming.

We left Sochi after two weeks and flew to Leningrad. Here we visited the Hermitage, museums, palaces, went to the ballet and the circus. The highlight of the visit for me was a trip to the Smolny Institute where we saw Lenin's office. We were in the care of a top Party official, a charming man, who taught David how to down vodka in one gulp. One evening he shyly asked David for his autograph.

'Of course,' David said, embarrassed.

'Oh, it's not for me,' Slava said. 'It's for my daughter. She's the little girl I introduced you to yesterday. I told her about you and that I was escorting you around Leningrad and she asked me if I could have a picture of you and your autograph. She said you were the first real revolutionary she'd ever met.'

Back at the Moscow hotel, we met Comrade Moses Mabhida, general secretary of the South African Communist Party. David discussed with him my non-admittance to the Party in London. Comrade Mabhida said I was a member of the Party in good standing and he would vouch for that. When David met him in London a few months later, however, Comrade Mabhida said that my membership could only be decided by Brian Bunting!

The ANC and TASS had arranged a three-week, countrywide speaking tour for David from 10 to 27 September. Even though he was fit and healthy, David did not like being without a member of his family for longer than a day. Solly Smith told him that if one of us accompanied him on the speaking tour, the ANC would pull out. David was in conflict. He agreed that we would not be part of the official delegation but said that if we attended the meetings as members of the public there could be no objection. Solly began shouting at David.

David came to see me at Red Lion after this meeting. He was distressed and unhappy. I took him to the doctor. His blood pressure was high and the doctor recommended rest.

But David's schedule was punishing. Within three weeks he spoke in Glasgow, Newcastle, Bristol, Liverpool, Manchester, Sheffield, Cardiff, Bournemouth, Nottingham, Harlow, and Southampton. Meetings were arranged in the evenings and during the days he travelled to the next venue, attended mayoral receptions, lunches, press and television interviews.

The tour was a tremendous success. He spoke magnificently, with a clarity and passionate commitment that moved people everywhere. No one could understand how he had emerged from twenty years in jail without bitterness, so fiery and intact.

The London chevra threatened to pull the ANC out of the tour on a few occasions. David felt that members of the London ANC office were making things difficult.

After much heart-searching, David telephoned the ANC in Lusaka, asking them to see to it that the tour continued successfully. They did so. A few thousand pounds were collected for the coffers of the ANC and people joined the Anti-Apartheid Movement wherever David spoke.

On 2 October David attended the Labour Party conference in Blackpool.

317

We flew to New York on 11 October, where David addressed the United Nations on the International Day of Solidarity with South African Political Prisoners. On 19 October he spoke at a public meeting in Leeds and he returned to New York on 30 October to attend a United Nations symposium on Namibia. On 7 November he spoke at a Labour Party meeting in Muswell Hill, on the 11th in Leicester, for the Interracial Group. On the 13th David spoke for the Third World First group, and on the 17th and 18th he went to Luton to address the South East Midlands Communist Party Congress. On the 20th he spoke in London for the Camden Trades Council.

On 21 November 1984, something occurred that was so bizarre that even now I cannot comprehend it. Five months after David's arrival in England, he and I were suspended from the London ANC for having agreed to stand for nomination to the Anti-Apartheid national committee! All ANC members are urged to participate in the Anti-Apartheid Movement. We were suspended for obeying this injunction.

We appealed against our suspensions – and received no replies.

The secretary-general of the ANC, Alfred Nzo, visited London and said he wanted the matter cleared up. As it was a regional matter all that would be necessary was a formal letter from both of us to the chief representative in London. We wrote immediately. There was no response.

In December I sold off half of Red Lion Setters and brought the remainder of the company to the house in Highbury. If I was to resuscitate the company, I would have to work day and night. David's job at Ruskin College had not begun – he was told that there was no money yet for his post. We were in financial trouble. Amandla was at college on a grant, studying community theatre and drama, and we were all relying on Steven's salary.

When David had first gone to jail, friends had approached a leading member of the South African Communist Party suggesting that they would like to set up a trust fund for David so that he would have money to live on when he emerged. This chevra advised David's friends that this was unnecessary, they would take care of David. He would want for nothing. Alewyn Birch, a constant friend to our family, arranged for David to be given a car by the Eva Reckitt Trust.

In January 1985, David joined the teaching staff at Ruskin College, Oxford, lecturing in statistics and mathematics. In addition, he ran a weekly seminar on Africa and was a member of TUIREG, a trade union organisation operating in Ruskin. After a term, students came asking David to lecture them in political ideas. He commuted from London, speaking at three and four meetings a week.

David had been offered a three-year contract, to be reviewed after one year – a far cry from the 1969 TASS offer of a 'job for life'. When the year was up, Ruskin College requested TASS to let David continue. They were very satisfied with his work and asked TASS to give him an increment in salary.

A few months later David received a letter from John Jones, Ken Gill's right-hand man at TASS, stating that if he had not reconciled his position with the London ANC by the end of the 1986 summer term, his position at Ruskin would have to be reviewed.

In the same week, David received a letter from the London ANC, stating, without explanation, that his suspension was to continue. The chevra would still not meet or talk with us.

'I must be an historic case,' David said. 'I must be the only man to be kicked out of an organisation I never belonged to. Why did they garland and hail me as an ANC member if all they wanted to do was publicly kick me out? They never even let me in.'

He was very upset – but not surprised. 'They've always wanted to keep their ranks small and exclusive. That's the only way they can control things. That's why they're scared of you, with your City Group. Look what happened in New Zealand. The youngsters, with their direct action, closed the embassy and got sanctions going there. Look, in the United States, the Free South Africa Movement has created a tremendous feeling that moved even Ronald Reagan to implement some sanctions. We just have to push on. Sidney's quite right. It's what we can do for the struggle at home that counts. That's what matters.'

The hostility mounted. The chevra made it known to the trade-union movement, the Labour Party and organisations throughout the country that they would not appear on a platform if David Kitson was speaking. He had acted, they said, contrary to ANC policy. And when people asked what policy, they were told that it was an internal ANC matter. British people were told not to interfere.

David continued to be invited to speak at meetings all over the country. TASS members in his Oxford region, noting his exclusion from their previous annual conference, elected him their delegate to the 1986 conference. David's urgent call to support the struggle for liberation in South Africa was answered wherever he went.

City Group membership continued to grow. Approaches to MPs and councillors by the chevra, telling them to have nothing to do with us, often led these people to phone, asking if they could join.

We campaigned for sanctions against apartheid South Africa, for the release of Nelson Mandela, for an end to the harassment of Nomzamo (Winnie) Mandela, against the death sentences of the Sharpeville Six, against the treason trials and the persecution of the United Democratic Front, against the hunger-striking children in jail. We picketed South African Airways and Barclays Bank, held ever larger meetings and rallies.

Red Lion Setters flourished and in a year we worked off the losses.

Amandla attended the Friday pickets regularly, stood on the police barricades and led the Pickies, singing to the tune of 'Twist and Shout':

> We're gonna shake up the embassy,
> Kick them out – Kick the fascists out,
> Come on, come on down Botha now,
> We're gonna boot you out.

We're gonna picket by day,
We're gonna picket by night
We're gonna picket until
Until we win this fight.

We're gonna picket by night
We're gonna picket by day
Picket and picket,
Till you hear what we say.

Steven was the City Group membership secretary, one of the
lead voices in the City Group Singers, the company secretary at
Red Lion Setters and he played a musical instrument in a samba
group. Whenever we could, we went to watch him perform.
David finds Steven's job fascinating – both are engineers. In
jail, David got a BA in economics and politics and a BSc in
mathematics and applied mathematics, a diploma in datamet-
rics and was finalising his honours degree in operational
research when he was released.

Steven and David have the same chuckle and mannerisms.
Whenever I can't find David, he is up in Steven's room
chatting.

We have Sunday lunches together. Last week, when David
was carving the chicken, he said, 'Who wants a game of Trivial
Pursuit after lunch?'

We all groaned. I said, 'You always win by miles. Well, OK
then, if the three of us can play together against you.'

'We'll have to discuss the nonstop picket,' Steven said. 'It
starts on 19 April. I've got to process the City Group
membership forms. On the Friday picket twelve new members
signed up and I've got to get the records straight so that the
newsletter goes out to everyone.' He threw Poopy a bone.

'You shouldn't give him chicken bones. They'll splinter and
stick in his throat.'

'Oh, Dad, that's just an old-fashioned saying,' said Steven.

'What has the committee said about T-shirts?' I asked. 'We
can't have RELEASE NELSON MANDELA and CLOSE DOWN THE
SOUTH AFRICAN EMBASSY on them. It's too many words.'

321

'Leave that to Carol,' Steven said. 'She'll think of a way to do it. I'm more worried about getting everything ready in time, the leaflets, song sheets, the Pavement University stuff – and we have to do something to protect all our gear from the rain. With the Public Order Act going through, the cops may not let us have a tarpaulin this time.'

'There's a working session tomorrow night,' Amandla said. 'We can raise all that there. I think the nonstop picket is going to be big. It was really good on the 86-Day-and-Night Picket in 1982, but now it's going to be tremendous. We have to reach out and get the support because I'm sure it's there.'

'Quite right,' David said. 'Wherever I go around the country, I can feel the support growing. Meetings on South Africa are getting bigger. More people have become aware in the past year. We have to build the strongest solidarity possible – show people that they can actually assist the liberation struggle.'

'Why don't you help me answer all these letters, Amandla? There's lots for meetings, some thank-yous and three from people who've joined the AAM and two who want to start groups. And one from Grannie Millie. She's planning to come over for a holiday soon.'

'Oh, Dad. You're always answering letters,' Amandla complained. 'I think we should discuss what's happening at home. Did you see Mrs Mandela spoke at a meeting in Kagiso and they've started a new campaign to release Nelson Mandela and to end the state of emergency?'

'Yes,' I said. 'That's why the nonstop picket was conceived. We're responding to the campaigns inside the country.'

'Also my college. I've got a term and a half to go. I have to think about what I'm going to do.'

'Have you contacted any agents to see your performance in *Blood Brothers*?' David asked.

'No,' Amandla said. 'I've been so busy rehearsing for *The Madwoman of Chaillot* and preparing audition pieces that I haven't got round to it yet. Pass me the salad, Steven.

'You should get Mom to run off some standard letters for you, Dad, so you just have to sign them.'

'What do you mean?'

'Well, you could have one that says, yes, I can speak at your meeting on such-and-such a date. Another one that says, no, I can't speak on that date because I have another engagement. Then there could be one that says, I'm pleased to hear that you have decided to start an anti-apartheid group in your organisation and that you thought my speech useful. And then you could have one that says, yes, I'll come to dinner but only if you invite all four of us and promise to serve roast beef and Yorkshire pudding with bananas and cream for afters.'

Steven and I laughed but David took it seriously. 'That would be terribly rude. I think if people take the trouble to write letters they should be properly answered. And anyway, your mother's too busy.'

Amandla threw herself on his lap. 'Oh, Daddy, I'm not being *serious*. Sundays are for discussions. You spend all week speaking at meetings, teaching at Ruskin, reading for hours, cooking and playing in the kitchen, writing letters, cuddling Mommy and Poopy. On Sundays you have to talk with us.'

'Oh, no problem,' said David. 'By the way, talking about bananas and cream, what's this?'

'It's an experiment,' I said. 'It's called apple tansy. I haven't made puddings for years.'

'When you were in jail,' Amandla said, 'and we were little, Mom made up a pudding out of rice crispies, cocoa, milk and egg. We call it Kitson pudding. We haven't had it for ages.'

'You don't have to make puddings on my account,' David said.

'Well, it's a sort of family thing, having pudding on a Sunday. But I remember when you were in jail,' I said. 'I remember being telephoned by a lawyer who said you'd been charged with possession of an illegal piece of pudding and I had to engage an advocate to defend you. I thought you were starving and had stolen it. I had nightmares about it.'

'Why? Did you steal pudding in jail, Dad?'

'Oh, no,' David said. 'I didn't steal it. In jail they make a sort of bread pudding – on the side, you know. In the early years when the food was really boring it was a real treat. It was an unauthorised piece of pudding – not an illegal piece.

'Jail bread pudding is made by taking the bread out of the crust and kneading it with coffee powder. You put it in a bowl and cover the top with a layer of margarine mixed with instant coffee and some sugar. One of the prisoners, Derek, had friends in the kitchen with access to the ingredients and he made a basinful every week.

'The four politicals in my section – this was when we were kept in Central prison with the general prison community while they were preparing a maximum-security jail for us – clubbed together to supply Derek with a month's toiletries and in return we got a slice each of bread pudding every Saturday.

'One Saturday when Marius Schoon and I were taking our portions to our sections, we bumped into Warder Vermeulen. He nicked us and we had to go with him to the front office.

'There, Sergeant Faan Jonker (who was sulking from his recent demotion from adjutant because he'd been caught smuggling) charged us with unauthorised possession of bread pudding.

'The prosecutor who was meant to hear the case went to Upington to prosecute jail cases there, and Vermeulen went on a month's leave. Our advocate, hired by our families, nagged the prison administration for a date to hear the case. But nothing happened, and then the cleaner responsible for the prosecutor's office put the evidence in the kitchen furnace.'

'I was terribly worried,' I said. 'I was told that if you were found guilty, you could get years added on to your sentence.'

'Well, when the charge sheets appeared before *Die Bok* – the captain in charge of the court – he blew a fuse! He was scared of looking a fool over the whole business – having leading advocates arguing over a piece of bread! All the inmates of the jail were simmering with outrage. The whole bread-pudding position was under threat in the jail.

'"Deal with it," Die Bok said to Bosveld, the prison superintendent. Bosveld asked us if we would accept his jurisdiction. After some haggling, we agreed.

'"Right, three meals each," he said.

'"Hey," I said, "I know a prisoner who got only one meal for unauthorised possession of tobacco."

'Bosveld nearly burst into tears. "I'm in deep enough trouble over this as it is. *Please* just take the three meals."

'So Marius and I spent twenty-four hours in solitary punishment cells, missing three meals.'

'Next week, you make the pudding,' I said.

They laughed.

Steven picked up a copy of the *ANC News Briefing* and leafed through it. 'I bet South Africa will manage to get a deal from the IMF,' he said. 'They keep going on about how they're reforming apartheid while they shoot up whole communities and even kids in schools.'

'Well, what d'you expect?' Amandla said. 'The Western countries want to hear the word "reform" so they can have an an excuse for not applying sanctions. They want to continue investing in South Africa – it's profitable. Every now and then Botha baldly comes out with a statement that things are getting better despite all the evidence that they're getting worse.'

'Now I see they're putting seven- and eight-year-olds in jail!' Steven said.

'I think this week has seen a very important development in South Africa,' David said. 'Did you see the report about Alexandra Township in the *Observer* today? Pass me that newspaper, Norm. Listen to this, everyone. This is a young black guy speaking:

We have made very great progress over the past two weeks. I think it can be said that we are now in control of Alexandra. The majority of the people are behind us. The police may control the streets, but we control the people.

'It goes on, and then says:

The comrades began organising in Alexandra only two months ago. They named their central organisation the Alexandra Action Committee. By the end of January they had formed 18 street committees,

325

aiming eventually to have one for each of the township's 44 blocks.

When we have conscientised them all, then at a word from us we can stop all these factories with a strike or cripple the shops with a consumer boycott. That is how the struggle is going to be fought.'

'That's tremendous,' I said. 'Alexandra is where I came in. When I went up to Johannesburg, after I joined the Congress of Democrats, I went to Alexandra Township and gave out leaflets there. There was terrible hardship and oppression. And now Alex belongs to the people. The people are liberating Alex.'

'But when is it *all* going to be liberated?' Amandla asked. 'That's the question.'

And that *was* the question. Our family was together now and we were waiting to go home.